The Midwife Mission

The Midwife Mission

John McDonald

WHITE SANDS PRESS

Published by
White Sands Press, PO Box 299
Liverpool, L15 7WY

Cover: Steve Aspinall
Printed by L. Cocker Ltd.
Unit A9, Erskine Street, Liverpool L6 1AU

This book is dedicated to all who extend to others, of whatever nationality, race, or creed, the respect they expect for themselves and their families

Amongst them were my old friends Pat Carmody and Pete Mackay, who sadly died before this book was finished

Contents

1

The Midwife Mission

IDRIS ROBERTS STOOD by the window and looked at the night sky. A few clouds hung there white and illuminated. The long sloping garden was bathed in moonlight and the trees at the far end could be seen almost as clearly as in the light of day. Beyond, abrupt and beautiful hilly country gave way to mountains with fern and tree and grass covered sides, which led to bare rock peaks. Hills, mountains and groups of trees all cast deep shadows to one side, yet themselves stood fluorescent in the light of the moon. Far off, along the side of a valley in shadow, moved the lights of a solitary vehicle on some nocturnal errand.

Idris looked at the stars. Distant and silent they held a host of secrets. If only he could close his eyes and upon opening them be in possession of those secrets. If only something beyond imagination could happen and enable him to transcend his earthly limitations. Above him was suspended the cosmos, in which all existence passed, each constituent part, finite and remote, barely gaining significance in a vastness without end. Idris felt his own mortality. What place could his life and his concerns claim within such a scale? Whatever he did the grass would grow on those hills, and when the snow fell they would lie, white and brilliant, on a moonlit night such as this. And in the spring that scene would become a garden of life. These things had happened and he had remained, unaware of this and much else, preoccupied with the human tragedies that hung over everything that happened at home. Eventually, realising that he was cold, he went to bed.

He was quickly asleep, and in sleep there was little to distinguish him from the other young people in the youth hostel. But *he* was on the threshold of an experience, which would set him apart not just from them, but from all other people, except for a very few – an experience to which the future of the human race would be inextricably linked.

2

Idris

I WAS BORN in Ballymoney, amongst the Protestants of Northern Ireland, my mother devout in her faith, my father an ex-British soldier, not so devout. I'm on a journey that started one afternoon in 1992, when I was ten years old. Before then, I had identified totally with the people around me, never questioning my loyalty to the things in which they and I believed. I did once wonder what it would have been like to be born a Catholic. But that merely led me to think about how lucky I was to have been born into the true faith. It certainly didn't lead me to understand that we aren't actually born Protestant and Catholic but that we learn as children to become one or the other, almost without thinking.

My faith and my loyalty were a passion to me. And the summer marches, when we Protestants celebrate all that we are, were the high point of my year. On the 12th of July the sight and sound of the flute bands and the drums and the spectacle of thousands gathered together with their banners and flags, was an utter thrill.

Soon after my tenth birthday, I went with my cousins to follow an Orange Order march. When the marchers reached a barrier that divided the local Protestants from the Catholics on the other side, policemen opened the gates in the barrier to let the marchers pass through, and we all cheered. But when I saw the faces of the Catholics on the other side, I didn't like it. They weren't cheering. They were grim-faced, and as the march passed through they shouted in anger.

I never forgot it. The incongruity of our pleasure and their anger stayed with me. I suppose that was the start of my journey.

The division between people of the two Christian faiths had always been there, and I didn't have friendly feelings towards Catholics. Especially because when father was in the army, his life had been in danger every day. I'd heard him talk about one of his friends who had become separated from the other soldiers and was surrounded by Catholic women who held him until the IRA arrived. Then the IRA took him away and shot him. Father had known that if he had taken the wrong turning and been captured he would have been killed. And while he was out on patrol he was always at risk of being shot. He'd been lucky, but many other soldiers hadn't. Hundreds had been killed. And the IRA killed policemen and members of the Ulster Defence Regiment too. Even when they were off duty, if the IRA caught one of them he was finished. More than once I'd seen the funerals of their victims. I loathed and feared the IRA. Because of them I felt under threat from Catholics.

Uncle Len, my cousins' father, had been caught driving a car with a bomb in it. He'd been on his way to "repay" Catholics for something that the IRA had done. That was how we felt about Protestant paramilitaries. Even when they did wrong, their motive was to pay back for the deaths in our community.

My cousins were proud of uncle Len. The fact that he was in prison was proof of his dedication to our cause. David, my oldest cousin, styled himself on his father, or rather on how he thought Uncle Len would have behaved. I was more than a little afraid of David. And so was Les, my other cousin, who was a year older than me. David would devise various ways of hurting us. More than once he persuaded us to play "knuckles". When it was our turn we never managed to hit him. His fist would be gone and we'd hit empty space. But when it was his turn he never failed to hit us hard on the edge of the knuckle. The "game" always ended with us in pain and David looking pleased with himself.

And David knew how to punch. When Les hit me I'd feel his strength and he'd knock me off balance, but when David punched, I just felt pain. Despite his being small for his age, he knew how to hurt: where to hit and how. It didn't surprise me that, by the time he left school, David had a gang of would-be hard-men around him. And anyone who annoyed him was in for a hammering. And it didn't surprise me that he went looking for fights with Catholics, or "Taigs" as he liked to call them.

I spent a lot of time in David and Les's company, so I was glad that there was one person who was decidedly harder than David. That was my father. One time when Dad saw David knee Les between the legs he came out of the house and hit him. There didn't seem to be much force in the punch, but it left David curled up on the floor gasping. David knew that father had once been a boxer. He knew about the time when father had been out jogging and had been mistaken for a Catholic and attacked and had "beaten-the-shit" out of his attackers. I knew that David respected father, and for most of the time that respect protected me.

Another step on my journey began, one Sunday, when I was staying with my cousins. We were playing football outside the house. I was in goal. Suddenly the game stopped and all of the lads seemed to be looking at me. It only took me a moment to realise that they were actually looking past me and I turned around. Walking towards me was a lovely girl with long fair hair. She was holding hands with her boyfriend. As they walked past she smiled at me. Then they went into a house, and just before the door closed, I heard her tinkling laughter.

"She's a Taig", David hissed as we continued the game.

I only ever saw her once more. It was a few weeks later. I was in my cousins' front room and, when I heard a horn honking, I looked out. There was a taxi on the opposite side of the road. She came out of her boyfriend's house, her fair hair tied back in a ponytail, bobbing as she walked. Followed by her boyfriend, she hurried to the taxi. Then the taxi drove off. She was the first Catholic I ever saw as an individual, and I liked what I saw.

The next time I heard about her, it was from Les: "They shot the Taig", he said.

"Which one?" I asked, trying to appear unconcerned. But inside I feared that he might mean her.

"It's *her*," he answered, and I felt sick in the stomach. It was worse than one of David's punches. And it lasted.

The man who was convicted of her murder was a "friend" of her boyfriend's family. She had been staying with her boyfriend when the "friend" crept into the house during the night with a gun. He fired a bullet into her head through one of her lovely eyes, for no other reason than that she was a "Taig". And then he fired three more bullets into her, just to make sure.

It was July, the "Marching Season", and the murderer had been involved at Drumcree, where the police backed by the army had forcibly moved Catholic residents out of the way to let Protestant marchers through their area. The sickening murder of the lovely girl and the fact that, despite the peace process, there were Protestants still killing Catholics caused me considerable distress.

By the time Les left school he had joined David's gang. I wasn't invited, and I wasn't surprised. Any chance that I might have been suitable material had died along with Bernadette Martin, the murdered Catholic girl.

Mother was infatuated with Ian Paisley. She regarded him as The Defender of the Protestant way of life. She loved his fiery speeches, and whatever he said was Gospel to her. But I was already seeing him as the inspirer of Protestants who wouldn't alter in any way to make peace with Catholics. I was frustrated. Everyone was horrified at the murder of Bernadette Martin. They knew that the sectarian killings were coming from our side. Yet most anger was focused on the IRA still having its weapons. That was being given as the reason for not supporting the peace process. To me, few were grasping the magnitude of what had happened. The IRA had stopped the war. They had given us peace. But we hadn't given the Catholics peace. Catholics were still being killed, and the IRA wasn't responding in kind. *They* wanted peace. But we were so one-sided.

When I tried to persuade my cousins that the Catholics were no longer the threat they imagined them to be, David became so angry that I thought he was going to hit me, and I prepared myself for my first fight with him. But it didn't happen.

I knew that he was against the peace-process simply because he didn't like Catholics, so I asked him how he would have felt if he had been born a Catholic. "Then I'd have been a Fenian", he said. "But I'm not a Catholic. I'm a Prod. So what's your problem?"

I started to ask, "Are we going to let the killing go on forever? How can it be right?" But I didn't finish the first sentence. I could see in his angry eyes the limit of his mind. He didn't know how not to hate Catholics. He enjoyed hating and he wanted them as the enemy. Fighting Catholics had become his purpose in life. I gave up. I knew it was hopeless.

David's head was full of the terrible things the IRA had done to Protestants. He could quote from the whole catalogue of Republican murders, from the IRA bombing of the remembrance service at Enniskillen, to the INLA shooting of a harmless Sunday school teacher. And he claimed that it was the IRA that started the pub bombings: that the famous bombing of Murphy's bar that killed six Catholics, had been a reply to an IRA bombing of a Protestant pub.

Years before when we little kids had our "shoot-outs" with the enemy I shot many an IRA gunman. But that wasn't enough for David. Once, when he joined in, he captured one of them, and he cut his head off. As we grew older, David's attitude was hardening.

Although I knew that most Protestants didn't share David's degree of hate, I began to feel that too many were always on the point of something like hysteria, seeing threats in things that elsewhere would be unremarkable. Catholic families moving into houses vacated by Protestants was seen as an encroachment on our Protestant way of life, or even as a slide towards a United Ireland. Catholics living in the "wrong place" provoked more imbecilic Protestants to violence and sometimes murder. For many, a reasonable settlement with Catholics would be "surrender".

Catholic resistance to Orange parades along their streets was another passion-raiser. But our claim to our right to go anywhere on the Queen's highway was a phoney claim. Everyone knew that the parades weren't benign affairs. There were marchers who held banners that carried the initials of paramilitary groups that had carried out many murders of Catholics. And there had often been violence when the marchers passed through Catholic places, and the shouted jibes about murdered Catholics were famous. And during the marching season there had been beatings and killings, of Catholics mostly. It was no secret that the parades along Catholic streets were expressions of our supremacy.

When I saw a Protestant politician on television defending *our* right to march along the "traditional" routes and mother nodding in agreement, I wondered if their heads were made of solid turnip. Once when I heard a Catholic on TV challenge the "right to march on the Queens highway" argument and asking why that "right" hadn't been extended to Catholic civil rights marchers, I wondered what he meant. It wasn't until the following year, when, for the first time, I socialised with a Catholic that I was to find out.

I was horrified when, during the 1998 marching season, Orange supporters at Drumcree tried to battle their way through police barriers and into the Catholic area. I felt it shamed our community. It would have been so easy to re-route the march as a gesture of conciliation. But the marchers were so full of what "we" wanted and cared about little else. Then, when three young children were killed by a fire-bomb on the twelfth of July, I was stunned. They were Catholics, the children of the Quinn family who lived not far from us, amongst Protestants.

By July 1998 I had left school, and it was Drumcree, with David in the thick of it and the murder of the Quinn children, that decided me to get away from Northern Ireland.

Before then, Uncle Len had come out of prison. I saw him on the day of his release, and he was just happy to be home with his family. It seemed to be all that he wanted. I wasn't prepared for the pleasant surprise that I was to receive the next day, from dad.

On his first evening of freedom, Uncle Len lived the dream he had had for years of going to the club for an evenings drinking. All of the adults in the family went. The next day, my dad told me that uncle Len had been angry about a song that had been sung in the club. The performing group had sung about shooting a "Taig" and watching "the bastard die". Those words had actually been sung, and the club had erupted in applause and cheering. Uncle Len, *the Loyalist paramilitary*, had been angry, and dad had been pleased by his anger: "He isn't the old Len", dad told me. "He's changed".

At the family get-together the following evening, Uncle Len talked about his wasted years in prison and how he had missed seeing his boys growing up. And he talked about Gusty Spence, the old leader of the UVF, the first Protestant paramilitary group and how Gusty had publicly apologised for the UVF's killings and that Gusty had actually used the words, "Abject and true remorse". Len said that he felt the same way himself.

To my delight, Uncle Len started to criticise Ian Paisley. But mother tried to stop him. I could see that she was careful how she spoke to her brother. I knew how happy she was that at last he had been released from prison. She said to him gently, "Now Len, some of us think Ian Paisley stands up for us like no one else does".

"I know Sis", Uncle Len answered, "but *I* think he brings out the worst in us …"

Dad interrupted, "Len, tell them the story you told me at the bar last night".

Len obliged. He said he had heard that years before, Donald Soper, a liberal/Protestant cleric, had come over from England to speak at an open-air meeting. He had been heckled by Paisley supporters, but had got the better of them. Ian Paisley himself was there, and half way through the meeting he had taken his hat off, and Donald Soper had said, "Keep your hat on there's a wood-pecker about". The crowd had roared with laughter. Ian Paisley had met his match. The next time Donald Soper came to speak, there were people who were determined to silence him. The clever man was shouted down for an hour and he had to give up. Even mother chuckled at the story.

Later, when I went into the kitchen, Uncle Len was there talking to his sons. I only caught the end of what he had been saying, "... they're always pointing the finger. Martin McGuinness only has to fart and they threaten to wreck the peace-process ..." When he saw me, he stopped. But he winked as he left the kitchen.

After he had gone, David shook his head, "Dad's over forty now. He's done his bit."

Uncle Len, for some reason, was given money by someone, and he used it to buy a computer for David and Les. David wasn't interested. He was too engrossed in his role as a Protestant hard-man and all that he considered went with it, including a daily session on his weights. But Les was interested. He'd been on a computer course since he'd left school, and he spent hours on the new computer every day, and I often joined him.

Les was a natural and, by the time I left school, his skills had won him a job in, of all places, Dublin, the capital of Catholic Ireland. On the weekends he came home, he was full of the place, and he gave me ideas. Before the Drumcree antics were over, I'd decided to follow him to Dublin.

Dad knew how I felt, and he had a similar idea. But it was to Liverpool he wanted me to go. His hometown. Mother preferred that I went there too. I preferred Dublin. Things were happening there. But when dad's brother, Glynn, let us know there might be a job for me in Liverpool, involving computers, as long as I was good at English, which I was, I took the chance. I needed to get away.

Before I left, barely a month after the murder of the Quinn children, imbeciles, who called themselves "The Real IRA", replied to our imbeciles with a bomb that turned the centre of Omagh into a scene of mass murder. Protestants and Catholics were killed. I couldn't wait to get away.

When mother and father saw me off they told me that David was leaving home too and that he was mixing with paramilitaries.

Mother told me that, although she'd miss me, she was relieved that I was going and leaving "it all" behind. And so I went to stay with Uncle Glynn, dad's brother and Aunt Dolly. Before I left, father had had a quiet talk with me away from mother. He told me that in Liverpool I would find that no one gives a damn about what anyone else's religion might be. It was what I needed. I could hardly wait for the change.

But on the very first evening, Uncle Glynn and Aunt Dolly took

me to their local club, St Cecilia's. It was a *Catholic* club. I wasn't
ready for it. I needed time. Yet they wanted me to meet a friend
of theirs, a Catholic, who, they told me, had left Northern Ireland
years before, for similar reasons to my own. I sighed inwardly and
went along, not suspecting the real purpose of the meeting.

Their friends, Edward and Eileen Harrington, were friendly
enough. Straight away, Edward, despite my being under-age,
bought me a pint of beer and started to ask me questions about
old haunts of his: a cinema, a swimming baths and a park he used
to go to. When I realised he was talking about Belfast, I told him
I'd only ever been there a few times.

"You're lucky", he said. Then he added, "What am I talking
about? *I'm* lucky. I've been in Liverpool all these years, while you
were growing up in Ulster. It can hardly have been a picnic ..."

I was going to tell him that it hadn't been too bad, but he
continued, "When I was a lad things were much better. Much
better ... and at one time, it looked as though they were going to
get even better ... do you know about Terence O'Neill?"

His wife, Eileen, looked at him disapprovingly, but he took no
notice.

I was surprised by the question, but I did have a kind of
memory of the man, and I pulled a face. It was a reflex action. I
was copying mother.

"Oh! What was wrong with him?" Edward Harrington asked
me.

I hadn't intended this. I felt like a non-swimmer who'd been
thrown into the deep end, as I made an excruciating attempt to
tell him why I had pulled the face. But I couldn't. I was so embarrassed.

To my surprise, Edward beamed at me. "That's what I'd expect
from any young man from Northern Ireland today", he said.
"You're too young to know. O'Neill was, by far, Ulster's best Prime
Minister. He tried to bring Protestants and Catholics together. If
he'd succeeded I'd still be there, and so would you.

"The trouble was a lot of Protestants didn't like what he was
doing, and they forced him to resign ... this was when the IRA was
defunct. It had given up ..."

"But there'd been an IRA bombing campaign hadn't there?"

"That was years before."

"How many years?"

"I don't know ... but the IRA had given up violence."

I could see Uncle Glynn mouthing a silent, "Shhh".

He didn't need to. I wasn't arguing. I'd grown up inside a one-dimensional family, and I didn't know enough to contradict Edward Harrington, "tipsy" though he was. So I asked him, "So that's why you came to Liverpool?"

"No. No. Not then. The civil rights marchers were on the streets. They wanted rights *within* Ulster: no discrimination ... voting rights ... they weren't after a United Ireland. It should have been welcomed. But mobs attacked them and ... next thing ... whole streets of Catholics were being chased from their homes ... and what would you expect? Armed IRA men came out to protect them." He slowly shook his head, "Things could have been so different. If O'Neill had got his way, there'd have been no Troubles."

The alcohol was having its pleasant affect on me. My background was telling me that I should be arguing with this man. But I was sitting in a comfortable seat in a warm club and the friendly Catholic, who was sitting next to me, wasn't arguing. He was telling me about the chance that had been lost.

"Do you know how they got rid of O'Neill?"

"Er ... no."

"He was blown out of power. Just before a meeting of the Ulster Unionist Council, Protestant paramilitaries bombed Belfast's electricity supply. Everyone assumed it was an IRA job, and O'Neill was finished.

I can still see him shaking his head in disbelief that such things had happened, "It was tribalism, pure tribalism", he said. "Decent, law-aiding people were beaten up, and decent people – my friends – rushed to join the new IRA. They said they had tried peaceful ways.

"And there was Ian Paisley ... I couldn't believe it ... a clergyman ... I'd always thought ministers of religion were wise people: people you could go to for advice ... I'd thought Christian morality was about doing unto others as you would have done to yourself. But here was Paisley ... he was making angry speeches attacking O'Neill. O'Neill was trying to meet the demands of the civil rights people and Paisley was calling him a 'Traitor' and a 'Lundy' ... I suppose you know who Lundy was?"

"Yes. He wanted to surrender Londonderry to the Catholic army."

"I'll bet you know the date?"

"Yes. In 1689 ..."

Edward laughed, "Let's agree that it was a long time ago ...

anyway, Paisley was accusing O'Neill of being a 'Lundy'. He was a
big name-caller, Paisley: the Catholic Church was, 'the ..."

"Edward, don't you think the young man has heard enough?"
His wife was telling him off.

Actually, I hadn't heard enough. If she had stopped him
earlier, I would have been grateful. But I had begun to like it. I
knew that had mother been there she would have argued with
him. I wondered how Uncle Len would have behaved? And dad,
how would he have responded?

We talked, instead, about the latest football sensation in
Liverpool: the local lad who had been picked to play for England.
I looked forward to going to the Anfield football stadium to see
him.

It wasn't until the next day that I discovered that it was Edward
who had the job for me and that he had wanted to meet me
socially to check me out. He rang Glynn to tell him the job was
mine if I wanted it. And he apologised for "going on" the way he
had, but he had, he said, found me so easy to talk to.

During the free week I had before starting work, I felt a
freedom I hadn't known before. There were no boundaries:
roads beyond which you didn't go because the Other People lived
there. There were no Us and Them and no concern with what
your religion might be. What people had here was probably all
the civil rights marchers had wanted in 1969: an indifference to
what your religion might be when you moved to a new home, or
went after a job, or simply went about your life.

But the civil rights marchers had met a hostile response. So
Edward had left for England, and it was my luck that he now
had his own printing company and he wanted me to be his new
"apprentice" compositor: a "typesetter", amongst numerous
other things, using a computer. When I went to see where I
would be working, Edward showed me old photographs of
himself with other compositors in a large workroom. The room
was full of racks of cases of lead type. Edward explained that
there had been hundreds of cases in the room containing many
typefaces, each in many sizes. Then he showed me the
computer that I would be trained to use. It fitted on a single
desk. He told me that it had the capacity of several rooms the
size of the one on the photograph and it did the work of other
departments too.

"It's sad", he said, shaking his head, "an old trade destroyed
within a few years. Apprenticeships are a thing of the past.

Anyone sets type now." Edward was an enthusiast for typography, and he still used the language from the old composing room.

For the first few weeks, he had me helping around the works and running errands, and I was sent out with the van driver to deliver finished work. Then one afternoon he asked me to take a package to his home and told me I didn't have to come back that day.

When I got there, his wife, Eileen, explained that it was their daughter's birthday on the day I was to begin my training on the computer. The coincidence had given her the idea that I might like to meet some young people of my own age. Her daughter and her friends were getting together that afternoon to plan a weekend in the Lake District. It might just be the right time.

I wasn't sure how to respond. Edward and his wife were extraordinarily thoughtful and I liked the idea of going to the Lake District. We'd had interesting lessons at school about Wordsworth and the Lakes, and I'd been inspired to write some poetry myself. But I didn't want to go into a room full of strangers. So when Eileen called "Jeannette" and I heard a loud voice say, "Ask him if he's brought his Lambeg drum", I decided I wasn't going into that room.

A pretty red-haired girl came out looking angry and said, "Take no notice of stupid Jones".

We shook hands, but I didn't go in. Instead, Eileen asked me how I was finding my new job, and we talked for a few minutes. Then I went home with a box of cakes and thoughts that I might visit the Lake District by myself.

And that's what I did. At first Glynn was going to come with me. He was full of the idea, telling me how great the Lakes were in late October with the temperature just right for walking and wonderful scenery, especially the trees, their leaves all kind of shades of golden-brown. But that weekend he had the chance to start work behind the bar at St Cecilia's.

That's another story: Glynn had been after the job since he'd lost his old job on the Liverpool docks. Before I'd left home, dad had warned me to make sure that I paid my way because Glynn and Dolly had been through a bad time. Glynn had written, some time before, telling him that a strike had been provoked and then that striking dockers had been sacked and their jobs taken by other men who were working for worse pay and conditions. But Glynn never referred to the docks in my company. I think he was trying to put it behind him.

I was pleased to be going to the Lakes by myself. A part of me was unhappy that I had left Northern Ireland, and being on my own for a few days suited my mood. I'd felt good after that first night in St Cecilia's. The talk with Edward had left me with a better understanding of the Troubles at home. But after that I'd increasingly felt that I had run away rather than face up to what was happening in Ulster.

It seemed to me that an explosion into a new round of violence, even war, between Catholics and Protestants was possible. If Protestants weren't careful, who knows what might happen? Even though I had a good job and a large part of me wanted to stay in Liverpool, I was troubled.

I left the bus some miles short of my Lakeland hostel and spent the afternoon walking. This was what I wanted: my pack on my back, away from everyone. My route took me along a path beside a lake with a tree-covered island in the middle. There were mountains all around. The countryside was everything that uncle Glynn had said it would be. Just beyond the end of the lake a track went steeply uphill towards some mountain peaks. It wasn't part of my intended walk, but I couldn't resist it.

I had a library book in my pack, a book of Wordsworth's poems. When I was at school, my teacher had praised my poetry. She'd said it was mature and had read it out in front of the class. I'd fancied that some day I might write poems good enough to be published. But the only time I'd been able to complete anything was after Bernadette Martin's murder. I'd written the poem after weeks of feeling down. I'd written lines like, "Life's an acid in my chest. Acid thoughts run through my rest … And daylight hours are not for me …" And so on. I hardly knew where the words had come from. I wasn't happy with what I had written, but it was how I felt. I thought that coming to the place that had inspired Wordsworth might lift me and inspire me to write something less personal. If it didn't, I had Wordsworth himself to read.

Going uphill, I didn't let up. I felt as though I was made for hill walking. I passed a few parties of walkers. They seemed to be dawdling. When I reached what I had thought was the summit, I wasn't even out of breath. Just over the "top" there was a mini-valley, and then the ground rose again to higher peaks. In the centre of the "valley" was a small lake, a tarn. I sat, my back against a rock and watched the wind send ripples across the surface, while I ate my sandwiches.

I reached the hostel, I thought, too late for the evening meal. But the warden had kept my food hot for me. I ate alone.

After I had moved into my room and washed, I went down to the main common room with my book. Someone was playing a piano. I looked in. The room was almost full, and sitting at the piano with her back to me was a red haired-girl. The day that I had gone to the Harrington house, I'd caught a glimpse of my boss's red haired daughter sitting by a piano just before she had come out to meet me. Surely it couldn't be her? She *had* been coming to the Lakes. But the Lakes covered such a large area. I retreated, wondering if it could really be her and her friends in that room. There was a smaller common room. It was empty.

I found it hard to read. I'd enjoyed being on my own for the afternoon and had expected to be satisfied with my own company for the evening. But after looking into the other room, I couldn't settle. The hostel kiosk was due to open at seven, and it was almost that time, so I made my way there. There was already a queue, and the girl who had been at the piano was in it. It *was* Jeannette, my boss's daughter, and she recognised me.

Wide eyed, she asked, "You're Idris aren't you? Why didn't you come into the common room?"

Feeling embarrassed, I told her I had been reading in the other room. She wanted to know what I'd been reading. I answered, "Wordsworth".

"I don't believe it", she said. "I meant to bring *my* Wordsworth. But I forgot."

After queuing at the kiosk, she wanted to see my book and came back with me. And we talked. She told me about her family: about her older brother, Brian, who lived in Australia and her younger sister and how she hadn't wanted to work for her father because she had intended to become a teacher, but instead would be going into the Civil Service. And she told me that her father didn't normally drink the way he had on that night in St Cecilia's, but he had been affected by meeting me.

I told her about *my* family and uncle Len and David and about Bernadette Martin and the Quinn children and the terrible Omagh bombing. With her, I could talk about those things. By the end of the evening I was completely at ease in her company and was sorry that we had made separate arrangements for the weekend and would be going our different ways. And when I asked her if, when we returned to Liverpool, I could see her again and she said, "Yes", I could feel the thump-thump of my heart.

I didn't go to bed straight away. It would have been pointless. The unexpected encounter had energised me. Instead, I stood by the window. There was an almost cloudless sky, and a luminous moon lit the landscape …

3

The Meeting

WHEN IDRIS SET out the following morning a strong wind was blowing and a low ceiling of cloud moved rapidly across the sky. From the blown branches of the trees, the autumn leaves were being swept and scattered by the wind. Idris was surprised by his own energy. He'd stayed up late the night before and although he yawned occasionally, he walked all morning without effort. Eventually, after stopping by the roadside to eat his hostel sandwiches, he turned off the road and along the path that would take him over the mountain and into the next valley. Shortly afterwards he felt the first raindrops and before long was walking in a heavy downpour. Ahead if him, dense columns of rain hanging from the clouds swept down the mountainside and along the valley, battering everything in their path.

That morning Jeannette had spoken to him briefly while he was eating breakfast. She had come up from behind and put her hand on his shoulder, "Don't forget to phone".

He had started to move his chair back, but she had stopped him, "Don't get up. I'm sorry. They're waiting for me." Then she was gone. "Don't forget to phone." Just as if. He couldn't forget if he tried.

He walked on and up and over the mountain, the rain beating on his face and his clothes soaked. Apart from being with Jeannette, there was nowhere else he would rather have been. "What if the weather had broken last night", he thought? He might have gone out into the wind and rain. That would have been something, walking in the dark in the wind and the rain amongst the trees ... "I'll go out walking, in the wet black night", the words had come involuntarily, "The wind blowing unseen trees and ..." Should he shut his mind off and suppress them, or ... "and sweeping heavy rain across the fields". Idris felt in his pocket for his pen. He turned off the path and up a track through the woods beside a moss-covered wall. He stopped next to a tree, and in the shelter of the tree and the wall, took out his map, partly unfolded it and started to write on the back.

The rain found it's way on to the map, however hard he tried to shield it. He'd just have to remember the words and write them down later. He folded the map and put it back inside his pocket and was about to step out from the wall, when he heard a shout, "Hello!"

Idris peered through the trees, startled to discover that he wasn't alone. Further up the track, under a large overhanging boulder, a man was standing. "It's dryer up here", the man shouted.

Wondering how long he had been watched, and feeling apprehensive, Idris made his way up the muddy path through the rain.

The stranger was small and slightly built. "I hope I didn't spoil your poetry", he said.

Idris felt a lifting sensation in his scalp. It was impossible that anyone could have known what he'd been trying to write. "How did …?" The heavy rain suddenly turned into a torrential downpour, and the rock was giving no protection.

"If you'd like to shelter", the man pointed up through the trees, "I'm parked not far away".

Idris hesitated.

"I've a caravan. If you want to get out of this?"

"Er …"

The man laughed. "Don't worry. I won't eat you."

Idris laughed too, "Thank you … yes please".

They left the shelter of the woods and walked up the exposed hillside in the drenching rain, then along a narrow grassy valley little more than a furrow in the hillside. The ground squelched beneath their feet. The furrow curved to the right, and there at the end where the hill rose sharply again, was a caravan: no car, just an unusual looking caravan.

"Here we are", The stranger said as they reached the door.

Idris followed him out of the downpour and into the caravan. Inside was unlike any caravan he had ever seen. Around the sides, at chest height, was a long shiny panel displaying scenes similar to television pictures, as well as graphs and columns of figures. They were continuously changing, scenes and displays of figures fading and being replaced by new ones. Except for the door he had come in by, he couldn't see any windows or doors. Strangely, above the scenes and displays, he could see right through the side and the roof of the "caravan" to the outside world. In the centre of the floor the only furniture was a table and two chairs. The man was already sitting and pouring coffee into two cups. He pointed to the vacant chair, "Why don't you sit down and relax?"

As he did so, Idris realised that his clothes were dry.

"My name is Ian", said the man.

"Mine's Idris."

"I know", Ian said. "I know a great deal about you." He pointed towards a scene on the display panel. A group of people were sitting around a table talking.

Idris looked and when he realised who they were he stood up, "Good God".

"Yes it's Glynn and Dolly and Eileen and Edward and you."

"Who are you?"

Ian pushed a cup of coffee towards Idris, "It's going to be hard for you to accept that I am who I say I am".

Wondering what could be coming next, Idris sat down again.

Ian continued, "Can you accept that some day there might be space exploration from this planet: manned spaceships going out into space?"

"Yes I can."

"Well I'm sure then you can accept that one day space explorers from out there might come here. Although I doubt that you would expect that they would choose to meet *you*. But if they did, and one of them invited you into his 'caravan', it would be so extraordinary, you would take some convincing."

Ian stood up and as he did, above him on the ceiling appeared an image of the night sky. He took a few paces and stretched and pointed. "My home is about there, to the side of the Gemini constellation. You can't see it. It's a long way away, and it's hidden behind dust clouds." He took another step and pointed again. "More than two hundred years ago, we came through here. We were visiting various stars looking for planets that might support life. As we drew nearer to your sun, our observations of one of its planets looked more and more promising. So we came straight here. It was a huge moment in our history. We had discovered an, to us, extra-terrestrial intelligence." He sat down again.

"Before then our probes had seen many worlds, some teeming with life, but where no intelligences had evolved. *And* we'd discovered places where great intelligences had once flourished, but had perished. Then we found your Earth. That's who I am."

Idris knew that something abnormal was happening, but to believe what Ian was telling him would involve a huge leap of faith. This must be a carefully prepared practical joke, "I find it hard to believe ..."

"That's fine. Think what you like. Treat this as a hoax if you like. But if you'll have patience ..."

"But, even if it's true, why would you be interested in me?"

"In as few words as possible, because you have the most valuable asset on this planet: a universal morality. But that's only the start of my answer. For now. You are one of a small number of people we're contacting ... I can see that you're very tired. While we talk, would you like to take a refreshing walk?"

Idris looked outside. The rain was still battering down. "Now? In that rain?"

"This will be a walk with a difference. Take a look in that room." Ian pointed past Idris to a door he hadn't noticed. "Try lying down in there. Close your eyes. Relax, and see what happens."

Feeling strange and very tired, Idris went through the door and into a small room. The walls and ceiling were a pale, restful, green. There was a low bunk against one wall. Almost without thinking, he lay down. He had a sudden vision of a beach and surf. All he'd done was blink. Then he closed his eyes properly, and he was walking along a beach with Ian. He could feel a warm breeze in his face, and the surf was rolling almost to his feet. Inland, there were sandhills and beyond them pinewoods. Except for a few people in the distance, the beach was deserted. Out to sea ships, some of them sailing-ships, passed to and fro.

"*How did we get here?*"

"Open your eyes."

"They are open. Look."

"No make an effort. Try."

Idris thought about his eyes. He raised his eyebrows and then opened his eyes. He was lying on the bunk again, looking at the pale green ceiling. He closed them, and he was back on the beach with Ian, "Good God".

"Don't worry, you are actually resting. This is Liverpool Bay. If we were really here today, your great-grandfather Glynn and his brother Gareth would still be alive." He turned and pointed, "They'd be fifty miles in that direction, working in the Bethesda slate quarries".

Idris stopped and looked. He hadn't known about a great-grandfather Glynn.

When they resumed their walk, Ian continued, "Apart from your earth, our probes have never found another surviving intelligence. They've existed, many of them. They evolve regularly across the cosmos, but they quickly disappear. They fail to overcome the condition *we* call 'barbarism'. Your friend Edward referred to it as 'tribalism'. It's the same thing. It's a terminal condition. Yet, without exception, those failed races", he pointed up, "considered themselves civilized. They had an aptitude for self-delusion. They mistook high-technology barbarism for civilization.

"I want to show you something. I'm afraid it won't be pleasant, but I do need to show you. If you'll open your eyes?"

It wasn't easy. Idris stopped and made the effort, and he was lying looking at the ceiling again as the pale green gave way to a scene: a car was surrounded by soldiers, and one of the soldiers was forcing a man into it. There were other people in the car. The soldiers backed away, and one of them fired a rocket straight into the vehicle, and it exploded into flames. The scene changed. A group of horsemen were riding down a mountain track. From the saddles of some of the horses hung human heads. The scene changed again. An ambulance was travelling along a street. Suddenly a helicopter appeared above and fired, and the ambulance exploded and crashed. The doors flew open and, for a brief moment, bodies were visible. One was a tiny girl. A blindfolded man is kneeling besides a ditch. Another man stands behind him with a sword ... Horrible scene followed horrible scene in rapid succession.

Idris heard Ian's voice, "Close your eyes when you're ready to come back". He closed his eyes and was glad to be back on the beach with Ian. What he had seen had left him shaken. *And* he was filled with a stunning, mind-altering acceptance: Ian looked ordinary; he wouldn't stand out amongst a crowd; yet he was who he said he was: a visitor from another world.

Ian intruded, "A whole lifetime wouldn't be enough for you to see all that we've recorded here. What you saw was the almost inevitable outcome of your cousin David's kind of thinking. That's why your disagreements with David were more than mere differences of opinion. Your cousin represents an evolutionary dead end, and you represent the chance of a future."

Still shaken, Idris asked, "Are you different ... from us?"

"We think we are ... now. But our history has been almost as bloody as yours. In one respect, it's been worse. We destroyed another human species."

"A human species? A whole human race?"

"We did. And the shame ..."

"How? Why did you do it?"

"I'll tell you how it happened. Our geography is different from yours. We have two polar continents, and the ocean between is filled with Islands. Our people had originated in the north but had been spreading through the islands for thousands of years. We didn't reach the southern continent until our equivalent of your eighteenth century, and we found another highly intelligent species living there. The land was unspoilt, full of natural resources. It had everything the northern trading companies were looking for.

"The imperial powers had parcelled out large areas of ocean and its islands to the imperial trading companies. Once one of these companies set foot on an island they could do what they liked with it. Tragically, it was the most rapacious company from the most predatory imperial power that took control of the Southland.

"They tried to turn the other advanced species into a race of slaves. But they found they had a fight on their hands. Just one of the Quats, as they were called, had twice the strength of a would-be slave-master, and they could be formidable opponents. So the company decided to exterminate them. The blood bath lasted for years ... 'Quat' by the way means 'smart animal'.

"Actually the people of my island, my ancestors, were virtually wiped out by the same company. We were regarded as primitives.

"Amongst the company soldiers hunting the Quats, was a young man called Aquiros. He'd become familiar with the Quats before the killing started. As the campaign went on, he became sickened and refused to kill any more. An ordinary soldier would have been tried and put into slavery, or shot. But because of his family's high social position, he was just shipped home.

"While he was on the ship, he wrote a pamphlet appealing for the killing to stop. He called the Quats 'human'. He said that despite their being physically different, they had all the essential attributes of human beings: they lived in communities; they had language; they passed sophisticated information on to their children, but above all they were capable of love and morality. What they didn't have, he said, was the capacity for large-scale war: they lived in small communities, and although they had some effective weapons, they had no firearms. At the end of his pamphlet he asked, 'Why is it that we always prey on the vulnerable?' Then he gave *his* answer: 'It is because our barbarous culture distorts our nature and leads us to betray our true selves: our natural love and humanity'.

"He managed to get his pamphlet published, but the power of the imperial companies was too great. Aquiros failed to save the Quats, and he never got over it. He couldn't forgive himself for his own part in what had happened and went to live on a remote island. While he was there, he studied the way of life of the people and compared it with how so-called civilized man lived. His major work, he wrote it while he was there, made him the outstanding figure of our Enlightenment.

"It began with the words, 'The pursuit of wealth and power erodes and often utterly destroys human values'. And he explained from his own experience how the powerful used their wealth and power to pursue even more wealth and power and refused to concede to anything but superior power.

"He argued that most people in 'civilized' society become de-humanised in one way or another and that as societies advanced, people with wealth and power came to regard the majority as inherently inferior, even as subhuman and treated them inhumanely. The rulers de-humanised themselves because they turned their back on their natural humanity, while the majority lost access to the full fruits of human culture.

"He said that whenever a vulnerable human group was lorded over by another group, both sides were de-humanised. Those who preyed on the vulnerable, de-humanised themselves by their behaviour, while the victims were denied their full humanity. He also said that whenever human groups were in violent conflict, a dehumanising process always took place.

"Aquiros's work was an appeal for a universal morality. He wrote about how, when he had worked for an imperial company, he'd seen entire peoples, including the Quats, being denied the most rudimentary rights as human beings. And he went back through history showing that this was common behaviour.

"In the North, it was a time of clamour for the Rights of Man. Aquiros argued that this was fine, but that everyone was a member of a human group of one kind or another and it was always being found convenient to exclude whole groups from full human consideration. He was the first to say that for individual human rights to be universal, there had to be group rights too and that all human groups had to be included. This was the argument that was eventually to have such an impact on our history

and perhaps made us different. Aquiros drew up an ency-
clopaedia of human groups and their integral rights, starting with
people sharing a geographic location: their right to their land was
inviolable, etc … he listed a whole range of human groupings and
what he claimed was their natural rights.

"It caused a storm. It didn't suit the imperial companies; they
had their writers claiming that a natural inequality underlay all
human affairs, with the most deserving rising to the top. But this
didn't explain why whole peoples had to be treated with
contempt, or why entire classes in the North lived a wretched
existence.

"Aquiros's influence eventually helped us to realise that we
couldn't carry on in the old way, and we changed. The change
wasn't easy. It wasn't smooth. We'd experienced many of the
barbarities that you've experienced. But we managed to avoid
the colossal barbarities of your world wars and of your modern
colonial wars. The comparable time in our history was probably
our turning point. Aquiros was long dead by then, but his ideas
had had huge influence. Other thinkers had taken them up and
developed them, and vulnerable groups had many allies, and
brutish behaviour became criminal. Colonists, especially the
giant companies, couldn't continue to behave as though the
world existed just for them. *And* the powerful knew that they
were liable to be brought to account before a world tribunal for
their behaviour.

"But we weren't moral Olympians and nothing was straightforward. There had to be many changes, small as well as large. But
we avoided", Ian pointed to the blue sky, "those genocidal struggles. Instead, we managed to lift our minds and think beyond our
little pond. And we turned our attention to the real problem:
surviving in an inhospitable universe …"

"The food's ready." The real Ian was calling. Idris opened his
eyes. He lay for a few moments, realising that he had been in a
deep sleep. Then he went into the main compartment. The table
was laid with food, and Ian was already sitting, and he was smiling,
"Come in. You must be hungry".

Idris sat down.

"How do you feel?"

"How do I feel …? Dazed."

"You'll feel fine when you've eaten … I know you'll like it …
Italian food. Let's relax." Immediately their surroundings
changed, and they were sitting in a restaurant. They were at the

same table, with the same food but surrounded by other tables. The people sitting at them had dark hair. The men wore suits and the women long dresses and jewellery. Above the clatter of knives and forks, there were foreign voices.

Ian leaned forward, "Turin, 1940".

As they started to eat, a man carrying a violin walked out on to a small stage. He stood still for a few seconds. Then as the talking fell away, he bowed and there was clapping. Raising his violin, he started to play. It wasn't the kind of music Idris was familiar with, but he found it beautiful and emotional. The man came down from the stage and walked amongst the diners, playing while they ate. A woman went on to the stage and sang while the violinist played his music. A lovely voice accompanied by beautiful music.

They had finished eating. The Italian restaurant was gone, but they still sat at the table. The night sky through the roof of the "caravan", now miraculously clear, was filled with stars.

"Why have we contacted *you*? We've a problem. We don't want this world of yours to go the way of so many others. But we don't know if your race has the capacity to move beyond your present condition. We'd like to help. But it would be useless even trying, in spite of people like yourself, if your race as a whole is incapable of changing. So, for now, we're limiting our contact to a few people, and you're one of them!"

"But what can I do to help?"

"Left to yourself, you would never appreciate your own value ... we'd like to accelerate your learning ..."

"You already have."

Ian laughed, "I suppose we have ... we want to see the effect on the people around them of individuals who represent the very best in human nature, and you are one of those people. But, first, we would like you to have a wide knowledge of the human experience. You can acquire that knowledge over this weekend, easily, if you want to. We can start tonight, while you sleep, by letting you see into the lives of others from around your world. You'll 'live' part of the life of each one of those people in turn. And then if you accept ..."

"I'll just have to lie on the bunk?"

"You've got it. You'll feel as though you're having the soundest sleep of your life; I'll let you sample a small number of people tonight, to see how you like it. I'll be able to tell at any time if you want to wake up. Then tomorrow, if you agree, we'll continue with many more people, *and* you'll absorb many books …"

When the evening was over, almost dizzy from his experience, Idris went into the green room and lay on the bed wondering how such a thing could be happening. Then he closed his eyes …

4

Thanasis

I'M LYING ON the grass with my rifle and ammunition beside me. Down at the bottom of the hill, my would-be captors are smoking. I can smell the rich sharp fragrance of their tobacco smoke. I can picture them sitting patiently behind the rocks, puffing on their pipes, knowing that, with a steep cliff behind me, I've nowhere else to go but down. I've shown them I'm a good shot. So it makes sense for them to wait. I keep getting the urge to creep down the hill to where Mikis and Stephanos lie, but there's little point. My friends are certainly dead. The Security Battalionists made sure of that. I'll try to escape after dark. I'll have to move over open ground, but I don't have a choice. My own end might or might not be imminent, but I know that the movement, the often-heroic movement, that I've been a part of, is irrevocably dead.

My old life before the bloodletting now seems unreal and remote. Was that life normal and the years since abnormal, or the other way around? I don't know. Mother and father were once real, live, flesh-and-blood people, who chastised me and loved me and coached me, for what they hoped would be a scholarly future. Mother was an experienced nurse and father a manager in an import/export bank. My brother Andoni too, was once a real, live, ever-present companion. Now, mother, father and Andoni: they've become dream-like memories.

I didn't realise it at the time, but the day I saw two strange children walking along the pavement below our apartment was the day that ended the old life. It's true that even before then, father had helped stranded British soldiers to safety. We'd have had them staying in our apartment, if it hadn't been for the senior policeman living in the flat below. And it's true that Andoni had gone by then. Greece had surrendered before he had a chance to fight the German invasion. With some of his army comrades he left on the day of the surrender, hoping to be a part of a future invasion force that would drive the Germans out. Apart from Andoni's absence, family life remained remarkably unchanged. Father's job had disappeared. But even before the trouble with Mussolini, he had used his savings to buy gold sovereigns, and we'd probably have been able to eke out the war eating off the black-market.

The two children were a puzzle. They were hardly moving. A small boy, little more than a toddler, was being led by the hand by a girl who was hardly older than himself. They were moving with such economy of effort that I had to watch for a while before I was sure that they weren't standing still. I called mother.

"There's something wrong with them", she said. "Keep your eyes on them. I'm going down."

It turned out that the children were starving and sick. I've felt guilty since, but I didn't want them to stay with us. I was desperately sorry for them, but I thought it would be preferable to return them home and give them the help they needed there.

Mother disagreed. She fed and bathed them and afterwards tried to interest them in some of my old toys and books. But it was obvious they were very tired. So she put them to bed.

Afterwards she talked to me, "Thanasis, you know our history. Remember Themistocles' time: the Persian invasion. Remember how Athenians put aside selfishness for the sake of Athens? Think of what happened. They could have enriched themselves by sharing out the wealth from the silver mines. Instead, they pooled the money so that Athens could build a new fleet. Without that fleet the people of Athens couldn't have survived the Persian invasion. Well, we're living in similar times." She pointed towards Andoni's bedroom where the children were asleep, "Greece is suffering. We can't stand aside. We must be part of whatever happens to our country."

I knew well that period of our history, and I knew that mother was right. Xerxes the Persian King had brought to Greece an army so large, Athenians had had to abandon Athens. They could never have survived if a few years before, Themistocles hadn't managed to persuade Athenians to put aside personal desires and build the fleet that would later save them by smashing the Persian fleet. I accepted what mother said, and anyhow, like it or not, my old sheltered life was about to end.

Mother and father had been horrified that a man like Hitler, with his belief that his own race was special and had greater rights than others, was the leader of the most powerful nation in Europe. Father predicted that with such an ideology, wherever Hitler's armies marched, life would become hell. So when the German army came to Greece and they were so orderly and normal, we were surprised.

Ultimately though, father was proved right for behind the deceptive orderliness, Hitler's extreme xenophobia was in command. Fortunately, Greeks weren't one of the peoples marked down by Hitler for slavery like the Slavs, or elimination like the Jews and Gypsies, and he hadn't wanted Greek land for German settlement, as he had with Poland and other Slavic lands. But Greeks weren't Germans, and within weeks the German Army had begun their organised looting of our country.

I watched the two children emerge from their apathy, as it slowly dawned on them that they were free to play around the flat. They moved around, sliding their hands across the polished furniture and feeling the texture of the curtains and the carpets and eventually chasing around the table and behind the settee. By then, we'd visited their home in the Dourgouti district and seen the grim life they would be returning to. Mother decided that, at the least, we would keep the children and their father in food. There was no mother in the family; Dougouti had a high mortality rate. It was through the children and Dourgouti that we discovered there was an organisation struggling to provide relief for starving Athenians.

Mother and father quickly became immersed in relief work, and I ran errands, delivering messages and medicines and was sent along specific routes through the city, noting the activities of German and Italian soldiers and reporting back. I saw sights I had never imagined I would see in Athens: skeletal Athenians dying on the pavements, municipal workers with carts collecting the dead.

Then one night in May 1941, something happened that captured the Nation's imagination. Two young heroes, Manilos Glezos and Apostolous Santos, removed the swastika from the top of the Acropolis. People talked about it for weeks: how an example had been set, how it had signalled that we Greeks wouldn't take the occupation lying down and that perhaps it was time for national resistance.

Nicos, a family friend, told father that the Communist leader, Giorgis Siantos, had already appealed to the leaders of the other political parties to come together to create a Resistance. Some of the smaller parties had responded, but the big parties, the prominent leaders, weren't interested. Some of them, including Papendreou, the Social Democrat, had been imprisoned and only recently released by the Italians. Jail seemed to have warned them off active resistance.

Mother was talking impatiently, as I walked into the room one evening, "We have to take things as they are. It didn't matter to us who was running relief; we joined in because we were needed ..." Nicos and Captain Othoneos had come to dinner to discuss whether to join the new resistance movement.

Father had answered, "But this is different. This is armed struggle. Can we trust the Stalinists?"

Mother was persistent, "Alex, the Communists have asked all parties to join in. It won't be their fault if they're left to run the Resistance. Do we resist or don't we? It's as simple as that."

Then Captain Othoneos said, "There's something wrong with Greece if only the Communists fight the Germans. They don't want it that way themselves. They're trying to get a coalition: a Popular Front. They've even said they'll work with Royalists. I want to fight, and if it's alongside Greeks who happen to be Communists, that's okay."

Nicos agreed, "That's my attitude ... and Churchill's. Didn't he say that to defeat Hitler, he would welcome the Devil as an ally."

Father laughed, "You're so persuasive". He turned to Captain Othoneos, "What about the other officers?"

Captain Othoneos pulled a face, "Too many of them expect to be paid ..."

Resistance wasn't left to the Communists. Thousands of ordinary men and women and youths and even children, joined the new movement, EAM. And we were amongst them. The relief organisation en-block joined EAM. Father and his two friends, Nicos and Captain Othoneos, joined ELAS, the military wing of EAM.

Father's time with ELAS was short. In the spring of 1942, he and his two friends were arrested as they arrived at a secret meeting. They were imprisoned and held as hostages, to be shot in reprisal for future ELAS actions. It was a worrying time, and it was brought to an end in a sickening way. The Germans carried out a mass shooting of prisoners, but didn't release the names of the victims. It was calculated agony for the families. Then, as a "concession" to Archbishop Damoskinos, they allowed the clothes of the dead to be hung up in the Archbishop's palace for identification.

Mother and I went to the palace. It was a heart-rending scene: hundreds of relatives searching amongst the bloody clothes, hoping their husbands or sons or fathers were still alive. Mother and I were amongst them, and we found father's jacket stiff with his dried blood. Captain Othoneos's clothes were there too and Nicos's trousers. Nicos had managed to secret a letter to his family into the pocket, even though he could hardly have expected it would ever reach them. It had effectively said, "Don't grieve for me. I am proud to die for such a cause as ours."

Mother took father's death very badly. She considered it was her pressure that had pushed father into EAM. I tried to persuade her that although father had been more deliberate than her in making his commitment, that was his normal approach. He liked to consider carefully what lay ahead. But knowing father's views, nothing would have stopped him from joining. And arrest and death were risks we'd all taken.

In spite of my arguments, mother remained preoccupied with what she considered to be her own part in father's death. That was until an evening a few weeks later when we were walking home. Our neighbour, the policeman's wife, came hurrying towards us and stopped right in front of mother, "Thank goodness I've caught you. They're waiting to arrest you."

Mother smiled and said, "That's okay Phillipa" and tried to continue home.

But Phillipa stood in her way. "You can't go home. You'll *both* be arrested." She pushed a parcel into mother's hands. "Take this. Food and money." She hugged mother and whispered, "I admire you. So does Vlanias." Then she turned and kissed me, "Thanasis, somewhere there's a girl … she doesn't know how lucky she's going to be". Then she hurried away. She'd taken a chance. If the wrong person had seen her, she would suffer the same fate as father.

It was the shock mother needed. *Her son was in danger.* EAM got us out of Athens and into the mountains, where ELAS was growing in strength. I didn't want to leave Athens. The spirit of the place: the courage of Athenians demonstrating and striking in defiance of the occupation.

In the mountains I resumed my old role as a conveyor of infor-mation. I become a "runner": a carrier of messages and my legs became hard from travelling the mountain tracks. I always seemed to be hungry. But it was understood that runners had to be fed adequately, and I'd never felt healthier. Travelling amongst the mountain communities, seeing the basic lives so many lived, brought back the feeling I had had, when I first went to the Dourgouti, that in my own life I had been very fortunate.

I considered it a stroke of luck that I had to deliver a message to Aris, our ELAS Kapetan. It gave me the opportunity to hear him address a public meeting. It was a time when the Nazi armies were successful everywhere, and we felt alone and in an unequal struggle. But Aris was able to see ahead. And in his speech, he told us that we weren't merely fighting the occupation; we were a movement of citizens, preparing for the democratic Greece we would have when the Nazis were defeated, and there would be no return to King and Dictatorship. He told us we must remember that we weren't alone in our struggle. Other nations were doing the same as we were. They too, were fighting for freedom, and when the war was won, we would have a better Greece in a better world. Listening to Aris, my spirits lifted.

Later, going up a steep track, I overtook a column of mules carrying supplies for the guerrillas. I could see from the mule-handlers' tired faces and the way they walked, that they had been on the road for a long time. *They* were part of the movement of citizens that Aris had talked about. In my heart I was with them. I wanted to lift them from this situation. Reward them. Give them the lives they deserved.

My admiration for Aris was shaken, when on another occasion I saw how he treated a cattle thief. The local villagers were brought to watch while he had the man beaten. Then Aris himself shot him. Later, my new friend, Mikis, seeing how I had been affected, "explained": "What Aris did wasn't thoughtless punishment. We are in a desperate situation, and anyone who preys on the people has to be made an example of. Aris hates violence. You can be sure of that. But he won't flinch from using it against an enemy of the people."

I didn't know what to think. I found it hard to accept that someone who could be so inspiring would have a man beaten who was about to die.

One evening a new arrival from Athens told us that the British were pressing a Colonel Zervas to create a rival liberation movement. I asked him, "What have the British got against us?"

"They want control", he answered. "Apparently they've paid Zervas a lot of money, but he's still hanging around in Athens."

Eventually the British pressured Zervas and other officers to go to Epirus to start their new organisation and supplied them well.

I was worried. I couldn't understand why, unless they had ulterior motives, anyone would want to create a rival organisation.

During weapons training, I discovered that I was a crack shot and was allowed to join the same guerrilla unit as my friend, Mikis. I went out on policing duties disarming over zealous government gendarmes and fake guerrillas and thieves who preyed on the farmers. And, to my surprise, I was allowed to go on the operation to blow up the Gorgopotamos viaduct. I was uneasy, because we were doing it for the British. British explosives officers and Zervas and his men would be part of the operation. I doubted the commitment of the Zervas people. But they fought well, and the British demolition team were impressive, although Zervas himself tried to call the operation off before the bridge was blown.

I fired on the enemy for the first time that night, and I can recall every detail. The fire of the Italian guards was holding us up and I went forward to a tree standing on its own in the open. I can remember thinking that it had probably been left standing to act as a range finder and that I might make an easy target. But I was prepared to die. I can still remember the dead leaves from a broken branch touching my cheek, as I held the rifle firm and ever so carefully pulled the trigger back. I managed to fire into the slit in the blockhouse, and the machine-gun fire stopped immediately. Others ran forward in the dark, firing as they went. Our end of the bridge was taken shortly afterwards.

While we had been engaging the guards, the British had been under the bridge at work with explosives and, as we were celebrating our victory, there was a tremendous explosion, and part of the structure of the viaduct collapsed into the gorge below.

I felt mixed emotions about what I'd done. I went into the blockhouse to see if perhaps the man I'd shot was only wounded. But someone had thrown grenades inside, and there was no one left alive. I knew that any one of the defenders might have been one of those Italians who hated Mussolini and Hitler and had been conscripted against his will and would have been as much an innocent victim as any slain Greek. After I'd seen the contorted Italian bodies, I couldn't join the jubilation. It was evident even then, that many Italian hearts weren't in the war and wanted no more of Mussolini and Hitler than we Greeks did.

But Gorgopotamos had been so necessary. The British were on the offensive in Africa, and blowing the viaduct had cut the German supply-line.

It wasn't surprising that the Germans, when they shot members of the Resistance, claimed they were shooting "Communists". And later when their puppet Government formed the Security Battalions from collaborationist Greeks, they said it was to hunt down "Communists". And when the perverse Colonel Grivas and his "X Battalion" took arms from the Germans to assassinate EAM members, he claimed he was killing "Communists".

What was unforgivable was that Churchill too distorted the truth. He called EAM "Communist" and ELAS fighters "Bandits". Raptist, the German's puppet Prime Minister, happily quoted Churchill to ease the conscience of collaborators who might have had doubts about their work. I've no doubt that Churchill's attitude expanded the ranks of the collaborators.

The truth was that we in EAM were a mixture. Regardless of any politics we might have, we had been thrown together by war. There *were* Communists, with their contradictory beliefs, who wanted to create the most just society the world has ever seen, yet regarded a tyrant like Stalin as a God-like figure. But they were a minority. There were also Liberals and Socialists and Conservatives and even Royalists, although many people I met in EAM couldn't be pigeonholed. We were Greeks and we displayed a range of outlooks and idiosyncratic views. But what was important was that we were all passionately committed to the struggle to free Greece, which was why we had joined the Resistance.

Compared to the power of the German military machine, our power was puny. We all knew that. That was why the larger struggle was so important to us and we were bitterly disappointed that, despite our commitment, we suffered Churchill's hostility.

But there was Roosevelt. *Everyone* had faith in him. The belief in Roosevelt was phenomenal. Before the war Aunt Yerania had often mentioned Roosevelt in her letters from Chicago. She'd been full of praise for him and his assistant, Harry Hopkins. Once she sent Roosevelt's photograph and a quote from one of his speeches. Mother had them both framed. They were on the wall for years, and I can remember the quote, "… it is literally true that the 'self supporting' man or woman has become as extinct as the man of the Stone Age. Without the help of thousands of others, any one of us would die naked and starved."

Aunt Yerania told us that Roosevelt and Harry Hopkins were looked on by some as dangerous radicals, even as Communists. So they had *that* in common with EAM. It *was* true that Greeks had been radicalised by the Occupation, and it was reflected in EAM.

I would have betted though that EAM would have voted for a Greek Franklin Roosevelt, but never for a Greek Stalin.

In order to establish their total control of Epirus, Zervas's forces over-ran EAM areas, and they had British officers with them when they did it. They had little trouble destroying our poorly armed, largely civilian, organisation and killing some of our members.

My unit received instructions to be prepared to join an operation to eject Zervas from his conquest. I was impatient. I wanted to strike back at once. But Sarafis our ELAS military commander was attempting to persuade the British to call Zervas back to his original area.

Unlike myself, Mikis was patient, "Learn to trust your leaders", he scolded. "Sarafis is concentrating on the Germans. He doesn't want Greek fighting Greek. Anyway", he shrugged, "that's how good leaders behave: diplomacy first".

I tried to argue, "But the British probably ordered the attack. Why talk to *them?*"

"They might have done. But Zervas might have ordered the attack himself. He's been sounding off about 'Communists' for a while now. You listen to the BBC don't you? If we attack Zervas, all the world will hear is that *we* attacked *him*. We'll be the villains."

Mikis's assessment of who would be blamed turned out to be right. Zervas continued his attacks, and when eventually we launched *our* offensive against *him*, all that the world heard was, "The Communist's attempt to take over in Greece". But the battle was a long time coming, and I felt Mikis was stretching the meaning of patience too far. I despised Zervas. His "Resistance" was causing the deaths of young ELAS fighters who had joined our movement to resist a foreign occupation, not to die at the hands of fellow Greeks.

I'd hardly seen mother since we had left Athens. After we reached Thessaly our work had separated us. While I became a "runner" she became a travelling medic, treating the sick and sometimes the wounded. I occasionally heard about her work and knew that she was popular. I understood why.

We came together again, when to my surprise, she sent a message to my unit asking if I could accompany her on a longer journey than she was used to. I don't know if it was just that she wanted us to be together again, or if it's possible that she had some kind of premonition that she didn't understand.

That last month together was a happy one. I could see that

mother was born for her work. We were short of most of the medical supplies she needed, but she had a rule she carried with her: hygiene. I seemed always to be boiling linen and bandages and needles and clothes and sometimes, sharp knives.

We eventually detoured to the small town of Komeno when mother received a message that there were sick babies there. The babies had badly upset stomachs, and mother decided she would set up a clinic and stay until they were all safely better.

There was fear in the little town. A few days before we arrived, a small group of ELAS fighters had visited Komeno to buy food. They'd left their rifles in the main street just before a German motorcycle patrol came in. The Germans saw the weapons and quickly drove out again. Naturally, the townspeople were fearful of what the consequences might be. The Mayor advised mother that it would be safer for her if she left. But she considered she had work to do. I hid my rifle and ammunition well away from Komeno.

One morning at the clinic, an incredibly beautiful woman brought her baby in, and I couldn't stop looking at her. I felt extremely embarrassed when, on her way out, she stopped in front of me. But to my relief she didn't scold me. She asked, "You're Thanasis aren't you?"

"Y-yes", I just about managed to answer.

"My oldest boy, Stephanos, he's very shy. He saw you with your rifle. He asked me to ask if you'd like you to go hunting with him? And if you and your mother are free, perhaps you'll come and share whatever we have in the pot?"

That was how Stephanos and I happened to be away from Komeno when the Germans came.

We were out very early the next morning, walking along the riverbank until we reached a reedy area some way from the town. Then we lay down and crawled slowly through the reeds towards the water. I didn't have my gun. I'd gone along to see the young hunter in action, and I was looking past him, wondering which of the fowl would later be on our dinner plates and Stephanos was waving with his hand, "Keep your head down", when there was an explosion from the direction of Komeno.

That was the start. As we hurried back, there was constant gunfire and more explosions. When we got closer, we could see many people fleeing across the river, and Stephanos went after them to try to find his family. I carried on with his gun in case I came across a German picket, but with such a light weapon, I'd have been fortunate to survive any encounter. I got close to Komeno but there was nothing I could do but wait.

When the Germans had gone and I entered Komeno, I wandered amongst the burning buildings and the bodies, looking in vain for someone alive, until I found mother dead. At the sight of her, I felt on the point of collapse, and it was only by sheer will that I remained on my feet.

The Germans had killed everyone, of any age, they found in the town. The only survivors were those who had escaped across the river. I kept telling myself that mother had made a choice and had known what might happen, and I was able to cope.

I can remember little of my journey back to Mikis and my unit. I'd left soon after the emotional service for the dead, where my own grief had been overwhelmed by the grief of Komeno, and my feelings were still there. But I was going back to fight; I understood why Sarafis had wanted to avoid Greek-on-Greek conflict: nothing should divert us from the struggle against the Germans. I felt angry at the thoughtlessness of the ELAS fighters who had left their weapons on view in the main street. But that anger was nothing to what I felt about "soldiers" who, because they had seen a few rifles that, admittedly, would probably be used against them, had conducted no enquiries or interrogations but had slaughtered hundreds of total innocents and had they caught them would have slaughtered hundreds more. Whatever the British were up to, they'd committed no Komeno.

I'd been back with my unit for a day. Mikis had said it was important that I make a detailed report on Komeno. We'd gone into Evyenia's little office. Mikis had poured me a full glass of wine and said, "Don't keep your emotions in. We want to hear everything. Evyenia will write down what's necessary."

I'd thought to myself, "You don't know me. I'll make a matter-of-fact report." But I found myself angrily telling him about the thoughtless stupidity of the ELAS men who had so casually left their weapons in the main street.

Then someone outside shouted, "Mikis, there's a lad here. He wants to see Thanasis." Puzzled, we went outside.

Stephanos was there, looking awkward and hot, carrying his rifle and a bag. The last time I'd seen him, he had been in shock and I had felt guilty leaving. He raised his arms a little and let them fall as though he didn't know what to say. Then, "I've been a day behind you all the way. You were travelling so fast, I couldn't catch up."

"Stephanos, if only I'd known."

"I want to join ELAS … with you."

"What about Komeno?"

"There's nothing to keep me there … I want to thank you."

"Thank me?"

"You kept your head. Then you came back here to fight. That's why I followed you." He raised his rifle a little, "I want to fight too".

Mikis walked over and put his arm around Stephanos's shoulder. "You've come to the right place. How would you like an Italian rifle? A crack weapon. Almost new. A Modello 6.5."

While Stephanos ate and drank, we told him about the training he would receive and what would be expected of him. "You know how to use cover Stephanos", I reminded him. "I saw you. You probably could have got close enough to catch one of those birds bird with your hands. Don't forget that skill. If you get the chance to fire at a German, keep hidden. Don't expose yourself."

Mikis winked at Stephanos, "The way Thanasis did at Gorgopotomas!"

Stephanos looked amazed, "Thanasis was at Gorgopotomas?"

"We both were …"

The next day, while Stephanos began his military instruction, I gave my report on Komeno.

Not long before Liberation, I was asked to act as a runner again, and one late summer afternoon, I found myself in unfamiliar territory with time on my hands. I went walking in the forest until, just after the trees gave way to open hillside, I came upon a ruined village. Every house had been either wrecked with explosives, or burnt. I sat in a seat built into a stone wall around an overgrown garden and let the afternoon pass.

I found myself thinking about Andoni and how marvellous it would be, if he had survived, to see him again soon and whether it would be possible for us to live Aris's vision of the future: a free Greece in a free world. To me, just a normal life without war would be *something*. But would that be possible? There had been so much division between Greeks, so much killing. There were thousands of Greeks in the Security Battalions doing the Nazis' dirty work. The latest fugitives from Athens had brought news that the Security Battalions and other collaborators had been rounding up the inhabitants of whole areas of the city. Hundreds of supposed EAM sympathisers had been identified, and some had been shot on the spot. The rest had been either kept as hostages, to be shot later, or shipped to Germany for forced labour. Young men were regularly hung from the Acacia trees lining the streets of central Athens. One girl had fled to EAM after seeing her boyfriend hanging in Omonia Square, guarded by Security Battalionists. The Battalionists did their work in the villages too. I loathed them, and my basic instinct was to pay them back in kind. But I'd tried to stand back and think about what was happening to us. I'd talked to Stephanos about how horrible it was that one measure of our success was the number of people we killed; although I did remind him that ELAS shot German prisoners *only* in retaliation for the hostages shot by the Germans. But Stephanos wasn't interested. He said he would have shot Germans anyway. *He* was a good example of the affects of the war on many people. When the Germans had launched a big offensive he smiled and said, "Now I don't have to go looking for them". It wasn't bravado. He meant it. He took part in some very bloody ambushes and never took prisoners. It was circumstance more than anything that had shaped Stephanos and myself and the other ELAS fighters and perhaps our opponents too …

"Are you okay?"

I'd forgotten where I was. I turned around. A young man, not much older than myself, was looking over the wall at me. I asked him, "Am I trespassing?"

"Don't worry. I'm Stathis. This is my father's house. I've brought my goats. Okay if we come in?"

"Of course. It's your garden Stathis."

Two goats came running into the garden. Stathis followed. "It's crazy I know", he said, "but I always look in first to see if there are any Germans here".

"It's best to be careful. I'm Thanasis. It's a shame about your house."

"Yes. We used to have a fine flock of sheep", Stathis pointed at the house, "but when the Germans came, they took them. We stay in the pen up the mountain now. The wife has just had a baby … do you think the British will be here before the winter?"

He didn't wait for an answer. Stathis went on to tell me how hard his family had worked to build up their flock and how they planned to build it up again when peace returned and how he was getting a small income from collecting resin from the pine trees and how full of life the baby was and much else.

After a while I left Stathis in his garden with his goats and his ambitions and his uncomplicated expectation of normality once the British came. Stathis gave me hope. Perhaps the desire to get on with life would prevail.

But so much was happening that caused me to fear it wouldn't be so. The German army was in danger of being trapped in our country by the advance of the Red Army across Eastern Europe. And as they were beginning their withdrawal, we were fighting our last battles with them. We in ELAS were taking part in Operation Ark, designed by the British to hurt the enemy before they withdrew. Yet we were always short of ammunition. The British were withholding fresh supplies, even at critical moments when our fighters were running out of ammunition and on the point of defeat. We had long understood in ELAS that our British "allies" wanted to weaken us. But now they were doing it with a vengeance and we were losing many fighters.

We had long since repulsed Zervas's attacks on us. But right at the beginning of Operation Ark, ELAS units were attacked by a small British-sponsored "Resistance" group, EKKA. Our Military Commander, Sarafis, asked the EKKA leader, Colonel Psarros, to arrest those who were guilty of killing ELAS members. But the attacks continued so ELAS responded by disbanding EKKA. During the fighting, both ELAS and EKKA men died, including Colonel Psarros. Even though they knew exactly what had happened, the British used the incident to accuse us of being terrorists and of murdering Colonel Psarros. Then, Zervas's forces attacked our 15th Regiment while it was fighting the Germans in a battle for survival at Kalamas.

I was in a state of rage when Sarafis came and addressed our Regiment and told us to be prepared for an offensive to crush Zervas. Sarafis had just come back from Lebanon where he had met senior British officers as well as Papandreou, who had been chosen by Churchill to be Greece's Prime Minister. Sarafis told us how, when our Greek army of volunteers in Africa had demonstrated and demanded respect and recognition for EAM and ELAS, they had been treated as mutineers and purged. The majority had been imprisoned in camps behind barbed wire. The remainder had been formed into a Monarchist army that could be relied upon to serve the British Prime Minister and put the King back on the throne.

Sarafis had even discovered while he was in Egypt, that Churchill had instructed the BBC to promote the Royalist cause and not present ELAS or its military operations in a favourable light and *not to criticise the German-controlled Security Battalions.* Our Commander left us with the warning that after Liberation, Churchill was likely to treat Greece as a conquered country and ELAS as his enemy.

Events moved so fast, that the planned attack on Zervas never took place. Contrary to accusations about our intentions, even though we controlled most of the country and by then had captured enough German arms to do it, ELAS never seized power when the Germans left. We cooperated with the British forces, and EAM nominees took only minor places in the Churchill-dominated Government. But our cooperation wasn't appreciated. Ridiculously, EAM wasn't invited to take part in the Liberation celebrations and was denied a serious role in the new civil power: the British were in control.

There were many unfriendly acts by the British military, including the treacherous instructions to the Security Battalions to keep their arms and not to surrender to ELAS. It was obvious that trouble was brewing. The specially selected Monarchist forces were arriving. Every single soldier had been interrogated by British officers for political reliability. And Grivas's "X Battalion" was still at large and armed. During the Occupation, the British had sent them at least one boatload of arms, which ELAS had intercepted.

Several individuals who had connections to the Security Battalions were appointed to the Ministry of War. And, incredibly, a collaborationist, Colonel Spiliotopoulos, who had coordinated the activities of right-wing anti-Resistance groups during the Occupation, was made military Governor of Athens. It should have been obvious that there was no point our trying to cooperate with the British Occupation. The newly appointed Greek Army Chief did resign in protest over what the British were doing, but our EAM leadership continued, pointlessly, to seek a friendly relationship with the new Occupiers.

With so many of our enemies about, we would have had to be suicidal to disarm. Yet that was what "our" Prime Minister, Papandreou and the British General, Scobie, were pressing us to do.

We ELAS fighters were in a state of limbo: our war record scorned, branded by the British Prime Minister "Miserable bandits" and our leaders desperately negotiating for an honourable and safe settlement, knowing we were the strongest force in the country, but not wanting to use force. At one stage Papendreou was ready for a settlement with EAM. But the British forced him to change his mind.

Then General Scobie brought matters to a head. He ordered us to surrender our arms. This was the situation when I received a message from Andoni that he was home, to my surprise, at our old apartment in Athens. I was granted leave and returned home.

I walked along the pavement where the two starving children had walked an age before. As I approached the door to the flats, it opened and the Janitor came out. He didn't close the door behind him, but held it open and nodded to me as I walked past. He'd recognised me. But he didn't say, "Where have you been?" or "I haven't seen you lately". He just nodded. Did he think I'd lived there right through the war? Perhaps he didn't think about me at all. After all, he had his own life and I knew nothing about that.

Andoni opened our apartment door wearing a captain's uniform. The same big Andoni, from the same mould as dad.

We sat in the armchairs opposite each other, while he explained how he'd learned where I was. As I watched him, it struck me that while he was around, dad would always be with us. Andoni already knew the bare facts: that mother and father were dead, but little else. So I told him what had happened since he had left home.

Naturally he was upset. He shook his head, "If I could only turn the clock back. If only I'd stayed ..."

I told him, "Andoni, if you'd stayed, you would probably have been with dad on the night he was arrested."

"I didn't dream there'd be resistance."

"Who did?"

"I didn't have the imagination."

"Andoni, *dad* didn't know there'd be a Resistance. None of us did!"

Probably because he was upset, Andoni went out into the kitchen. When he came back he was carrying the Big Plate. It used to come out after dinner and during social evenings. On it were biscuits and cheese and nuts and two glasses. In his other hand he had two bottles of wine.

It was dad's old wine, "Wow. Is the wine still here? *The Apartment!* How come we've still got the apartment?"

Andoni put his finger to his lips and pointed to the policeman's flat below, "The least said the better. Vlanias knew where I was. He looked after us. We 'Royalists' aren't all bad you know."

"Are you really a Royalist? They made you Captain."

"Don't be taken in by that. Shit, I was never a Royalist. That was my reaction to dad. My loyalty is to people like you, who fought the Germans. Not to the King or to Papandreou."

"*What?*"

"It's true. When I heard that there was a guerrilla band in Thessaly ..."

"That was Aris, our ELAS Kapetan."

"I know ... I applied to be sent back. I'd have gone in as a Royalist, Republican ... anything, so long as I could have a crack at the Germans. I didn't know about dad, but I knew what the Germans were doing. But the King forbade resistance. Can you imagine how I felt? Do you remember that day at dinner when I said I admired Metaxas and dad rounded on me?"

"Yes. You had a big bust up."

"That's right. That's when it all started."

"Metaxas was putting people in jail. Some of dad's friends had been arrested."

"I understand *now* how insensitive I was. Later, I heard dad saying to mum, 'Andoni isn't the brightest member of the family'. That did it! Christ, I was only sixteen. I'd been romanticising. I'd been reading about Philip and Alexander and Napoleon. I just saw Metaxas as a man who might get things done. When dad reacted like that, I dug my heels in. I said that the Republican politicians were a shower. Remember?"

"Yes. That really got dad going."

"Well that's one thing I *was* right about. I saw them close up in Cairo, and they're worse than I'd thought possible. I looked after security and I was always around the politicians. At first they impressed me. They tried to get Churchill to understand that the King couldn't return without a properly run plebiscite. They explained how the country had once voted the King out and how he'd come back again on a rigged plebiscite and how he had made Metaxas Dictator. But Churchill doesn't listen. He just knows what he wants, and he wants *his* King back. They'd been members of the same Masonic Lodge in London."

"That's all Greece means to Churchill?"

"You're joking? Greece as part of the, so-called, British Sphere of Influence, with the King on strings: that's what Churchill wants. There's no more room for an independent King or independent politicians in Churchill's mind, than there is for an independent Resistance. Anyway, the politicians got the message: Churchill makes the decisions.

"Hold on." Andoni went out to the Kitchen and came back with more wine, "You should have seen the antics of the politicians when Sarafis came out from Greece to meet them."

"Was this the Lebanon Conference?"

"That's right. Everyone knew that Sarafis's men were fighting the last battles with the Germans, but no one showed even curiosity: what were the casualties; how many dead? Not the slightest interest. Instead, Papandreou led an orchestrated attack. ELAS were 'Terrorists'. They were 'Murderers'. They'd murdered Colonel Psarros. Then Sarafis got to his feet, and they all shut up. They knew that he'd been risking his life when Papandreou had been fattening his arse in Athens.

"Sarafis went into the details of the attacks and the killings they'd suffered from Zervas and Psarros. He named individuals who had murdered ELAS prisoners. He went through the requests he'd made for an Allied Commission of Enquiry. No one said a word. But when he tried to tell them about the soft life Zervas's officers lived: anything but fighting, they wouldn't listen. They knew that they themselves were the political equivalents of Zervas: Churchill's servants ..."

We talked for most of the night.

I had been lying awake for some time, unable to sleep, when I heard Andoni leave the apartment. He had to be on duty. Despite my tiredness, I stayed awake. Nothing Andoni had told me had relieved my fear that some kind of attack from the British was coming. He'd even heard Papandreou talk openly about the need to take on ELAS and force them either to disarm or revolt and then let the British deal with them.

The day Andoni had returned to Athens he'd had an argument with a group of British officers. One of them had told him how he'd rescued Colonel Grivas and some of his 'X Battalionists' after they'd been cornered by ELAS fighters and were either about to die in a firefight or be taken prisoner. Andoni had blown up, "Whose side are you fuckers on? Those bastards deserved to die."

During the argument that followed, the officers made it clear that they didn't regard ELAS as a legitimate force. *That* summed up the official British attitude to our country's national Resistance.

I had arranged to meet Andoni in Omonia Square. From there, we intended to go and watch the planned EAM demonstration in Constitution Square. Athens EAM supporters were going to protest against the high-handed British attitude.

As I walked down the stairs and was about to pass the flat below, Vlanias came out. He had obviously been waiting: he held out his hand. But before he could say anything, I thanked him, "Vlanias, all that you've done for us ..."

"Compared to you, it's ..."

"You saved mother's life ..."

"Come inside Thanasis. We've got to talk."

I looked at my watch, "Vlanias, I want to. I'll call later ... I've arranged to meet Andoni."

"Okay, call when you come back. We must talk. But don't go anywhere near the demonstration. It's been banned."

"When was it banned?"

"Last night. Papandreou withdrew permission."

"But it's too late to ban it. People won't know."

"I know. And the order's gone out to use force to stop it. There'll be bloodshed ..."

When I reached Omonia Square, Andoni was already waiting for me. He pointed along the crowded avenue, "They've just forced their way into the Constitution Square. The police have been trying to stop them."

Walking up the avenue, we could hear the crowd cheering. Then, "Crack-crack-crack-crack ..." the firing was too rapid to count. The cheering changed to screams.

As we entered Constitution Square, just in front of us, a British officer was carrying a bleeding girl to a car. Many had fled, but there were still people in the Square. Some were lying on the ground dead or wounded. Some were standing, obviously in shock, hardly believing what had happened. Others were angry and trying to get to the police building, where rifles still pointed from windows. Two British tanks were moving to block the entrance.

A few yards to one side, a woman was trying to help a boy who was bleeding from a wound to his head. The British officer returned from the car and knelt beside the boy. Then he carefully lifted him and carried him away.

Andoni went over to the woman and helped her to her feet. She was pale and thin, and she was angry. All she said was, "They think they can do this to us. What kind of people do they think we are?" Then she stood looking at the pool of blood where the boy had lain.

After the car had driven off carrying the casualties, Andoni walked over to the British officer, "Brigadier Jones?" The officer looked at him but didn't answer. "Brigadier, did you see the shooting?"

"Yes. Yes," he seemed to wake up. "I was standing over there." He pointed towards the police building. "There was no reason for it. It was a good-humoured demonstration. There were whole families. They were happy because they'd made it into the square. EAM was having its day. Then the shooting came from up there." He pointed to the upper stories of the police building.

"Did anyone fire back?"

"No. There were no guns." He moved close to Andoni, "Papandreou will have to go or Athens will go up in flames. I must get back." He hurried away.

We moved through the square to see if there was anything we could do. Suddenly Andoni stopped and pointed, "I think that's John Cole".

"Who?"

"An army doctor. A friend of mine."

When we reached the officer he was kneeling next to a casualty, a young woman and tying a handkerchief around her arm. There was a pool of blood on the floor under her hand. When Andoni said, "John", the doctor didn't seem surprised. He just looked up and answered, "She's losing blood. Will you carry her, and I'll take care of her hand?"

As they were lifting her into the ambulance, John Cole said to Andoni, "I'll see you when I can. I know where you live."

To my surprise Andoni became angry. He answered, "That fucker Churchill". John Cole grimaced and closed the ambulance door.

The whole of Athens knew we were at a critical point. Papandreou's resignation or even an apology, or an announcement of a Commission of Enquiry, would almost certainly have averted further bloodshed. And Papandreou did attempt to resign, but the British wouldn't let him. Then Papandreou blamed EAM for the bloodshed in Constitution Square.

To our surprise, John Cole came to see us that evening. He told us that the Greek medics had such expertise at treating gunshot wounds he had been of little help. It was an evening I wouldn't have missed. Meeting John Cole gave me something to think about.

John was upset by what had happened that day. But when Andoni cursed the man behind it all, to my surprise, John made an emotional defence of Churchill. What he said boiled down to, "Without Churchill's fighting spirit, the Nazis would have ruled Europe for fifty years; someone like Churchill comes as a package, warts and all." I knew, because Andoni had already told me, that John hadn't liked Churchill's imperious behaviour in Africa, ordering Generals into offensives against a well-equipped German army before they had the right equipment. John had counselled officers who had implemented the foolish orders. So I knew he was no naive worshipper of Churchill.

It was a strange evening. We knew that a major clash between ELAS and the British was imminent. John wasn't happy but was trying to be loyal to his leader, and Andoni was angry, but making an effort to control his emotions. And I was preoccupied, wondering if John's loyalty to Churchill was beyond reason.

Andoni and John had been close friends in Egypt, and their differences didn't alter that. Before he left, John asked us if, once the war was over, we would visit his cottage in Somerset in the heart of rural England. If only it had been possible.

During the Occupation, ELAS in Athens had been limited to quick guerrilla actions. Anything more would have resulted in annihilation. With the Germans gone and no sign of the Constitution Square gunmen being brought to justice, a sustained attack was certain to come.

For days the city was filled with the sound of gunfire as ELAS battled with the police. I didn't want it to be happening. I thought the killing in Constitution Square had shown that ELAS couldn't safely disarm and had put the Resistance in a strong moral position. I simply wanted EAM to continue insisting that Allied observers, Americans and Russians, come to Greece in strength and enforce fairness. What I didn't know then, was that Stalin was in collusion with Churchill. They had agreed that Churchill would "have Greece" and Stalin would, in exchange, "have Rumania" and the dominating say in other eastern European states.

I didn't know then, although I might have guessed, that President Roosevelt was against that kind of thing and had actually protested to Churchill about his deal with Stalin. But the chain of events that was to follow the Constitution Square shooting ended the chance of serious American involvement.

Andoni and I didn't even consider taking part in the fighting until after the British Army and the Royalist Mountain Brigade *and* the rearmed Security Battalions, joined together to fight ELAS. Before then, I'd heard the BBC broadcasting to the world that EAM was trying to seize power in Greece. It was nonsense. The least battle-experienced and least trained section of ELAS was attacking the Athens Police. Crack ELAS fighters in the mountains were being withheld. And ELAS aims were limited to replacing Prime Minister Papandreou and bringing collaborators and the Constitution Square murderers to justice.

For me, it was the involvement of the Security Battalions and the Royalist Mountain Brigade that made me realise that ELAS had little choice but to fight for survival with everything it had. Andoni agreed.

The last time he wore his uniform it was to report, apparently, for duty. But he returned within a few hours, driving a staff car loaded with rifles and ammunition and a Bren gun. And he brought a Brownling pistol for each of us. We reported together to ELAS.

If Churchill believed his own expletives about ELAS, he must have been shocked at our success in taking most of Athens, despite the forces he had ranged against us. The fighting was savage and we took many casualties, Andoni amongst them. He had been trained in house-to-house fighting by Commando instructors, as part of his security job in Egypt and had been able to help the young ELAS volunteers to fight more methodically. But his knowledge hadn't helped him when spitfires attacked our positions. Some kind of projectile came through a wall and exploded. Andrei, who had shared the Bren with him, was killed, and Andoni was wounded in the chest. He was taken to a medical centre and although he had lost a lot of blood and had a number of smashed ribs, nothing vital was damaged.

Faced with the failure of his offensive, rather than agreeing to do something about the Constitution square killings, which would have ended the fighting, Winston Churchill continued the lie, that we were seizing power, and he ordered two fresh army Divisions, which should have been fighting the Germans, to Greece. They attacked us as soon as they arrived.

I expected that Churchill's misplaced priorities and the twisted motives behind them would bring a fighting response from the EAM leaders. But instead of recognising that we were engaged in a decisive fight and that we had to take Athens, they pointlessly appealed for compromise and sent our most experienced fighters under Aris and Sarafis to destroy Zervas. And so we lost the chance to take the city.

When our sector was attacked, against so many trained soldiers and their weaponry and straffing planes and some artillery, we had little chance and were pushed back. Our medical centre was quickly overrun, and although the wounded were left alone by the British soldiers, behind them were armed Greeks, possibly Grivas and his gang. *They* took Andoni and the other ELAS wounded from their beds and shot them.

After Andoni's death I didn't want to go on, but I didn't know what else I could honourably do. I felt as though some malevolent force had skewed reality. Andoni had wanted only to serve his country and had fled with the British Army, hoping to return as part of an invasion force. Instead, he had returned disillusioned and met his death resisting his "allies". Thousands of other young Greeks had made their way to Egypt with the same idea as Andoni, but had ended up imprisoned somewhere in the Libyan desert. Our British "allies", who should have been attacking the Germans, had diverted whole divisions to fight us. Fighting by their side were collaborators who had done the Germans' dirty work during the Occupation. The straightforward, understandable world, I had once known had disappeared.

It was madness. And *we* became part of the madness. We were trying to establish a new front line. My unit were directed to a commercial building that was built as solidly as a fortress. It had a small gap in the wall, a battle scar. It was an ideal position to set up the Bren gun. I put it just inside the hole where it couldn't be seen and watched as our battered forces retreated through the new defensive positions.

It was then that I saw the first sign of *our* madness. Dozens of prisoners were being hurried past my position by armed ELAS youths. I'd seen prisoners captured in battle many times. These were different. They were obviously civilians. As they went by, I saw a familiar face amongst the prisoners. Shocked, I left my position and ran after them.

"Stop. Stop."

One of the guards, a girl with a rifle hanging from her shoulder, shouted for the column to halt. She and another guard walked back, "What's the matter?" She asked.

I pointed towards Vlanias, luckily he was in civilian clothes, "You've got a totally innocent man".

To my surprise she answered, "You're name is Thanasis isn't it?"

I looked at her, struggling to place her face.

"I'm Chrysa, Captain Othoneos's daughter. I came to your apartment. Remember?"

I looked, but didn't recognise the face.

"With my paint book. Remember?"

"*Chrysa!*" I pretended to remember.

"I heard that you and Andoni were back."

"Chrysa, I'm glad to see you, but," I pointed at Vlanias, "He's my neighbour, Vlanias. He saved my mother's life ... and mine. He risked *everything* for us."

Chrysa turned to the other guard, "Thanasis' father was shot at the same time as mine. Someone's made a mistake. Okay if we let Thanasis' friend go?"

"Of course. We only want collaborators."

Chrysa walked over to Vlanius and put her hand on his shoulder, "You're free to go friend".

Vlanias stayed with me for a while. He told me that the British were arresting suspected members of the Resistance and in retaliation, ELAS were arresting suspected collaborators. He said that he understood why they had taken *him,* but they were casting their nets too wide.

It was then that he told me, I hadn't known before, that he came from a republican family and had started his career in the police force *before* the King had returned and, of course, before the Metaxas dictatorship.

When the shooting started, I made him leave and I returned to my post. I didn't want to waste ammunition, so I changed from automatic to single-shot and my Bren gun became a sniper rifle. I fired single rounds into the recesses of buildings from where I thought fire had come at us.

The most horrible moment of that day was when we were hit by heavy machine gun fire. Luckily I saw the gun-flash and fired directly at it. Just as at Gorgopotomas, the firing stopped immediately. I knew they wouldn't fire from there again.

Then I became aware that there had been a scream during the gunfire and that my companion, who was supposed to be refilling my empty magazines, had left the room. I ran down the stairs and met him coming up. He had an arm around the young girl, Marika, who had just joined our unit. She wasn't hurt but she was pale and trembling. Inside the room below, I found Vasilis and

Erikos, two brothers, dead on the floor in a pool of blood. I'd seen the results of large calibre bullets on the human body before. So, although the sight was sickening, I was able to pick up their blood-spattered German machine-pistols and carry them upstairs and then go back for the spare ammunition. I would need them if the "Tommies" entered the building.

Marika told us that when the machine-gun had opened up, her two companions, thinking it was covering fire for an attack, had gone to the window with their weapons and been hit straight away.

The direct attack on us never came, but we could hear the sounds of shells exploding and spitfires releasing their rockets a few blocks away. I knew that *there*, there would be scenes similar to the one in the room below. We weren't surprised when we received the message, "Pull back, or you'll be trapped".

There was much physical destruction in Athens. Food and water supplies had been disrupted and the power cut off. It was winter, and the population was suffering. The Government continued to claim that ELAS had started the shooting at the Constitution Square demonstration and had been making a bid for power. Many believed the story.

What was worse was that a British Government agency was constantly putting out reports of ELAS murders. I never believed *most* of it. But I was fighting alongside young men and women who had lived in Athens during the most brutal time of the Occupation and had been lucky to survive. From their grim state of mind, having found themselves again fighting for survival, I had no doubt what some would have done had they captured Security Batallionists. And there was little doubt that our side had taken prisoners without proper discrimination. Vlanias had told me that amongst his batch there was an actress who had been the mistress of Rallis, the Germans' puppet ruler: *she* was a non-combatant. And other prisoners had claimed they had no idea why they had been seized.

After a hard fight in Athens the British had to face up to the fact that ELAS in the *whole* of the country would be too strong a force for them to crush. And so they agreed to talk and terms for an end to hostilities were agreed. Staggeringly, they included ELAS disarming and putting itself at the mercy of our enemies. I couldn't comprehend at the time why our leaders had agreed to disarm. Beyond Athens *we* controlled Greece. It was only after the war, when the Churchill-Stalin arrangement became public knowledge that I understood: Stalin must have pressured Siantos, our Communist leader, into accepting the British terms. Everyone knew Siantos was clever and that he was a very brave man: he had led the Resistance *from inside Athens*. And so he had the authority to carry most of the leaders with him. Aris, our ELAS Kapetan, wasn't impressed. Knowing that the settlement was suicidal, he kept his weapons and stayed in the mountains and was disowned by EAM.

What made it worse was that when ELAS agreed to release the hostages they weren't all alive to be released. Some had died from the ordeal of marching into the mountains through the winter snow. Others had been shot. Whether or not the dead numbered thousands as our enemies claimed, *there had been murders*. Siantos claimed that neither EAM nor ELAS had given orders for any executions. But the killings left a stain on our reputation.

I returned to the apartment deeply depressed. I hadn't known a single ELAS volunteer who had been happy with the ceasefire arrangement. Every one of us had had our lives fundamentally changed by the Occupation, and we had become committed to the struggle to free our country. Then, when we should have been jubilant, celebrating Liberation and full of hope for the new Greece, we found ourselves fighting a bloody battle for survival, in which many died. Yet our loyalty to ELAS and our willingness to defend Greek independence remained undiminished.

I went over in my mind many times how things would have been different if Sarafis, with his high standards, had been in command in Athens. I was sure that there would have been no hostage-taking. And had he arrived before the British reinforcements, we would have taken Athens. Then, in victory, instead of the bitterness of undeserved defeat, our idealism would have inspired Greece.

I wasn't allowed to be depressed for long. One night, a few weeks after the supposed settlement, I was lying in bed unable to sleep when I heard a noise in the apartment. Before I could do anything, the bedroom door opened and I heard Phillipa's voice, "Quick, come with me". She pulled me out of bed, "Don't turn the light on". I took my pistol from under the pillow and followed her out of the flat. She closed the door quietly and we hurried down the stairs to her apartment. Once we were inside, she whispered, "Shhh … men with guns downstairs". She took a coat from a hanger – she was hardly dressed – and covered herself. "Vlanias is arguing with them." Then she hugged me, "Thank God I got to you first".

Vlanias, because of who he was, was able to refuse the gunmen entry. But I was never able to live there again. I was lucky to have friends like Phillipa and Vlanias. Vlanias provided me with a false identity and a new apartment, and while EAM members were being hunted across Athens, I started a new life.

I spent the next two years tutoring children whose education had been disrupted by the Occupation. In exchange for my new identity, Vlanias made me promise not to contact anyone who had known me previously. So I was unable to discover what had happened to friends who I had fought alongside during the Battle of Athens.

Sometimes I would stop and think, "Can this really be happening?" I had never thought that joining the Resistance would result in my having to assume a false identity once the war was won. But that was only a small part of a skewed reality. The settlement was being disregarded and Security Battalionists and Grivas's men were being taken into the army, while ELAS men who, according to the disarmament agreement, should have been, weren't. And the arms that ELAS had surrendered had been given to monarchist bands, and by that first summer, hundreds of Resistance fighters had been murdered and many thousands were in prison, and thousands more who had been picked up by the British, were still being held in camps outside Greece. If the Government had brought to justice both collaborators and those responsible for the deaths of the hostages, that would have been fine. But power was in the hands of enemies of the Resistance.

The news that Winston Churchill's Government had been voted out of power in Britain electrified Greece. While he was British Prime Minister *he* had decided who would and who would not be *our* Prime Minister, and under his tutelage, three Prime Ministers had come and gone. It looked as though there were going to be big changes in Greece. But little altered. The new British Prime Minister handed Greece over to his Foreign Minister, Bevin. Bevin was an ignoramus on Greek affairs and simply adopted Churchill's "anti-Communist" attitude, which meant doing nothing to stop the reign of terror.

I lived for two years with a feeling of guilt. Some dissident ELAS units had kept their weapons and taken refuge in the mountains and, as the terror spread across the country, increasing numbers of fugitives joined them, and a low-key guerrilla war began. At the back of my mind was always the lingering consideration, "Should

I be with them?" But they had little choice, while I had and I held back. I held back while elections were held under conditions of terror. I held back for the plebiscite on the return of the King and almost voted "yes", thinking that at last the Terror might end. I held back when, Manilos Glezos, one of the two brave youths who had removed the swastika from the Acropolis, was imprisoned. And I held back when Zervas became Minister of Public order and the executions soared. And I held back when the security forces finally caught up with Aris and displayed his head on a pole. That is how Aris, who had inspired me with his vision of a better Greece in a better world, met his end. Whatever his faults, the death of this hero of the Resistance, and the mutilation of his remains, for me, symbolised the Greece that followed "Liberation". But still, I held back.

It was only after President Truman responded to Bevin's appeal for America to take over Britain's role in Greece, that I finally went to the mountains. It was partly the accumulation of wrongs and my conscience, but largely my shock at the patently false justification President Truman gave for American intervention that decided me to go: President Truman made a wide-ranging speech about the threat from international Communism, without talking about what was actually happening in Greece. And all kinds of apocalyptic statements were coming from America about what would be the consequences of the "fall of Greece": "The Iron Curtain would move to the Mediterranean"; "There would be widespread collapse of resistance to Soviet domination"; "Greece would be the starting point of global conflict between freedom and Soviet domination", and so on. But I knew, and every rational Greek knew, that this wild talk misrepresented what was happening. The resurrection of resistance had been triggered by repression and nothing else. And when the American President said that it would be American policy to support free peoples who were resisting subjugation, he was doing the opposite. It was warped reality again.

What was real was that the Resistance had repeatedly tried to negotiate a settlement, but Bevin had never responded. He regarded every peace offer as a "Communist trick", and when there was a call for an International Commission of Enquiry, Bevin had responded, "I will have no commission of any kind go to Greece". The last incredibly stupid remark of Bevin's before I left Athens was, "If only other countries would stop interfering in Greek affairs".

I was able to find Mikis and Stephanos again. They had stayed under arms. Mikis had become an officer in the new "Democratic Army" and Stephanos an NCO. Mikis made sure that I would serve in a unit under his command alongside Stephanos. They told me of the dejection in ELAS ranks in 1945, when they had heard of the agreement to disarm. Most had given up and gone home to an uncertain future. But some had kept their weapons and waited.

Mikis was no longer the model EAM loyalist he had been during the Occupation. He was unimpressed by the new leader, Zachariadis. Zachariadis had spent most of the war in a Nazi concentration camp and had no idea of what it was like to face regular army formations. Instead of keeping our fugitive army in bands, which could attack and retreat quickly, he was preparing for positional fighting. "A recipe for disaster", Mikis told me.

Over the following 18 months, we fought according to the Zachariades formulae. If anything, we fought more desperately than during the Occupation. But we lacked the resources to fulfil Zachariades ambitions. When we tried to take the town of Konitsa, we failed. When the Government forces attacked us in our stronghold on Mount Grammos, we had to withdraw to Mount Vitsi. But when we were attacked there, *we won the battle* and we counter-attacked and retook Mount Grammos.

Many times during those battles, I saw the same kind of horrible, bloody scenes I'd seen during the Battle of Athens. Sometimes the dead were my fellow soldiers. Other times, especially during our offensive from Mount Vitsi, they were Government troops, mostly conscripts. My constant feeling was, "They deserved better than this". But I knew that, far from the battlefield, there were men who *knew* how to deal with "Communists". And they would continue to send their dive-bombers and napalm and artillery shells and "advisers" to get the job done.

The inevitable, unstoppable assault eventually came. The Government army had thoroughly defeated our forces elsewhere in the country and were able to concentrate everything against us on Mount Vitsa and Mount Grammos. At first we were determined in our resistance. But the continuous attacks from the Spitfires and Helldivers with their napalm and cannon and rockets and the tank and artillery fire inevitably broke our defences. Then, in too many places, the foot soldiers overwhelmed our survivors, and we had little choice but to flee.

One of the disadvantages of our having Communist leaders, was that they became embroiled in the disputes of the Communist world. And Zachariades, despite Stalin's wartime betrayal, supported him in his dispute with Tito, the Yugoslavian leader. Consequently, Tito closed the Yugoslav border to us, and we had only one direction in which to go, towards Albania. Understanding this, our adversaries rushed to block our retreat. So our army had to march by a more circuitous route.

During the night march, Mikis called Stephanos and myself to one side. "Do you want to spend the rest of your lives in Albania", he asked? Then he told us he was going back to try to escape through enemy lines and invited us to go with him. And that was what we did. We were lucky. We were at the height of summer. We had to spend many hours patiently lying on the ground waiting for night to come. We knew it would be an accident if we were caught because no one was looking for us – our beaten army was going in the opposite direction.

And so we found ourselves out of battle, free to go where we wanted and considering our futures. At first Stephanos said he was going back to Komeno, and I decided to go with him. Mikis planned to go to Piraeus and work his passage on a boat to Australia. Stephanos must have been thinking about this option, because the next day he said he would go with Mikis. Then I remembered a message that Vlanias had given to me from John Cole, after he had heard about Andoni's death. He had offered to arrange for me to study in England. I decided I would write to John and ask if the offer was still open. But first, I would go to Komeno. There would be people there who remembered me, and I might find sanctuary and work of some kind.

But, there was our condition. We could hardly go anywhere until we had cleaned ourselves up. The Democratic Army had once occupied the area we were in, and we were near to a village Mikis knew well. He decided to go down and contact a villager he knew. He would see if we could get fresh clothes and scissors and soap and a little food to replenish our rations. We waited until the end of the day and, as the shadow of the mountain moved across the valley, Mikis went down to the village.

When he returned, he got us to our feet and walking straight away. As we walked, he explained that where his old friend had lived, he had found only the fire-blackened shell of a house. He said he knew he shouldn't have, but he had stopped and looked through the window of a café, hoping to see a familiar face. A man had come out and asked him what his business was. Mikis wasn't the kind to be intimidated, and there was an argument before the man hurried away.

As Mikis was about to leave, the proprietor had come out and given him a bag of food and warned him to get away because he'd aroused the suspicion of a notorious Security Battalionist. Mikis had my Brownling pistol in his pocket and had been tempted to go after the man, but he thought it would make more sense to get back to us.

We walked through the night, and when day broke we stopped and slept in the forest. In late morning we started out again. For a while we walked beside a stream, but as it turned and ran steeply downhill we followed the path to higher ground – we wanted to avoid people.

A little later, as we walked along a ravine, Stephanos whispered, "There's someone up ahead", and Mikis casually started walking up the slope to our left. Stephanos and I followed. Almost immediately from behind rocks about a hundred metres away, men stood up and started firing at us. I ran to the top of the slope and threw myself to the ground, but neither Mikis nor Stephanos was with me. They hadn't reached cover. And the gunfire continued. I crawled to a better position and fired quickly without taking aim, and the men ducked down behind the rocks. One of them wasn't quite hidden. A tiny bit of him was still showing. I fired again and heard a yelp as he withdrew. Then I took a look at Mikis and Stephanos. My friends were certainly dead.

I guessed that the Battalionist, whom Mikis had argued with outside the café, must have gone for help and tracked us down.

They have been waiting for some time now. They're waiting for me to move. I'll be as patient as they are. After dark, I'll make my move.

"Nikos", someone is shouting from along the ravine.

"Stay with the horses", a voice answers, "This one's wily. And he's a good shot."

"*Wily.*" "*A good shot.*" That's respect ... of a kind. When they fired at us, we were carrying rifles. If I go down unarmed, perhaps they'll be satisfied just taking me prisoner. Perhaps they'll just beat me up, not kill me. Whatever I do I'll be taking a chance. Even if I manage to slip away in the dark, they'll catch up; they've got horses. Shall I go down?

I'll try it. I'll try to talk to Nikos.

"Nikos!" No answer.

"Nikos, I'm coming down. I'm surrendering." I'm standing with my hands above my head. They're coming out from behind the rocks pointing their rifles, but they're not firing so I walk down the hill.

As I reach opposite Mikis and Stephanos, the leader shouts, "Stay where you are Communist".

"I'm not a Communist."

He's not responding. He's walking towards me. I've never seen such hate in a man's face before. His intention is obvious. I'll try to get back to cover. As I turn to run, I feel a hard blow to my back and I'm knocked to the ground. I try to roll, but I'm hit again and again.

From somewhere far away, I can hear the familiar sound of gunfire ...

5

Petrona

WHEN MY YOUNGEST sister died, father didn't cry. But that didn't surprise anyone. Like many Indian fathers, he'd had much sorrow in his life and had learnt not to show his emotions. Yet I'd heard that, years before when President Arbenz was overthrown, father had cried. I wondered about that but couldn't understand it. I was too young then to know, amongst other things, that President Abenz had been the elected leader of our country. But I never forgot that father once cried over President Arbenz.

Much later I learnt that between 1945 and 1954, two fine men, first President Arevalo and then President Arbenz, had tried to make Guatamala a better place.

Some time after 1954, mother and father and other Quiche Indians followed Vincente Menchu and his family up into the Altiplano to clear land and grow maize. The soil wasn't as good as in lower regions and it took time clear the forest. To get by we had to go down for months each year to work on the cotton and coffee Fincas. They were places I hated. We slept in huge sheds with hundreds of other Indians, many speaking dialects I couldn't understand. Instead of the freedom of the Altiplano, we were under the control of overseers: Ladinos who worked for the landowners and watched how we worked and had the power to fine and cheat us. One particularly nasty overseer had thrown mother and myself off a Finca, without pay, because we had missed a day's work after my brother died.

Luckily, friends from our village were disgusted by the overseer and walked off the Finca. *They* had their pay and were able to help us home. That was the kind of thing that was likely to happen when you went to work on a Finca. Your work was wanted, but *you* were of no consequence.

After years of effort, our village was beginning to grow enough food for us to live on. Then a landowner's agent arrived with a team of surveyors and began measuring our land. They were going to claim it for the landowner. That was when Vincente Menchu really became our leader.

The village decided to fight, but it was Vincente who had to go out into the Spanish-speaking world to argue for us, even though he spoke only our own language, Quiche. To get someone to speak for us in Spanish, we had to pay. And this cost our community dear.

Vincent found that he wasn't dealing with honest people and was surrounded by trickery. Rich landlords bribed *everyone*. That was how they worked. The interpreter misrepresented what he said, and twice Vincente signed away our land, after being assured by officials that he was guaranteeing our ownership. But despite his apparent simplicity, Vincente was a fighter, and somehow in the end he came through. A court awarded the land to us. It had taken years and drained our resources. And the village had suffered violent attacks. *And* Vincente had become a marked man. But the land belonged to us, and Vincente had won friends who would join him in future struggles. It was towards the end of *that* struggle that I left our village.

I hadn't been well since the spray plane flew over us while we were working on the Finca. Everyone felt weak that night. Some weren't able to eat. And Vincente's son died. He must have taken more of the spray than anyone else. I was ill for weeks, and even afterwards I didn't fully recover.

One evening a friend who understood some Spanish told mother that she'd heard the landlord's son and a woman she'd never seen before talking about me while I was working.

The next day the same woman came with her husband and an interpreter and asked mother and father if I could go to live with them.

Father instantly refused. Sometimes when an Indian girl was asked for, it was for the wrong reasons. Even when a girl was genuinely taken on as a maid, she was likely to be treated without respect and might be fed leftovers. But the woman said, "I can appreciate how you feel. But we're not landowners. Please give us a chance. You can keep in touch with Petrona and we'll take care of her. I could teach her to speak Spanish, and perhaps she could help me to learn Quiche? We'll treat her like a daughter. We don't want her as a servant."

My parents had never before been spoken to so respectfully by a Spanish-speaker. They were won over.

That was how I came to live with Geraldina and Francisco. They weren't the greed-filled kind that mother and father feared they might turn out to be. Yet I found them very strange at first, and their house was strange too. I'd never dreamt I would live in such a place. At first, I was afraid to touch anything. To know there was a tap where, at any time, I could get instant hot water was a wonder. And to have an oven where I could immediately get the heat to cook tortillas and other foods was strange. And the refrigerator was filled with foods of such variety. And there was beautiful furniture, and there was *my bedroom*. I felt so out of place.

Geraldina showed me how the bath and toilet worked. Then she filled the bath for me. Afterwards, she had clean new Indian clothes ready. Indian clothes! She'd taken the trouble to provide the kind of clothes I would want to wear.

Then I went down to eat. We sat at a table and ate strange food. I felt out of place and didn't want to be there. If I could have left then and instead been with mother, even at the Finca, I would have gone.

Fortunately for me, on that first evening a friend of Francisco visited the house to meet me and to act as interpreter. He didn't speak Quiche very well, but at least I could understand what he was trying to say. He explained that Geraldina and Francisco had never had a daughter themselves and had always wanted to know more about the Quiche Indians, but didn't even understand the language. And then they'd seen me on the visit to the Finca.

Luckily, he happened to say that he knew Vincente Menchu, and from that moment we talked for the whole evening. And as we talked the strangeness fell away. That was the real start of knowing Geraldina and Francisco. At the end of the evening, before I went to bed, *they* thanked *me* for all they had learnt.

Francisco's interpreter friend called a few times a week, and I spent my days in the company of Geraldina. It was amazing how quickly we learnt to talk to each other, using sometimes Quiche and sometimes, Spanish words. We went together to the market, and I would choose food and when we returned, show her how we Indians cooked. Unfortunately, in return, I had to eat the meals she cooked. But after tasting *my* tortillas, they wouldn't have any others. The allowance they gave me every week allowed me to send money home and buy cloth from the market to make clothes.

I got to know Geraldina so well that we talked for hours every day. I told her about how every baby was special to the Quiche people and how neighbours would bring food for the pregnant mother and how for the first eight days of the baby's life the community would continue to provide food and how on the eighth day we would hold a ceremony to celebrate the integration of the new baby into our universe and tell the baby of the sorrow and hardships of the family and how the child would be brought up to respect her community and its customs. And I told her how, when the child is ten years old, he or she is told of how the Spaniards dishonoured our ancestors.

To my surprise, I found that Geraldina knew as much as I did about the disaster of the Spanish conquest. And she talked to me about the many Indian and other, native peoples, far beyond Gautamala, who have suffered conquest. Geraldina explained, "There is nowhere in the world, not any place, where native peoples have been treated honourably".

I would never have thought it possible for people like Geraldina and Francisco to exist. They occupied a place in life I hadn't been aware of. They weren't struggling to make a living, or living at the expense of others. They had enough money to buy the food they needed and to live in a comfortable home, yet they looked beyond their own lives. They were preoccupied with what was happening to others. They were concerned with the effect outsiders were having on the Indians and were especially concerned with what the army was doing and with America, because the American Government supplied our army with it's weapons and trained its officers.

Francisco came home from his work at the university one evening and said he had heard that Vincente had been arrested: the landlord's bribery had been at work again. Francisco told me that Vincente's friends beyond the Quiche community were doing their best to help. And I knew that my community loved Vincente like a father, and they would be doing their best to help too. Yet it was a year before Vincente won his release. Then he was kidnapped while he was working in the village fields.

Luckily the villagers were alerted in time and took their machetes and surrounded the area. They didn't catch the kidnappers but they saved Vincent's life. He had been badly beaten and tortured. But he was still alive. He was a bloody mess, and many of his bones had been broken. He had to go into hospital.

Then it became known that Vincente wasn't safe in hospital, and he had to go to a secret place.

Vincent survived. He was a physically diminished man, but the damage he had suffered made him even more determined. His leadership inspired people beyond the village and even beyond the Altiplano. Once he was able to move about again, he was often away helping other Indians. And his family too became involved in his work. Sadly, in my country such a family is marked for tragedy.

Vincente was arrested again and charged with being a "Communist subversive". It was ridiculous. It was a blatant attempt to get Vincente Menchu out of the way. He would probably have had difficulty explaining what a Communist was. But Vincente had allies who helped him, and he won his release and went into hiding.

I missed so many things that happened at home, even though much of it was unpleasant. I escaped the time our would-be landlord sent armed men to expel the entire village and destroy our homes. I escaped the times the army came and found an empty village because we were prepared and had fled. I missed so much of the life of my community.

And I missed the sad time when the community threw a fiesta in honour of the Menchu family and said "goodbye" to them. Their long fight for the Indians had made them too many powerful, violent enemies. Others had felt so threatened they'd left to join the guerillas, but the Menchus felt they had other work to do. From then on, each of them had to live separate, furtive lives moving amongst Indian communities.

The Menchu family had given so much to others, and I knew there would be no one at home who wouldn't be deeply affected by their fate. The older Menchus, the father, the mother, the brothers and the daughter, my old friend Rigoberta, weren't just leaving home, they were splitting up and going their different ways and didn't know when they would meet again. And they were leaving behind a teenage son and two young daughters.

I missed village life so much. From time to time I'd dream of returning home for good. But what mother and father had said when they persuaded me to leave was true: since the spray plane, Indian life had been too much for me. With Geraldina and Francisco I'd have a chance of improvement. And it turned out to be true. I ate meat or fish most days and vegetables and fruit. And

I felt healthier. Also, I was learning things I would never have learnt at home, such as reading and writing in Spanish.

It struck me one day, that apart from my Indian clothes and my tortillas and some of the other food we ate, the only thing that reminded me of the Altiplano was the staircase. Going up the stairs, if I closed my eyes, I could be walking up steep steps that had been cut into the rock just below the village.

I'd grown plump from eating rich food and no longer having the effort of daily work. I remembered once seeing a Finca owner, who was enormously fat, struggling to get out of a car. A woman from home, who had worked in his house, told me that the man ate enough food to feed a village. I didn't want to be anything like that Finca owner. So I made it a practice, whenever I was on my own, to walk up and down the stairs in my bare feet for a while and feel my heart beat from the exertion.

During an intimate talk with Geraldina about my reaching puberty and some of the things that should have happened, not happening, I told her I didn't think I would be able to have babies. She looked extremely surprised, "Well if it's true, we're in the same boat", she said. "I can't be a mother either." Then she added, "I'm sad for you, Petrona, but I'm not sad for myself. It suits me. I love children, but I wouldn't want to have any here. Yet I have my plans: someday we might *have* to go to Mexico. There, I'd like to have children … or to America, or Canada, or Europe. Then I'll see a doctor. And if you come with us who knows what might be possible for you?"

"You might have to leave the country?"

"It could happen. Francisco has had to flee once, before we were married. *They* were cracking down on students and lecturers. They killed hundreds, but Francisco managed to escape to Mexico, and when they turned their attention elsewhere, he came back."

"You think *that* might happen again?"

"Its likely. Nowadays, they keep track of their enemies on the computer system they've been given …"

"By America?"

"No. By Israel."

"*Israel?*"

"It's a country … in a way, Petrona, it's best that you don't know about these things."

I was puzzled. Geraldina had always answered my questions before, "But why shouldn't I know?"

Geraldina looked embarrassed. "It's not that you shouldn't know, Petrona. It's just that I don't want to draw you too much into our world. Some of Francisco's friends have been killed." Geraldina thought for a moment, "I suppose we could *talk* about it ... there have been so many murders its becoming a scandal, and the American President is afraid of getting the blame ... Israel is a small country that gets a lot of American money, so she steps in when she's needed and helps regimes like ours.

"Some of Francisco's activities are dangerous. They shouldn't be. But they are. And it's getting worse. The less you know, the safer you'll be. So I'd rather leave it at that."

It was as though talking about it had brought it about. One morning the phone rang. Geraldina answered and after putting it down, she'd altered. She was very tense when she said, "Francisco's got to go away". Then she hurried around the house filling a bag with Francisco's things. "Please come with me?" she asked, when she'd finished.

"Just act as though we're walking to market", she whispered as we left the house. And so we walked along our regular route trying to look normal, although anyone who knew Geraldina would have realized that something was wrong.

We turned off the usual route into a road we'd previously passed. A little way along a car was parked, and as we reached it, a door opened, and Geraldina got inside, and I followed. Francisco was in the front seat next to the driver.

As we drove to the airport Francisco explained to me, "They've arrested my friend Ramon. I don't know if they're after me yet, but I can't take a chance. I'm going to California to discuss some computers the university's after. If I can't come home, I hope you'll follow with Geraldina."

After returning home, Geraldina swallowed some tablets and, while she rested, I prepared coffee and doughnuts. Then, as we took our refreshment, she sat with her head resting back on a cushion and slowly explained that the Government had been arresting Trade Union organizers, and Ramon, who was a Union organizer, had gone into hiding. But somehow he'd been caught. Because of Francisco's close connections with him, he was automatically in danger. "'Arrest' is the wrong word for what's happened to those men", Geraldina said. "Guatemala doesn't have political prisoners. If they're heard of again, it'll be a miracle."

I had once thought that with Geraldina and Francisco I had

found a refuge from violence, but I had discovered that people in the cities were in danger too. Francisco returned a fortnight later. There had been no sign that he was in danger, and by then Ramon, Francisco said, "would be beyond anything, let alone talking".

On the anniversary of the handover of the Presidency from Arevalo to Arbenz, Guatemala's two Great Presidents, my new "parents" gave a dinner for special friends. After the dinner, an American woman, Eileenkilleen, spoke to us in Spanish about what had happened during those Arevalo-Arbenz years. It seemed strange, an American talking to *us* about Guatemala. But she had knowledge we would never have been able to get in our own country, especially about the Americans who had organized the overthrow of President Arbenz. I liked the woman's name, "Eileenkilleen", and kept repeating it to hear the lovely sound. Her name gave her a special aura.

From this American woman I learnt that many years before, America's President, Franklin Roosevelt, had inspired the democratic movement in our country that overthrew a dictator and brought about the election of President Arevalo.

She told us that the General in charge of our army hadn't liked our new President, and there had been attempts to overthrow him. And President Truman, who became the American President after Franklin Roosevelt, hadn't liked Arevalo either, and when Arevalo told the American company, United Fruit, to act with decency towards its workers and meet and negotiate with them about their wages and conditions of work, Harry Truman stopped sending weapons to our army. It was meant to turn the soldiers against President Arevalo.

Then in 1951 when Arevalo handed over to the new President, Arbenz, in a speech he said that when he himself was first elected, he was full of fire about what he wanted to do for our country, but he had been obstructed by people without morality or law. And he warned that the new leader would be in danger because Hitler's and not Roosevelt's, ways had won in the world. President Arbenz must have learnt from President Aravelo, because the first thing he did was remove the most dangerous army officers.

He had plans to build a modern power station and a port and a new road along the Atlantic coast. Eileenkilleen made the plans sound wonderful. But the American President, Eisenhower, hadn't seen them that way. He hadn't liked them because they would compete with the American owned power station, port and railway.

And when President Arbenz defied Eisenhower and went ahead with a scheme to buy unused land from the American company, United Fruit, for settlement by landless farmers, Eisenhower became very angry. It didn't matter to him that the land had been unused, or that thousands of Guatemala's poor were starting to farm their own land.

What mattered was that without land, the farmers had had no choice but to work for the landowners, and the American company, United Fruit, was the biggest of them all. Eisenhower ordered that our leader be overthrown.

I didn't hear much of the rest of the talk. I was thinking about how mother and father had lived through those times. Thanks to President Arbenz, thousands of Indians had started to farm their own land. It must have been a time of joy until our Great President, Arbenz, was overthrown. Father must have understood immediately what it meant for the Indians. At last I knew why father had cried over President Arbenz.

I only half heard Eileenkilleen talk about how the farmers had been thrown off their new land and how trade unionists had been shot. I already knew about those kind of things.

She finished her talk by telling us how, after the overthrow of President Arbenz, the American Government had sent someone to interview captured prisoners who were supposed to be Communists. He reported back that few, if any, of the prisoners knew anything about Communism.

On Guatemala's National Day, I heard the news: a demonstration, mainly of Indians, had carried out a surprise occupation of the congressional building in Guatemala City. My village had actually organized it to protest against the kidnapping of Petrocinio Menchu, Vincentes son. Petrocinio had been kidnapped by the Army. Although he was only sixteen, Petrocinio was Community Secretary. He also helped nearby villages. Many other Indians had joined the occupation to protest against the army's treatment of Indians.

A few days later I went home. I had to be there. I had always admired Petrocinio. He had taken on the responsibilities of leadership, despite the danger and I wanted him saved. Geraldina and Francisco feared that if the sit-in failed to win support from outside the country, reprisals would follow. And that's exactly what happened.

After the failed sit-in, the army announced that they were going to make an example of some captured "guerillas" and commanded Indians from a large area to attend the punishment. Everyone knew that Petrocinio would be amongst the "guerillas" to be punished.

The place of punishment was a long way away. Remembering my old exhaustion, father tried to persuade me to hide rather than travel such a distance, but I insisted on going, and the journey wasn't a problem. But I wasn't thinking of myself. The Menchu family had come together and was just ahead of us. I was afraid they might be recognized. And I was hoping that somehow Petrocinio might survive.

At the place of punishment the Army was waiting, and they had armoured cars and helicopters watching us. There were many Indians.

An officer spoke to us. He said that a group of guerillas had been caught and they were about to be punished for being Communists and Cubans and subversives. Then he ordered the prisoners to be taken from a covered lorry. When they were brought down, none of them could remain standing for long and were repeatedly forced to their feet by soldiers. I wondered what was wrong with their mouths, until I realized they had had their tongues cut out. They had no fingernails or toenails and their hands and feet were covered in blood. There was a girl amongst them whose ears were gone. All of their faces and heads were battered and bloody. I couldn't recognize Petrocinio amongst them. The Menchu family obviously could, they were so distressed.

When the prisoners were lined up, the officer made a speech about how Communists from the Soviet Union had moved first into Cuba and then Nicaragua and now they'd come to Guatemala and how what was being done to the "guerillas" was how all the Communists would end up. The prisoners were repeatedly being forced to their feet with kicks and blows from the soldiers.

This was all being done before a gathering of families, and the children were crying and clinging to their parents, terrified. Some of the parents were crying too. Others had faces fixed with anger and hatred. Vincente Menchu was one of these. For all his gifts of leadership, he could only stand and watch what was being done to his son.

Then the officer told the soldiers to take the clothes off the "guerillas", so that all of their punishments could be seen. The girl had had one whole breast and the nipple from the other cut off. Dogs must have been set upon her, because she had bite marks all over her body. As the officer described the tortures that had been carried out, I could feel the growing anger around me. Then, when the soldiers poured petrol on their victims and set fire to them, the whole assembly surged forward to try and save our companeros, and the soldiers withdrew. They retreated with their weapons ready, shouting, "Long Live Guatemala. Long Live the President".

The prisoners were covered with coats and blankets, and the flaming petrol was doused. But it was too late to save anyone. Petrocinio's mother held him in her arms, kissing him.

When I returned to Geraldina and Francisco I knew it would be for the last time. I didn't put a time limit on my stay, but I felt I had to be with my people.

Yet with Geraldina and Francisco, there was so much I could learn. Those who sat on the Indians, squashing us, limiting us, treating us like mindless animals, they were Spanish and English speakers. They conducted their business in Spanish and English and violence, and however hard we struggled, they were always on top of us. Yet the best hope we ever had, had come from the Spanish and English speaking world. Arevalo and Arbenz were from there. Geraldina and Francisco and their friends came from that world. And there was much from there that I needed to learn. I'd learnt Spanish, and Geraldina was teaching me English, and I hoped that would be just the start. I'd listened to talks about neighbouring countries and even countries further away, where a similar struggle to our own was taking place. I'd listened to discussions on how oppression could be fought, and I knew I had much to learn. I also knew that Geraldina and Francisco and their friends were the willing allies of the Indians. And I knew they were in danger. People like them regularly "disappeared".

Many Indians were desperate to publicize our plight and were prepared to risk their lives to do it. But I didn't know about the planned occupation at the Spanish embassy. If I had known, I would have been there. It was a non-violent, no-weapons sit-in. Anything else would have been suicidal. Yet the attack on them, when it came, wouldn't have surprised them; they would have anticipated it, but decided to go unarmed anyway. There was one survivor from the massacre of the embassy sit-in. He was later kidnapped from hospital and killed.

After days of anguish, what I had suspected was confirmed. Vincente and other friends from home were amongst the dead. But I knew such things were *normal* and life had to go on.

Geraldina and Francisco gave one of their dinners, and afterwards everyone talked about what had happened at the Spanish embassy. My interpreter friend was there and to my surprise asked me to say some words about Vincente. Yet, once he'd asked, it seemed the most natural thing for me to do. I talked to them in Spanish about Vincente's hard life and how I had been impressed by his clear mind and understanding of what we had to do to resist our enemies and how he had successfully defended our right to our land. I told them he had known he would eventually die in the struggle but had accepted it, as part of being an Indian leader. And I told them how my friend Rigoberta was being hunted and how her sister, who was only seven, had gone to the guerillas and how I feared for the surviving members of the Menchu family.

But what I couldn't have known was that Vincente's wife, Petrocinio's mother, was shortly to be captured and was to die almost as terribly as her son had done. I was told the details of her death, but I prefer to remember her as I knew her, the mother of a fine family.

The regime goes after the finest people. So it was probably inevitable that they would eventually come after Geraldina and Francisco. A warning came that they must leave the country immediately, and they went the following morning, leaving everything behind. Why some meet terrible ends, while others are allowed to live, I don't know. But I was thankful that Geraldina and Francisco were given the chance to live.

Before they went they pleaded with me to go with them, saying how life would be much better outside Guatemala. I told them I loved them and was grateful for all they had done for me, but I had to be with my people. And before they went, I was able to tell Geraldina that my periods had begun. She was delighted that I was going to be a normal, healthy woman. I wasn't so pleased myself. Like Geraldina, I hadn't included children in my plans.

I went home carrying presents and money. I stayed for a full month. Then I left and joined the guerillas …

6

Amir

I HAVE NEVER been so filled with hope as I was on that bright, bitterly cold day in February 1979. I was there in the immense crowd, under a clear blue sky, that welcomed Ayatollah Khomeini back to Iran. No one had to ask how anyone else felt that day; there was collective euphoria. We were rejoicing because the remarkable man, who had been exiled by the Shah years before and had orchestrated our revolution from abroad, was returning to us. We believed that a great change was taking place. The Shah had already fled and very soon we were to have an Islamic Government and a time of honesty and justice.

Greeting the Ayatollah were many who had helped to bring the change about. During the past year we had repeatedly marched towards the Shah's guns, surviving only because the bullets had struck our comrades and not us.

But the person I most wanted to be with me, hadn't come: Ashraf, my friend from the School of Social Work. She wasn't on any of the demonstrations during 1978. She is a Bahai. And Bahais, she told me, don't take part in politics. Besides, the Bahais were on the defensive: there were some who were using the unrest to attack them.

One morning Ashraf had come into the lecture late and was obviously not her normal self. The teacher asked her, "Is something wrong Ashraf?"

"Yes", she answered, not loudly, but her clear voice reached the whole class. "My cousin was hurt, and he was refused treatment at the hospital, and he died before we could get him to another one."

"Are you sure ...?"

"Yes. A man rode him down on a motor bike."

"I'm so sorry. You had no need to come in. Why don't you take the day off Ashraf?"

"No thank you."

The class continued, for me, pointlessly. I couldn't wait to be with her to find out exactly what had happened. And I wanted to re-assure her that most Muslims would be horrified by what had happened. I knew the danger the Bahais were in. I'd been at her home when their pastor called with the news that their fellow Bahais in Shiraz were being turned out on the streets and their homes looted and burned. I was surprised by her family's composure and at first I thought it was "face", to impress me. But I was to find that Bahais were stoically prepared to face any ordeal for their faith.

I had good reason to be grateful to Ayatollah Komeini. When I was a baby, he had raised funds for the dependants of the victims of the anti-Mossadeq coup. Mother and I were amongst those dependants. Father had been shot for being a Mossadeq supporter. So Khomeini helped us through some very difficult years.

Mother and I had our lives dramatically affected by the coup. But we weren't alone in that. Mossadeq had been our constitutional Prime Minister, and before he was overthrown was struggling to limit the power of the monarchy. His defeat had left the Shah free to rule as he pleased, and amongst the things that pleased him was suppression of civil liberties.

Before his overthrow, Mossadeq had been trying to bring Iranian oil out of British and into Iranian ownership. But the British Prime Minister, Winston Churchill, persuaded the American President, Eisenhower, to arrange Mossadeq's overthrow. During my childhood, hatred of the Shah and Churchill and Eisenhower was part of the air I breathed.

Mother and I eventually went to live with Uncle Mashti, father's younger brother and Aunt Shery. Mother helped out by keeping the accounts of Mashti's construction company. Mashti refused to get involved in the corruption of the Shah's regime, so he won no Government contracts and his company stayed small.

I can remember when we first went to live in Mashti's house, being baffled watching my cousins Farhad and Bijan playing complicated board games. They threw dice and counted at a speed that bewildered me. And I marvelled at the number of books they had. I didn't realise then, that they were living the kind of life I would have had, if father had lived. During my school years I never caught up with them. After school, while they went on to higher education, I went to work for Uncle Mashti. I never regretted it. I felt I was meant to do what I was doing. Whatever I did, carrying bricks, lifting heavy sacks of sand or cement, digging trenches, or any of the other physical tasks, I wanted to do it. I enjoyed using myself. After work, Aunt Shery would say, as I ate my oversized dinners, "You're just like Mashti used to be, you've got hollow legs".

I'd say, "And a hollow head". But really, I didn't have a complex. I could hold my own with anyone in conversation, or in banter. That was one aspect of work I loved.

During break one afternoon I asked Salim the plasterer, "How many pull-ups can you do?" (Salim liked to show off his strength.) Before he could answer, I added, "With one hand".

"You need two hands for pull-ups", he said.

"I'll bet you whatever you like, that I can beat you in one-handed pull-ups … only one hand holding the bar."

We made our bet and with everyone watching, Salim had his try. I pretended not to notice that he hadn't chinned the bar. I counted, "One". He tried, but couldn't manage another.

Then it was my turn. I hung by my right hand and asked, "Ready?"

"C'mon, let's see what you can do", Salim egged me on. I knew what I could do. I'd practised. I clutched my right wrist with my left hand and heaved. I managed seven.

Salim refused to pay up. He claimed I'd used two hands and cheated. Everyone else said that I only held the bar with one hand, so I'd won. Then we called him names.

The reason I can remember our antics that day so well, is that while we were arguing, mother came on to the site and called everyone together. She announced, "Mashti wants you all to take the week off. I've got your money here. He said he'll see you next week". Mother's eyes were red. She had obviously been crying and something was clearly very wrong. No one asked any questions as she gave each man his pay.

It wasn't until we were in the car that she told me what had happened. Cousin Farhad had been killed in a raid on a military armoury. Unknown to us, he had been a member of the Mohajedin and was on one of its operations when he was shot dead.

Mother explained that Savak agents had come to search the house that morning. At first they were unfriendly and didn't said why they were there. Then when they'd completed their search and found nothing incriminating, they revealed what had happened. After seeing how shocked Aunt Shery and Uncle Mashti were, the Savak officer changed completely and tried to console them. He said that time and time again, he'd seen boys from good families come to grief after falling under the influence of the "Communists".

I tried to figure out why Fahad hadn't given me even a hint that he was with the Mohajedin. We were so close. Apart from my sorrow, I felt hurt. It took a while for me to realise that Farhad must have been bound to absolute secrecy. The Mohajedin's fight against the regime was taking a terrible toll of its ranks, and discipline must have been crucial.

One result of Farhad's death was that Mashti told me he wanted me, eventually, to take over the business. I asked him, "What about Bijan?"

"Can you see Bijan up a ladder?" he asked me. "Besides, he isn't interested in anything but Medicine, and he's in love with Europe. I'm not sure he'll be coming back after he qualifies."

And so it was that, to prepare me for running the business, Mashti gave me time off work for study. Ironically, the qualifications I eventually got were, later, to give me the confidence to leave the business and be admitted to the School of Social Work. That was to be years in the future. But the steps that led me there started almost immediately.

A family friend asked Mashti if he would help the Head of the School of Social Work who was organising repairs to, what had recently been, the Teheran Mental Asylum. Mashti took me along.

When we arrived we were sickened by the stench. Students were hurrying about carrying buckets and mops and shovels and cans of disinfectant. The woman in charge turned out to be Princess Sattareh Farman Farmian, from the old royal family, supplanted in the coup that had brought the Shah's father to power. She explained that she'd had the asylum patients moved to more suitable premises and was preparing the building to receive children she had found starving in the Aminabad Orphanage. Mashti agreed to co-operate, and he left me behind to supervise the repairs.

The students told me that the Princess was a dynamo of energy. In a whirlwind of activity, she'd raised the funds and accumulated a library of books and recruited the teachers to start the School of Social Work. Then she'd taken on the students and was giving them a mixture of an academic and an activist education. The students were being trained to go out and tackle Iran's social problems. I was impressed and drew a great deal of satisfaction from the work.

But my pleasure was cut short after a few weeks, when I was conscripted for military service. Although I was angry and regarded my being in the army as a complete waste of time, to my surprise, I did enjoy some of the things we were forced to do. Most of us did. The physical training and learning to use various weapons and the military manoeuvres were so far removed from normal life, it was hard not to get a kick from them.

But I didn't like sitting through lectures and being told that under the Shah's command, we were the main defence against "communism" in our region. I didn't like the example we were given of this "defence": how our army, along with British Special Forces, had defeated a "Communist" uprising in Oman. The lack of democracy in Oman, or in our country, wasn't mentioned. I didn't believe a word of it, and my sympathy was automatically with the rebels.

I was one of perhaps 200,000 who were the Shah's personal playthings, equipped with expensive modern weapons and on call at his command. A large slice of our country's oil revenues were being squandered on us. I finished my military service convinced that the Shah, "The King of Kings", as he liked to be called, lived on his own personal cloud.

Some years later as we were driving home from work one evening, Mashti said, "The Social School Secretary was asking about you the other day".

"About me?" I was surprised that she even remembered me.

"She said you're the kind of person they try to attract."

"How did she come up with that?"

"I think sometimes they get the wrong kind. You know, the type who puts on airs and wants to sit behind a desk and look important. Anyway, someone's interested in you. Are *you* interested?"

I told Mashti I'd never thought of my future apart from being with his company.

"Well the offer's there. I don't want to lose you. I told her that. But we should do what we want with our lives. Not what others want us to do. You've got my blessing, whatever you decide."

The possibility of an entirely different kind of life opened up. I certainly wasn't Mullah material. I didn't have that kind of calling. But I have always passionately believed in the social ethics of the Koran, and I felt revulsion towards the Shah and those around him. To me, they were selfishness personified. It wasn't just the crooked way they made their money. It was their self-indulgence, the extent of their luxury: their houses and estates on other continents and fat foreign bank accounts. To me, those people, when they could have been doing a lot of good with their money, wilfully chose to ignore the ideals of our faith; I'd never wanted to emulate their kind. But to be trained professionally at Princess Sattareh's school, to do the kind of thing her students were trained to do? Yes, I felt, that is how I would like to live.

Later that year I started at the Teheran School of Social Work. That was in 1976. The following February, the first demonstrations that led to the Revolution began.

After Khomeini came back, I was sure our school would have a great future in the new Islamic Republic. But I knew we would have to wait until the Shah's last Government, the Bakhtiar Government, had fallen. Bakhtiar was the Shah's choice: appointed by the "King of Kings", before he fled. Bakhtiar seemed to think his moment had arrived. He had spent time in the Shah's prisons, and I am sure he had good intentions, but he didn't seem to grasp that, because he *was* the Shah's choice, he was unacceptable to the people. There was a Revolution in process and with it, a profound desire for change that couldn't be satisfied by just another Prime Minister. The people wanted an end, immediately, to the American connection that had sustained the Shah and wasted our oil revenues, an end to Savak and its jails, and to the Shah's army, an end to the Israeli connection, an end to virtually everything the Shah had stood for.

The people now had Ayatollah Khomeini. *He* was the moral authority in our country. But there were still Bakhtiar, and behind him, the Shah's generals.

When huge numbers of people come together for a common purpose, something extraordinary happens. I felt it first on the day Ayatollah Khomeini returned, and I felt it again on the day the Air Force came over to the Revolution: we were on the streets, over a million people, calling for Bakhtiar to resign, when the blue helmets of the Air Force appeared amongst us. There was instant soaring emotion as we welcomed our new friends and lifted them to our shoulders.

But what everyone feared, happened. The Imperial Guard left their barracks and attempted to crush the "rebellion" and what had been a peaceful demonstration turned into a bloody battle.

Everyone remembered the 1954 coup that had returned the Shah. This time, the Mullahs had weapons, and too many were prepared to fight, for the Shah's forces to succeed. There were so many clamouring for guns that I didn't get my chance to join the battle until the Guards were retreating. By then I'd seen too many casualties of the battle, many of them shot in the head, not to respect the expertise of our enemy. Eventually, as the casualties mounted, my turn came and a Mullah issued me with two of my old army weapons, an American M16 and a grenade launcher. He directed me to a room opposite the enemy positions.

I was horrified by what I found there: there was a machine-gun at the window, behind it, in a pool of blood, lay the men I'd been sent to help. Each was lying with his feet towards the window, each apparently killed by a single bullet. One was a cleric. Another, I could see from his calloused hands, was a manual worker. The third looked like a teenage boy. He was still slowly bleeding from where his forehead had been. I guessed that they had been shot in rapid succession as they tried to fire the machine-gun.

Feeling vulnerable and fearing I was visible from across the street, I crawled along the wall opposite the window, moving slowly, looking for some sign of where the shooting had come from. It was simpler than I'd expected. There was a wisp of smoke drifting from the window of a room directly across the street. It wasn't gun smoke. No one had fired since I'd arrived. Incredibly someone was smoking in there. Being presented with such easy targets must have made him over confident. I gripped the grenade-launcher, crouched as low as I could and aimed carefully. I knew that if I didn't get the trajectory right and the grenade went too high and hit the window frame, or wall, it would be the end of me. On the other hand, if I went too close to the window, *that* would be the end of me. As I pulled the trigger, I saw a movement. I'd been seen. But too late, and as the room opposite filled with flame and smoke, I crawled out into the corridor.

The Imperial Guard was retreating fast, and I didn't get another chance to engage them that day. If military victories were counted only in casualties, we would have lost. But we had defeated our enemy's purpose. The Air Force had stayed and fought on the side of the Revolution. We had won the day.

The Shah's plot had been uncovered. His leaving was a ruse.

Before going, he had left instructions for a military coup and had expected to return. But most of the army had deserted and given up their weapons. The Imperial Guard was isolated. Yet they still tried. And they were to try again the next day. And the next. Perhaps they believed the US marines would come and reinstall their Shah.

I'd been home to let mother see I was okay. I was on my way to the fighting the following day, when a motorcyclist with a wounded man slumped on his pillion stopped and asked me to help. The man was loosing consciousness. I awkwardly sat on the carrier and held his passenger fast to the pillion. We got him to the hospital and then returned to the fighting together. It turned out that the motorcyclist was a member of the Mohajedin. That's how I came to spend the weekend with a mixed group of Mohajedin and our new friends from the Air Force.

I'll never forget the experience. Their discipline under fire was awesome, and the Imperial Guard couldn't advance against them. They would carry wounded comrades to the rear and then return to their positions, sometimes only to be shot themselves. Their mounting casualties didn't deter them. My motorcycling friend explained that the Mohajedin had long accepted that they would have to trade their lives for freedom. Later, he was shot through the head.

Over that weekend, the Imperial Guard was defeated, and the Shah's last Government fell.

Khomeini had repeatedly broadcast that he wanted a return to work on Saturday, February 17th. I returned to school on that day. I was enthusiastically looking forward to the support we would receive from our new government.

Before I could get through the door into the school, Zabi, the old Janitor, whom I used to chat to, called me to one side. He looked distressed. "What's the matter?" I asked him.

"You've known the Princess for a long time haven't you?"

"Yes I have. What's wrong?"

"Some of the students came in with guns."

"Guns?" I couldn't believe it. "What have they done?"

"They've taken her away to be executed!"

"That's crazy."

"It's what they've done. Hakim drove them. They've gone to the Majlis police station … by the old bazaar."

I ran into the school and along the corridor and through the hall. There were students everywhere standing around. They turned and watched as I ran past. I took a set of Land Rover keys from the office.

I drove as fast as I could, but the streets were littered with the wreckage of the fighting, and it seemed to take an age. When I reached the police station, Hakim was standing by his vehicle. He saw me and raised his fist and started to shout some kind of slogan. But I took him by the collar. "You bastard", I shouted in his ear. "She gave you a job and you do this to her." I dragged him around the vehicle to the entrance of the police station. I told him, "You're going to tell them about all the things she's done".

He pointed, "I'm just the driver ... it's them". Coming out of the door were four students carrying automatic rifles. I recognised them, but wasn't sure of their names.

One of them, apparently the leader, asked, "What's going on?"

He was so calm and apparently pleased with himself, I thought, "Oh, there must be an explanation for all this", so I asked him, "Why the guns? What's happened to Sattareh?"

"She's on her way to Ayatollah Khomeini to be executed."

I looked at the four of them. They looked as though they were expecting me to be happy.

"Have you all gone crazy? Don't you realize her school's been doing the kind of thing Khomeini wants."

"She was trained in America. She's been working for the imperialists. It's time to throw them out."

I tried to talk to the others. "Its the Shah's generals Khomeini wants. Savak agents. People like that."

But they let their leader talk, "She was the director of one of the Shah's institutions".

"Yes", I said, "and you were a student at one of the Shah's institutions".

"I had no choice."

"Neither did she. Even Mossadeq had to deal with the Shah. Should we have stopped breathing because the Shah ruled the country?"

"Mossadeq wasn't corrupt. He didn't take money."

"What are you talking about. I saw the Princess start the school. She had to use her own money to get it off the ground. She's out of pocket. The school has been her life. She put it before her family."

They looked unimpressed so I continued, "One of the first

things she did … there were starving orphans … like skeletons. They were looked after by convicts until Sattareh found them …"

"What was she doing visiting Israel?"

"What! Someone's made that up!"

"No one made it up. She visited Israel. We saw it in the school files. Israel and the CIA, they were behind the Shah. They taught Savak how to torture."

"Don't you *know* her? If she went to Israel it must have been for a good reason. There's lots of Muslims in Israel. You know how they're treated. Aren't they part of our Islamic community? Don't they deserve our help?"

I tried hard, but couldn't shake them. I felt it was all to do with Sattareh being a woman, a confident, highly educated woman, who had what they must have felt was power over them. Perhaps these students were the kind Mashti had talked about, who wanted a job behind a desk and resented Sattareh sending them to work amongst the city and village poor. Whatever their motives, they had taken the first opportunity to remove her.

Sattareh had always left the school files open for the staff and students to see. She never hid anything. She put the entire business of the school open to scrutiny. It looked as though the four students had gone through the files trying to build up a case against her. And they were prepared not just to punish her for what they claimed was wrong, but to have her executed.

For them, the Revolution meant something different than it did for me. To me, it had been about doing away with injustice. Probably to them, injustice was something that the Shah and America and Israel dished out. They seemed to have no standard of right and wrong for their own behaviour. They had guns and would do what they wanted, and there was someone they resented.

I'd wasted too much time on them and when I went inside the police station the Princess had gone. She'd been sent for judgement to the Alavi Girls' School, where the Ayatollah had his headquarters. The charges were being taken seriously.

It wasn't too far to the Alavi School, so I decided to walk. It would give me time to think. So far I'd been dealing with prejudice and hate. When I reached the school I'd try to have Sattareh released and have someone mature look at the school files.

I soon discovered I wasn't the only one on my way to the Alavi School. There were many others going the same way: they formed excited crowds. Something big was happening in their lives, and they were hoping to see the person mainly responsible. I looked at them, men women and children: the women in black chadors. All were single-mindedly walking to where the object of their adoration was. They believed absolutely in Khomeini. They saw him as being close to the people, a man who lived a frugal life and would act in their interests.

In his time Mossadeq too had won the support of the people. He had opposed foreign ownership of our country's oil. He had refused to endorse the Shah's rule and had demanded that money wasted on renovating palaces be invested in building factories to employ people and create wealth. Mossadeq had become a hero. But the hero had fallen. Now the people had another hero, Khomeini. He had made an enemy of the Shah: he had criticised the pomp and the lavishness and the strutting and had said, "The Shah is just a man". He had become the Shah's most prominent critic. But *he* hadn't fallen. It was the Shah who had gone. And now this hero, Ayatollah Komeini, had power.

The crowd was so dense it took me until evening to actually get into the alley that led to the main gate. I'd realised how difficult it would be, so I'd stopped and bought myself a meal and phoned home to let them know where I was. And I'd phoned Sattareh's office, just in case she'd been released and returned to the school, but the line was dead.

After a struggle, I eventually made it to the main gate, but it was impossible to talk to the guards on the inside. When someone on official business arrived, the guards almost fought the crowd to get the visitors inside. So I had a long frustrating wait amongst the ecstatic crowd.

Once, a line of Imperial Guards was led through the crowd and taken inside the gate. Their captors explained to us that the Guards were about to swear allegiance to Khomeini. They were putting themselves in his service. I was astonished. I had thought that anyone who had been prepared to shoot the people would never be allowed to handle firearms again.

Later, a man carrying a bleating sheep fought his way to the gate and fell through when it opened: even the revolutionaries organising the new Iran needed to eat.

Most people had gone before the end of the day, but it wasn't until after dark that the alley emptied, except for me. It was freezing cold and I'd been waiting for quite a while before my chance came. The gate suddenly opened, and a cleric stepped out into the alley. Before it could close, I stepped inside. The guard shut the gate behind me. "Can I see someone in authority?" I asked him.

"It's late. Are you a Guardsman?"

"Me?" I felt insulted. "I spent three days fighting the buggers."

He laughed. "We all did. What is it you want?"

"I'm from the School of Social Work. Sattareh Farman Farmaian was brought in earlier. She's been accused of all kinds of stupid things."

The guard put his hand on my arm, "Don't worry. Everyone knows about her. The Ayatollah isn't happy about all these people taking the law into their own hands. They're looking at her case now. If she's innocent she'll be released."

"But she is innocent. She shouldn't have been brought here."

"Okay. Okay. Listen it's late. I shouldn't have let you in. If you say she's innocent, she'll be okay."

"Can I speak to whoever's taking her case?"

"It's not allowed. Listen, I shouldn't have let you in. You'd better go now. I'm sure she'll be okay." I had no option. I had to leave.

So she was still there. I thought that if her case was being looked at she might be released at any time.

Time passed, and I walked up and down the alley to fight off the cold. Suddenly there was a volley of rifle shots from somewhere inside the compound, followed by absolute silence. I tried not to think, just to wait. But it was impossible not to consider the possibility that Sattareh had been shot. Yet I knew that some of the Shah's generals had been taken prisoner, and it was virtually certain that it was them who had been executed. A while later, I heard someone sliding a heavy bolt to lock the gates from the inside. I decided to go home.

Mashti woke me next morning with the news that Sattareh had been released. He'd spoken on the phone to one of her relatives. She'd been kept all the previous day and half the night, waiting in the freezing cold in the schoolyard, before being interrogated. The interrogator had let her know that Ayatollah Komeini wasn't happy with the youngsters who were acting on their own. Nevertheless, she'd been interrogated and had felt that her life was in danger.

But she was eventually told that Ayatollah Taleqani had spoken up for her to Khomeini. He told the "Court" about her work in the prisons and on the streets and had actually said that the

Revolution wouldn't succeed if it consumed people like Sattareh. Khomeini was impressed and wanted her to go back to her work. In spite of his blessing, an aide quietly warned her that her life would be in danger from some of the students.

The Revolution ended the Princess's life's work. She never went back to the school, and militant students confiscated her car and, even worse, someone she employed, who had a connection to the local Revolutionary Committee took over her home.

Sattareh was in hiding. I wondered why she didn't go directly to Ayatollah Taleqani and ask for his protection. But I was just an anonymous person who wasn't in danger. And I didn't appreciate, as she must have done, that the local Committees and their gunmen had power to hunt down whoever they wanted and that Khomeini took their views seriously. Probably Sattareh understood the nature of the change then taking place. I certainly didn't. Weeks later Sattareh fled the country. Possibly, it was the only way she could stay alive.

I never went back to the School of Social Work. Neither did my friend Ashraf. I was able to rejoin Mashti. But it was harder for Ashraf. For her, the work of the school had been of even greater religious significance than for me. Besides, she'd socialised with Sattareh and had never missed the princess's weekend hill-walking expeditions.

My feelings towards Ashraf were more than friendly. We'd become close and I wanted to marry her. But I had a host of worries. Although the new Islamic constitution carefully guaranteed that no one would be persecuted for their beliefs, I knew that Khomeini regarded Bahais as heretics. I also knew that amongst the Mullahs, there were some fanatical anti-Bahais, and I was worried about Ashraf and her family and the rest of the Bahais.

The Bahais were unusual people. Their religion could be summed up with the words "love" and "tolerance". Ashraf would come out with memorable little sayings like, "In the garden of the heart, plant nothing but the rose of love", and "The earth is one country and mankind its citizens". And she believed them with all her heart. Other faiths had inward-looking, intolerant sects, who thought themselves especially selected by God and who treated others according to narrow, selfish creeds. Not the Bahais. They were anything but narrow. They accepted that Islam, Christianity and Judaism were true faiths. Yet, they had their own original core aim, which they saw, I think, as uniquely theirs: World Peace. They made it their, central and, to them, achievable aim.

I admired them for their optimism because, palpably, no religious creed, or set of beliefs, had so far managed to end the world's interminable violence. The old religions, or at least many of their followers, had led the world through endless bloodshed.

My own faith, Islam, was no exception. Mohamed's teachings had held the promise of different communities respecting each other and living in peace. Yet not long after his death, his followers were at war killing each other, and the early promise was never fulfilled. And Christianity? Despite its message of love, and its supreme Commandments, "Love thy neighbour", and "Thou shall not kill", Christianity had a history of intolerance, persecution and wars. One of its first lessons to Islam had been the slaughter of the Muslim population of Jerusalem. And Judaism? Judaism had been the source of Christianity's admirable Commandments. Yet Judaism had had no better results. The Palestinian people were still reeling from the violent theft of their land, in the name of God, carried out with the support of the Christian West. As far as I knew, other old faiths had fared no better.

Might the Bahais be more successful? Their faith was a young faith, and Bahais had never wielded power. So they hadn't been tested. Yet, they were the only body of people I knew who were totally true to the ideals of their faith.

My immediate concern was that the Bahais were about to become victims of the intolerants let loose by the Revolution. The evening Ashraf and her parents came to my house, to meet my family, they brought news that their holy place, The House of Bab in Shiraz, had been taken over by the Authorities. What was meant to be a relaxed occasion turned into a nervous, worried evening, as we talked about what might come next.

By the end of 1979, I had ceased to believe in Khomeini. By then the House of Bab had been levelled to the ground and nearby Bahai families evicted and their homes given to others. And hundreds of other Bahais had been made homeless, jobless and penniless. Many had lost, not just lost their homes, but also their shops, offices and farms. Bahai centres and holy places and even cemeteries had been confiscated. And some Bahais had been killed.

Khomeini disappointed me. When Israel had done exactly these things to Palestinian Muslims and Christians, he had been outraged. Despite his years of struggle, he was ending his days concerned only with injustices done to Muslims. I remembered reading about a courageous Jewish dissident in Russia who, after he had been allowed to go to Israel, had joined one of the extremist political parties, which stubbornly denied equal rights to Palestinians. I came to see Khomeini as an Islamic version of that Jewish dissident.

I had once heard the expression, "Not by bread alone". Now I understood it. Our construction company was doing well. The Government were getting many things right, and there was plenty to be done in the new Iran. But, for me, the atmosphere had become as unbearable as it had been during the Shah's time. We had made a Revolution. For what? Forces had been released that were beyond anyone's control, except perhaps, Khomeini's. But the man wasn't up to it. I was frustrated, I couldn't think of anything positive I could do.

But there were some who acted. Without telling Mashti or me, mother and Aunt Shery joined a women's demonstration against compulsory wearing of the chador. The first we knew about it, was when we returned home from work one evening. Mother and Shery were preparing a meal with every sign of normality, except that mother had a black eye.

The demonstrators had been attacked. Their male attackers had used fists and clubs, and some had used knives. Two women were knifed. Khomeini condemned the attackers. But I never heard if the culprits were caught and punished.

Not long afterwards, I was involved in violence myself. I was walking through central Teheran and as I turned a corner I nearly walked into a melee of club-wielding goons attacking Mohajedin newspaper-sellers. I ran the few paces that separated us and hit one of them. I continued running, feeling sure he wouldn't be wielding his club again that day. His fellow goons chased me, but they couldn't run at top speed carrying clubs. I lost them easily.

Afterwards I was elated. I'd done *something*. But I didn't like what those people were doing to me. I was full of anger. So many who had so much to offer were becoming their victims: even the heroic Mohajedin.

The Mullahs who had so often criticised the Jewish state, were creating Israel's mirror image: an Islamic state where those who weren't Muslims, or weren't considered sufficiently Islamic, were ridden over, roughshod.

We attended a memorial service, Mashti, Shery, mother and I, for the son of the Anglican Bishop who had been murdered, by fanatics, guilty of being a Christian. We went to show our sympathy for the young victim. We were pleased to discover that most of the mourners were fellow Muslims.

Before long we were paying our respects to other victims, Bahais, friends of Ashraf, executed in Adelbad prison: guilty of being Bahais and refusing to give up their faith.

One spring evening in 1980, I was working at Ashraf's home when *they* came. They carried an arrest warrant and their inevitable guns. They had orders to arrest Ashraf's mother and father. Luckily, I was alone in the house, so was able to lie to them. I told them the family were away from home.

After the gunmen went, I phoned Ashraf's father and warned him not to come home. "Don't you worry", he said, "we've done nothing wrong. Our consciences are clear."

When they returned I tried again. "Listen Husayn, it doesn't matter that you've done nothing wrong. They're after you. You need to go into hiding to protect yourselves."

He turned his open, honest face to me, "We'd rather face them", he said.

I tried again, "You know what happened to your friends ..."

It was hopeless. They waited at home until they were arrested and went as though they were going on some pleasant excursion.

That's how Ashraf and I came to marry earlier than we'd intended. We were married by the time we visited her parents in prison. There were two glass partitions separating us, and we had to speak by phone. They actually looked happy. Yet I knew that Bahais in Adelbad prison suffered all kinds of indignities and could be tortured and threatened with death, which was no idle threat. How harshly they were treated, depended partly on the whim of the interrogator and partly on how senior a Bahai the prisoner was.

While we were talking, I overheard the visitor on the next phone saying, "You're lucky to be in prison for your faith". The comment reinforced my impression that the more resolute Bahais, drew great satisfaction from facing the inquisitors and not weakening.

That was when I first thought about getting Ashraf out of Iran. I was sure that if she were arrested, resolute in her faith, she would bravely face whatever might happen.

Over the months, Ashraf's parents kept their cheerful faces, but their paleness showed their deteriorating condition. Then one day during our visit they were strangely happy. And while they were being led away they never took their eyes from Ashraf.

We were told the next day that they had been executed.

Although Ashraf was obviously affected, she didn't cry in my presence. Her faith gave her strength.

I spent the next few weeks trying to persuade her that we should apply for visas to leave the country. But she was arrested before I could get her to agree. When I arrived home from work one evening, I found they had taken her. I spent that night wide-awake, all kinds of schemes running through my mind mostly involving guns and violence. But eventually I managed to think more rationally. The next morning after a sleepless night, I'd made my plans.

It took me a few days to get my interview with the investigator who was dealing with Ashraf.

"So you think you can do better than us?" he asked.

"I don't think you'll succeed. I'm her husband. She loves me. If anyone is going to convince her, it's me."

"I'm not sure."

"Look, you say all you want is for her to become a Muslim. Does it matter how you achieve it?"

"Any Bahai who converts, however it happens, can go back to living a normal life."

"Then please trust me. All I ask for is a month."

"It's the Israeli connection I don't like."

"There's no Israeli connection."

"Surely you know about the Bahai centre in Israel?"

"Surely *you* know it was there before Palestine became Israel? It's an accident of history. What about *our* holy places In Israel ..." I could see that he didn't like what I was saying, so I played my card of last resort, "Look, if I can't convert her within a month, I'll divorce her".

"You'd do that?"

"Of course. If I can't convert her, I'm finished with her."

He gave me two weeks. I couldn't believe it. She was free.

She came out of the prison gate and saw the car. I wanted to get away as quickly as possible. I pushed the door open, "Ashraf. Quick. Get in." And we were away.

"Amir, what's happening?"

It wasn't a time for explanation. "Are you happy to be out?"

"I can't believe it. To be back with you." She took my free hand and held it to her cheek. At last she was crying.

I wanted to say comforting words, but I didn't. Instead, "You're brave Ashraf. You would have taken whatever they did to you, wouldn't you? Well, they want you back in a fortnight." I didn't wait, as I had intended, to let her think about *that*. Instead, I immediately added, "I'm going to do everything in my power to stop them getting their hands on you again". I was desperate and before we reached home, I had verbally bludgeoned her into agreeing to escape with me, over the mountains to Turkey. It was probably from concern for my state of mind that she agreed to my plan.

We drove straight to my family to discuss our plans. Understandably, neither mother nor Shery liked the idea.

Mashti wasn't sure, "Can't you go into hiding?"

Since I'd suggested the same thing to Ashraf's father, I'd reconsidered that option, "We want to get out before we go on any wanted list".

"Ashraf. Couldn't you pretend to give up your religion."

"Mother, Ashraf's faith is her life."

"I'm sorry Ashraf. I shouldn't have asked."

"It's okay."

Mashti asked, "Do you realise what you'll be taking on? Physically, I mean."

"We're both in good condition."

"But finding your way through those mountains?"

"I've got maps."

"You'll need to know all the side tracks", Mashti answered. "They don't show on the maps. Only local people know about them. You'll need to know checkpoints … the way border patrols work."

"We're going to travel in the dark. We'll be very careful. Can you think of an alternative?"

"I've been thinking … you don't have much time. I know someone who lives in Tabriz. He was a Mossadeq organiser. Sadeq Vahdat. He left Teheran after the coup. The last I heard of him, he was living on his own in Tabriz. There's just a chance he knows someone who can help." Mashti spoke to Sadeq by phone that evening, and from the start he wanted to help us. The next day he phoned back, "They must be prepared to leave at short notice". We made our preparations.

Four days later he phoned again, "Be here tomorrow night".

We spent our last evening with mother, Shery and Mashti. We talked about what might happen when we reached Europe.

Where would we end up? Germany? Sweden? Bijan was studying in France. Perhaps we could go there? A lecturer at our college had once spoken glowingly about the School of Social Studies in New York. Was it possible that some international body would fund our studying there? Perhaps I could start a construction company somewhere; I knew construction inside out; I'd just need to read up on local regulations.

The next morning we set off in Mashti's pick-up truck on the long drive to Tabriz, our tools and building materials in the back. Mashti and I wore our working clothes. The idea was that should we be stopped, Ashraf wrapped in a Chador, would feign sleep and Mashti would do the talking.

I was afraid that someone from the local Committee had seen our early morning departure, but we were never stopped. On the highway we were indistinguishable from other traffic, and when we went into a cafe for food, no one gave us a second look. And so we arrived at Tabriz and met Sadeq.

Sadeq told us about his contacts with Kurdish activists and the two young Kurds, friends of his, who would be leaving for Turkey the following night; they were willing to take us along.

Mashti had taken his leave, and Ashraf and I were eating the meal Sadeq had prepared for us, when he said to me, "I couldn't remember Mashti, until he mentioned your father. Then it came to me, Mamhoud had a younger brother. When I realised who you were, I was determined to help you."

"Who I was?"

"I knew your father well. We were friends. I spent a lot of time with him during the last months of his life."

"Mashti never told me."

"Mamhoud didn't let him get involved. He knew how dangerous things might get. Your father was a very able young man." He grimaced, "To be shot down the way he was ... you know about it?"

"Mother told me when I was little."

"You don't mind me talking about it then?"

"I don't mind. I've known about it all my life. Mother wanted me to know."

"Did your mother tell you the reason? Oil."

"Yes, that was part of it."

"That *was* the reason. Churchill wouldn't accept Mossadeq's take-over of the Anglo Iranian Oil Company, and it was always only a question of when he'd do something. He wasn't one for half-measures. That's why Mossadeq was trying to come to an arrangement with the Americans. Some of us thought he was playing with fire.

"There was a lot of feeling over Westerners owning our oil, and Mossadeq could fill the streets anytime he wanted. Then – he baffled us – he banned demonstrations. He banned *his own supporters* from coming out on the streets. You know about the demonstration that was put down? Over a hundred killed."

"Yes. Mashti told me."

"The killing wasn't Mossadeq's fault. It was probably part of the American plot. Anyway, Mossadeq disarmed himself by banning his own supporters. That's how the coup was able to succeed. It came out later that the American Ambassador had offered Mossadeq a deal, 'Keep the people off the streets, and I'll be able to get you American aid'. *That was the deal.*" Sadeq shook his head, "And Mossadeq agreed.

"Before we could do anything, Mossadeq had been overthrown, and the Shah was back, and we were being hunted down. Your father was recognised on the street and shot. That's why I came to Tabriz: to stay alive ... have you read Kermit Roosevelt's book?"

"Who?"

"He was the American agent who organised the coup, and he had the nerve to write a book about it. Anyway, straight after the coup, he flew to London to see Churchill. That bastard wanted to know all the details of the coup. About that time, while they were gloating together, that's when they shot your father. Then Kermit Roosevelt flew to Washington to report to the other bastard."

Later that evening Sadeq took us on the first leg of our journey. After dark, a "taxi" picked us up and took us out of Tabriz to the north, then along a winding road into the hills to the west. Before we left, Ashraf had a minor triumph with Sadeq. She saw him put a pistol into his coat pocket and pleaded, "Please don't take the gun".

Sadeq answered, "I don't think you realise the kind of people ..." Then he stopped and just stared at her: to me, an image of innocence. I thought Sadeq was probably recalling the reason she was fleeing.

Ashraf said, "I'd rather be caught than have someone killed".

Sadeq didn't argue. He left the gun behind.

We'd been travelling at speed for some time, when the driver warned us, "We're being chased. Leave the talking to me. Go to sleep."

We were soon overtaken and stopped by a car full of Revolutionary Guards. They surrounded the car pointing their guns. "Out. Get out." We pretended we were asleep. I felt the car sway as the driver got out. Then, "Sattar", "Payam", followed by talking and laughter.

We stayed "asleep". After a while, miraculously, the driver got back inside and drove off honking to the guards as we left. "Payam's my brother-in-law", he explained. "He owes me a favour."

We drove on through the night, still at speed, until eventually we turned off the road and along a bumpy track. After a few hundred metres Sadeq said, "We're here". We got out and gave the driver our heartfelt thanks.

Sadeq led us on. We were at a higher elevation than Teheran and walking uphill. The air was clear and cool and visibility was good. There were no clouds and the stars sparkled with a brilliance I hadn't seen before. We seemed to be in the middle of a wilderness. In every direction there were hills dotted with occasional trees and sparse vegetation. After going uphill for a while, we crossed the brow of a hill and then descended into a dark ravine. We emerged into bright moonlight, and Sadeq turned and put his finger to his lips. Soon we were walking along the side of a cultivated field, then past an orchard. From somewhere not far away dogs started to bark. Sadeq walked faster. I felt like taking Ashraf's hand and running on past him. But the fast walk was enough, and before long the barking became a faint sound in the distance.

We walked on, sometimes seemingly ever upwards, until we found ourselves descending rapidly to lower ground and cultivated fields and human settlements. Once we saw a pair of illuminated eyes, watching us from within the darkness of a copse. We had no idea what they belonged to.

The sky was glowing with the first sign of morning, when Sadeq turned for the last time and put his finger to his lips. We followed him quietly. He led us through an orchard, right up to a large shed. The door was slightly open, and Sadeq went inside. We could hear him talking to someone in Kurdish. They talked for a while, then a big man with white hair came out. He nodded to us and waived us inside.

Sadeq looked happy, "Well, we've arrived". He looked around, "You can rest here until tonight".

"A Kurdish woman brought us coffee and food and left us to our ourselves. She hardly said anything. Sadeq had already explained that our helpers were putting themselves at risk and simply wanted us to pass through their hands as quickly as possible. After eating, he left us to catch up on our sleep. We lay down fully clothed on the straw and slept."

I woke up to the smell of tobacco smoke. Sadeq was on the other side of the barn sitting with his back to us and smoking his pipe. He must have heard me standing up, "Everything's arranged", he said without turning. "They're glad you don't need horses. Horses are so conspicuous ..."

After Ashraf had come around and we'd chatted for a while, the woman brought us more food: a full lamb meal and cheese and tea. She spoke to Sadeq in Kurdish. He translated, "She wants you to eat as much as you can. You'll need the food inside you once you get going."

I already knew that the Kurds were seeking autonomy and had been on the verge of an agreement with Khomeini's negotiators, when Khomeini, himself, blocked the deal; he had no concept of national rights. According to Sadeq, the two Kurds who were to be our guides had been involved in the fighting that followed the breakdown of the talks. They would be carrying guns and would use them rather than be taken by the Revolutionary Guards. I didn't mention it to Ashraf and thankfully, when they came for us, she didn't comment. She seemed to accept that Kurds had guns.

We said goodbye to Sadeq and tried to thank him. I won't forget his answer. "*You* are doing *me* a favour", he said. "Doing this for you helps me believe that my life hasn't been a total waste."

"Sadeq, how could it have been ...?"

"No. Listen. When I was your age, I believed in human progress. I didn't think we could go backwards. I had Beliefs. I thought I would be part of doing great things for our country. Look what happened! Look what we've come to! The most I can do is help you to escape *from your own country*."

Sadeq put his hand out to Ashraf. He hesitated and looked at me.

"Sadeq, it's okay."

He took Ashraf's hand, "Don't change. You might be wrong in the detail. But, don't change ..."

The two youths, Mosehn and Mahtob, led us off at a fast pace.

There were more clouds than the previous night, and it was darker. It wasn't a problem. Within an hour we'd reached a surprising height. We were well into the mountains and with luck, wouldn't emerge until we were inside Turkey. I had to admire our guides. They were "professionals". They never took us over a ridge without looking carefully at what was beyond, and never let us walk erect going over. Once over, they'd hurry on as though we were in a race. We walked for hours, resting only when one of our guides went to check the way ahead. Sometimes we had to go up very steep slopes. Then they let us go up first in case we needed their help. We never did.

We had one bad fright. Mahtob came racing back down the track. Armed horsemen were coming. We seemed to have nowhere to go. We ran down the mountain until we reached open ground. There we hid amongst the boulders to one side of the path. There were clicks of safety catches as our friends readied their weapons.

The horsemen passed by. The danger over, we pressed on. Mosehn warned us that our riskiest time would come when we approached the border. There would be armed guards about.

Luckily we saw them in time. We needed to cross an area of open ground and pass through a gap in the cliffs. Three guards were standing on top of the cliffs silhouetted against the clouds. It seemed we would have no chance of reaching the border. Mosehn pointed at the ground and whispered, "Let's rest", and we lay down.

I couldn't guess what we'd do next. We were actually at the border, almost in Turkey, but there were armed men blocking our way. Ashraf looked at me with raised eyebrows, asking, "What now?" I didn't know.

Mahtob nodded and smiled. "Just wait", he seemed to be saying. And so we waited.

Eventually Mosehn pointed to his watch and whispered, "When they pray, go as quickly as you can".

I realised what he'd been waiting for. A few minutes later the guards disappeared below the cliff top. I could hardly believe our luck. We hurried across the open ground and along the path through the cliffs. Mosehn carefully led us out. We were at the beginning of a path that would, within a minute, take us out of Iran. The path itself seemed easy enough. But below was such a drop that if you tripped, you'd fall to your death. That wasn't what worried our friends. They held their guns ready and told us to cross quickly. We went, and they followed. We hurried on, until we were out of sight of the border. Then we danced a jig. We were in Turkey. Ashraf was beyond the reach of the inquisitors ...

7

Lucas

I FIRST BECAME aware of Patrice Lumumba when I was a schoolboy. Patrice was older than me, but I and everyone else in our school, knew his name. He was very bright and sure of himself. I had no idea then that he had qualities that would one day enable him to become the outstanding leader of my country. But if someone had asked me to guess which of the boys I knew would eventually become our Prime Minister, I would have immediately answered, "Patrice Lumumba". Patrice didn't stay at our school. Even at that age he had an independent attitude that led him into disagreement with the school, and he was expelled.

I didn't see him again until 1959, when I went to work in the Post Office in Leopoldville. Patrice was a fellow-worker and also our Union Secretary. And he was one of the leaders of our Congolese independence movement. I felt proud of my connection with him. His passion for a unified country, without tribalism and his ability, made him stand out from other leaders like Kasavuba and Tshombe and Albert Kalonji. They were more concerned with tribal and regional matters.

We Post Office workers had the privilege of seeing Patrice frequently. I remember one time, after someone had complained about our manager who was a bully, Patrice talked to the man and altered his behaviour. That the man changed didn't surprise me. He had been on the receiving end of Patrice's reasoning. And when Patrice talked to you, it was no ordinary experience. He had a wide mind and could see aspects of a problem that hadn't occurred to anyone else. He enlightened everyone who listened. And it was the same whatever circles he moved in. It was no wonder that the American Ambassador is reported to have said that if Patrice had been a waiter and had walked into any gathering of Congolese politicians carrying a tray, he would have come out as Prime Minister. Perhaps if Patrice hadn't been so able, an American President wouldn't have wanted him dead.

Thankfully, in my Post Office days, I didn't have an inkling of what was to come. Independence was in the air. Everyone knew it was coming. We thought it would be a time of joy. Few would have guessed that it would bring a resumption of a sordid past.

The extent of President Eisenhower's antagonism to Patrice still baffles me. Possibly, his agents had tried and failed to *buy* Patrice. Whatever the reason, Patrice's opinions should have been accepted as reasonable by any modern democratic politician. I heard him speaking many times, in private and in public and there was no hidden Patrice. He wanted the Universal Declaration of Human Rights applied to Africans. That was at the centre of his views. He was against racism of any kind, black or white. He spoke continually against violence and against tribal antagonisms. And it was certainly unjust that, after he became Prime Minister, he was blamed when Congolese troops settled tribal scores in blood in South Kasai Province.

Patrice wanted ordinary Congolese to be the prime beneficiaries of economic development. And he wanted the friendship of Belgium. He even appealed to young Belgians to come and live in the new Congo. But Patrice had self-respect, and he made it clear that the relationship had to be one of equality and respect and not of master and servant.

At Independence, we Congolese didn't have a national consciousness. In the nineteenth century, when the Belgians came, we weren't a nation. We were a conglomeration of tribes, who were unfortunate to live in the area King Leopold II coveted. But if anyone should understand the reality behind the talk of Western leaders, it is us. We learnt it from Leopold. He was a master of West-talk. He wanted to "civilize" the Congo. And he won the approval of the most powerful states for his "civilising" mission. *We Congolese* lived and died the reality behind his talk.

We were people, just like the Belgians, with husbands and wives and with love and hope for our children. And we had our skills and grew crops and fished and hunted and traded, and we had our own precious traditions and languages. And we had no less love of life or right to life, than the Belgians or Leopold himself.

Leopold didn't see it that way. His greed led him to care only for the ivory and rubber and copal, he could force us to deliver to his armed agents. He saw us merely as expendable creatures that could be put to work to make fabulous profits for his companies.

Once his power was established over our land, Leopold made it a crime for us to hunt and trap in our own forests. He stopped our traditional planting and imposed taxes, which we had to pay in rubber, copal, grain and labour. Meeting these "taxes" was no incidental matter. It became the main object of our existence, desperately searching the forests to fulfil quotas.

"Tax" probably sounded civilised to Western ears, an aspect of modern life. But for us, if we couldn't meet our "tax", we could have our villages destroyed or even be killed. It became normal practice for the soldiers to deliver baskets of human hands to Leopold's agents, to prove they had properly chastised defaulters. One agent even decorated the border of his garden with the heads of defaulters.

When news of Leopold's methods first became known in Europe, instead of feeling shame, he paid journalists to lie to the European public about what he was doing in the Congo. And he paid them to discredit the honest men who were telling the truth. Then he turned his attention to the French Congo.

The French Congo was just across the Congo River from our territory. But it might have been on the other side of an ocean it was so different. Its Governor, the creator of the French Congo, Brazza, was totally unlike Leopold. He considered the tribes in his territory to be the owners of the natural wealth of their land and to have the right to trade with the Western companies who wanted their goods. And that's how things were done in the French Congo under Brazza. An indication of the difference between Brazza and Leopold is that Brazzaville city, after all the years that have passed, is still called "Brazzaville", while the word "Leopoldville", has long been erased from the map.

When Brazza came to the Congo, he must have seen us as we were: people who were different from himself: but people. Brazza spent months getting to know each tribe. He had a reputation for patience and for talking to Africans with respect. He took time to negotiate with each tribe, rather than march through their territories the way Stanley did, by force of arms. Besides, Brazza exposed himself to the infections that killed so many Europeans, while Leopold never risked setting foot in the Congo. As an American might say, "Leopold probably considered his own 'Ass' too precious".

Brazza's Congo was so much of a contrast to Leopold's that Leopold used his paid journalists in Europe to smear and discredit

Brazza, until he was removed. Then the Leopold admirers were able to move into the French Congo.

Eventually, the Belgian Parliament took the Congo out of Leopold's hands. The shame of depopulation through physical abuse, hunger and disease and direct killing had been too much. But Leopold did one last thing before he lost control that was, long after his death, to help destroy Congolese democracy and independence: he created the mining company, Union Miniere.

Patrice ceased to be our Union Secretary after he was jailed for, allegedly, stealing Post Office money. There was no way of knowing whether he was really guilty, or the victim of an attempt to discredit him. I certainly didn't think any less of him. My feeling was, "If he's taken some money back, good luck to him". *And* I was convinced that his main motive would be the cause of Congolese Independence. The jailing did him no harm. He was soon released by popular demand and quickly became recognised as our most able political leader.

Patrice's party gained more seats than any other party in our new National Assembly, and he became our first Prime Minister.

Our Independence Day was 30th June 1960, and at the celebrations the Belgian King *praised King Leopold* and, to us, made it sound as though granting independence was an act of generosity. We Congolese didn't like it. But it was Patrice's speech, not the King's that created an explosion of Western anger.

Patrice was angry when he stood up to speak. President Kasavuba had already replied to the king's speech, in less warm terms than he had originally intended. But it was still a respectful reply. That probably heightened Patrice's anger. He himself was too forthright to pretend, and he talked honestly about the suffering of the Congolese under the Belgians. It was the truth. We Congolese knew it. But it wasn't diplomatic and the Europeans were angry.

To me, the episode was one more instance of how the West, the official West, lives in a world of make-believe: a world of assumed respectability, a fantasy world where crimes, if committed by West-favoured individuals, are of little importance. Diplomatic language, ceremonies, shows of civility and ladles of West-talk, transform the criminals into respectable pillars of the Western scheme of things. Third-World leaders who describe things as they really are become demonised, as Patrice was.

After Independence, "our" Black Congolese army mutinied against the authority of their Belgian officers, and Patrice's words took some of the blame. But the truth was that even without Patrice's speech, the mutiny would have happened. Our soldiers, or rather the soldiers who had served the colonial regime, weren't prepared to serve under white officers any longer. It's also true, that if we Congolese hadn't lived as a black underclass with constant humiliation, the mutiny would never have happened.

Some mutineers were satisfied with simply arresting their commanders, but sometimes officers were beaten up. And, in some areas, the mutineers attacked and arrested white civilians. Probably hundreds nationwide were attacked, and some women were raped, and tragically, some whites were killed. Understandably, there was panic amongst the Belgians and they rushed to leave the country. I was ashamed of what was happening and knew it would do us no good.

Patrice moved quickly and agreed to a new Black-officered force. He had intended to do this anyway, but gradually. The Leopoldville soldiers came back to discipline. After a meeting with Patrice they actually went out and tried to halt the white exodus, but the harm had been done. The flood continued. Yet the trouble seemed to be ending. There was every prospect of the country settling down.

Then Moise Tshombe stepped in. Tshombe was well financed, reputably, by the Belgians. And, using the money, he had been narrowly elected leader of Katanga Province, where Union Miniere's mines operated. Tshombe was the Belgian's Black puppet, and just when it looked as though we might be able to begin a peaceful Independence, Tshombe's paid-mouth began to make a lot of noise about Katanga wanting to stay free from "Communist" slavery and misery. It made no sense. It bore no relation to what was actually happening. But it served as justification for Tshombe's next two acts. First, he invited the Belgian Government to send their army to Katanga. Then he declared Katanga independent. *This was Belgian intervention.* They wanted to keep control of the Union Miniere copper mines.

So within a fortnight of independence, the Belgians had returned and seized our country's mineral wealth. They also seized the airport at Leopoldville. No sovereign Government could have tolerated such intrusions into its territory. Patrice had little choice but to send his troops against them. First they went to take the airport, and the invading Belgian paratroops retreated to the town of Matadi. And from Matadi we received news of a massacre of Congolese civilians. The response was predictable. Blacks attacked whites, and over fifty were killed.

The mood amongst blacks until then had been, "We have had a terrible start to our Independence. Let's put it behind us and face the challenge of managing our country ourselves." Belgian intervention dashed that hope; especially as rich Katanga Province had been our country's treasury.

One of Patrice's first responses was to ask the Americans, *not the Russians*, to send their soldiers to get the Belgians out. It wouldn't have required any fighting. If the Americans had consented, the Belgians would have just gone. But President Eisenhower refused. He said it would be best to keep the two major powers out of the situation. He suggested instead, that we ask the United Nations to send a force. Patrice must have listened to Eisenhower, because he did ask the UN to intervene. Everyone knew that America and Russia were competing to influence each newly independent country, and so Eisenhower's response seemed an example of unselfish statesmanship.

Little did we realise that it was West-talk again, behind which the American President was deploying his own quiet, sinister intervention. If anyone had tried to tell me at the time what was really happening, I would have thought they were deranged.

While he was acting the statesman, President Eisenhower was sending an agent with a poison, produced in an American Army laboratory, to murder Patrice. And there were two separate assassins sent, but none of them managed to get to him.

Unfortunately, Eisenhower had other means of undermining Patrice. He must have decided to get to Patrice through key tribal and regional leaders. Probably few people know the details of what happened, but before long, Albert Kalonji had declared South Kasai Province, home of our diamond mines, an autonomous state, and the Belgians flew arms to Kalonji. Another two key public figures, President Kasavuba and second in command of the army, Mobutu, both of whom had Belgian and American connections, stayed their hands and waited for the right moment.

At the time, UN involvement seemed an acceptable, bloodless, way of ending foreign intervention. But when the United Nations' force arrived, instead of moving against the Belgians, it moved to take power away from Patrice. Hammerskjold, the UN General Secretary, went beyond his authority and ordered that all aid to our country go through him. This order, if obeyed, would have prevented Patrice getting the arms he needed to try to end the intervention. But Patrice ignored Hammerskjold and got weapons from the *only place he could*: the Soviet Union. And he sent his newly armed troops to re-take South Kasai and Katanga. At first they were successful. Then Belgium's hired mercenaries defeated them.

It was immediately after this defeat, on September 5th, barely two months after Patrice had been elected, that President Kasavuba announced he was dismissing Patrice from office. And he publicly blamed Patrice for the chaos in the country, not Belgium and Union Mineire, not Tshombe, not Albert Kalonji, not America or Hammerskjold, but Patrice. Kasavuba, whose party had won only 12 seats in the National Assembly and owed his position to Patrice, was dismissing the Prime Minister whose party, the largest in the National Assembly, had won 42 seats.

Two days later, President Eisenhower announced to the world that he was taking a serious view of the Soviet Union's "intervention" in our country. Like much else, it didn't make sense. Patrice seeking Russian aid had been a last resort. And it had been completely legal, from one Government to another and open for all to see. The aid was essential for the defence of our national sovereignty. The American President was of course indulging in West-talk again, as a smoke-screen for what was really happening.

Yet all of Eisenhower's countrymen weren't taken in. One American television newsman, comparing Patrice's situation to President Lincoln's, questioned whether President Lincoln might not have accepted Russian help to save the union of America, if he had been prevented by outsiders from ending the secession of the South.

Not surprisingly Patrice won the support of our National Assembly and Senate. But the forces of intervention ranged against him were far too strong. Hammerskjold's three main UN officials in our country were Americans. One of them, Andrew Young, was a Black American. He was an honest man and was constantly shadowed by American agents. Another of the three, Andrew Cordier, I would guess, was part of the plot. He used United Nations troops to take control of Leopoldville airport. And when Patrice's loyal army commander, General Lundula, tried to land he was turned away. Cordier also used UN troops to take control of the radio station and prevented Patrice talking to the Congolese people. There can be little doubt that it was this misuse of United Nations authority by Cordier, which defeated Patrice.

There were so many strands to the plot: General Lundula's second in command, Mubuto, played his part. Miraculously, he happened to come by enough money to pay the whole Army and secure his control of the soldiers. Then he was able to use "his" army to disband the elected National Assembly and Senate; *they* had remained loyal to Patrice. And he arrested Patrice.

There was probably a consensus between the American and Belgian leaders that Patrice couldn't be allowed to live. Imprisoned and alive he would be a danger always threatening to lead popular opposition to their stooges. Eventually, President Kasavuba and Mobutu sent Patrice, our elected Prime Minister and his two Aides, Joseph Okito and Maurice Mpolo, to Katanga for disposal.

After being brutally battered for many hours, Patrice and his Aides were delivered to Tshombe. Care of Tshombe, they were murdered by mercenaries. The last I heard of Patrice's whereabouts, was that a member of the American Embassy staff claimed he had carried Patrice's body in the boot of his car.

I know that all men are fallible and vulnerable and that we shouldn't put all of our hope in any one leader. Yet, when Patrice died, my hope died too. I knew that my wretched country was entering a long, dark night. I left Leopoldville for Oriente Province and took the rural teaching post I hold today.

It's the start of another school year tomorrow, and I'll be teaching a different class. In our small community, everyone knows everything about everyone else, and I expect that during the morning some child's hand will go up, "Please Sir, tell us about Patrice Lumumba …?"

8

Saionji

I'VE REACHED OLD age and in my life have experienced much that has been rich and rewarding. But I've been lucky. I've survived nightmare times that took away so many people I knew and some I loved. When I was a boy I imagined I would be able to do more or less as I liked with my life. But I was soon disillusioned. Father took us "back" to Japan and I lost my feeling of freedom. It wasn't just the small daily constraints of Japanese life that affected me. It was also that in Japan it was obvious in a way it hadn't been in America that our lives are ultimately governed by large forces. And before many years had passed, I found myself surrounded by a violence I could never have imagined when I was a boy.

But I've survived. And survived with many of my early beliefs intact, I believe, because of my mother and father. I learnt so much from them. For instance, father had been a boxing fan when we lived in America and he loved using boxing language. He'd more than once said that it was wrong to go through life simply fighting one's "own corner" and that you had to learn to appreciate how things looked from other corners. By that, he hadn't simply meant that we should be unselfish. He sometimes used the analogy when he was talking about large conflicts between nations. I came to believe, long ago, that father's attitude should be applied to the whole web of relationships between people. My belief has helped me to witness the passions and prejudices I've lived amongst and be sure that *that* is not the way to live. In the face of people who knew no better than only to fight their own powerful corner, doing much harm, I've kept my sureness of that.

Of course, like mother and father, I'm Japanese and so I know all about the American, Commander Perry, with his squadron of black ships, who came to Japan and forced our country to "open up". And I know about the British "black ships" that forced the opium trade on China and took Hong Kong from her. And I know about the other European powers that came to Asia and inflicted endless indignities on China, once Asia's greatest state. So I know that in some circumstances, one has no option but to fight one's own corner.

I was lucky. Father had studied under Yuckichi Fukuzawa and, perhaps because of that, he had sought a woman like mother. I was born too late to meet Fukuzawa. But I would love to have known him. He must have been a fascinating character. To our family he was a hero. He was born in feudal Japan under the Shogun and grew up hating the rigidities of feudal life and resenting the obeisance lower ranks had to pay to their supposed superiors.

Fukuzawa was a Samurai who thought swords should be done away with. During the nationalist ferment at the time of the Imperial Restoration, when many Samurai would have liked to use their weapons on foreigners, he actually sold his own swords. He then went about with a short sword in place of his long sword and a little blade, more like a knife blade, where the short sword should have been. Hidden in their scabbards, no one could tell. So he was able to appear a normal Samurai and at the same time satisfy his own pacific outlook.

Fukuzawa's distaste for feudal life led him by accident to take the first step to becoming a great educationalist. Commander Perry's infamous visit that woke up Japan led to an immediate concern with national defence. Fukuzawa seized the chance of getting away from his feudal clan by going on a gunnery course. In order to master gunnery he had to learn Dutch, the language of the gunnery manuals. His knowledge of the Dutch language made him aware of the strange new world of Western culture, with its advanced science and technology. And this led him on to learn English.

And so when the Shogun sent emissaries to Europe and America, Fukuzawa, the rare English-speaker, was with them. Fukuzawa wasn't one to see and merely be impressed. He came back with his mind wide-open and determined to learn and to bring Western knowledge to Japan. But the hundreds of books he brought back from America were impounded, and he couldn't get his hands on them until after the Shogun had fallen.

Because of his interest in the West, Fukuzawa's life was in

danger from other Samurai. But despite the risk, he did establish a school and educated hundreds of Japanese youths. And as the sheer power of the West made it obvious that, to be able to defend itself, our country would have to learn Western ways, Fukuzawa, from being a notorious character, became a prestigious figure.

During the Civil War, he didn't take sides because he didn't agree with either the "keep-the-foreigner-at-arms-length" policy of the Shogun or the "keep-the-foreigner-out" attitude of the Emperor's forces. And when the Imperial armies won and he was asked to take charge of the country's education, he refused.

Sometimes father would talk about the Japan that might have been, had Fukuzawa not thrown away his great opportunity and how Japanese children had lost the chance of an education under the anti-macho Samurai. And he'd tell me how at the time, Fukuzawa had been so obsessed with our country's helplessness, he had believed his children would grow up to become slaves and became deeply depressed. His self-administered therapy had been teaching the new knowledge from the West. His single-minded work resulted in the creation of Keio University. That's where father met him, and it was on Fukuzawa's advice that he went to study in America.

America influenced father even more than Fukuzawa had done: it was different in so many ways. There was the astonishing mixture of peoples. When father went into a shop, or a restaurant, he might be served by someone from any one of a dozen nationalities. And Americans were direct and without the exaggerated deference father had grown up with: people were easy-going and informal. The women too. And there was huge wealth. And the country was vast. In America, it was a different existence, and it opened up my father's mind. I know that there was much more to America than father saw, or remembered. But these were the things that impressed him and won him over.

It was after visits to the homes of American friends, that father decided he wanted an American home for his family. So mother went out to him before he finished his studies. Then, when he graduated, he stayed and worked for an engineering company that was exporting to Japan. That's how I and my brother, Juniichi and sister, Takiko came to be born in America.

More than once, father told me that it was Fukuzawa who taught him how to think, but it was in America that he learnt how to live. I understand how much he appreciated America because when we moved to Japan, I suffered the reverse experience and found the constrictions hard to take.

That was when our family split up. Juniichi stayed in America to continue his studies. And Takiko was so unhappy in Japan that she became ill and was allowed to go back. I had mixed feelings. I longed to be with Juniichi and Takiko in America, but not without my parents. I was too young to leave them anyway, so I had no option but to stay and learn to fit in with Japanese ways.

But I did it my own way. When I bowed, I thought of Fukuzawa with his hidden cut-off blades and compared myself, with my hidden thoughts, to him. Yet I was in for a bigger culture shock than any set-piece behaviour could give me.

In the classroom, I found myself surrounded by boys who thought it would be a great thing to go to war, especially against the "dirty Chinks" and even to die for the Emperor. It didn't take me many lessons to realise that they thought that way because of what they were taught. I'm sure every nation's schools tell their own history from a one-sided view. But this Japanese education was so overwhelming. The boys soaked in the lessons about the glorious Japanese victories of 1895 over the Chinese and 1905 over the Russians and about the annexation of Korea. And they revered the names and exploits of heroes who had given their lives for the Emperor. They saw death in battle, fighting for the Emperor, as the highest attainable honour for man. And they eagerly anticipated future wars. They were full of Japan's Greatness. I found the school atmosphere alien.

I didn't like the idea of Japan attacking other countries, and the thought of willingly going to war and throwing my life away, didn't seem an attractive idea. Even without my parents influence, I think I would have rejected *that* notion. But I did talk to mother and father, and they helped me to understand my new country.

It was usually mother I talked with because father was so often out late, or even away from home, working for his American company. She explained that Japan throwing her weight around was normal behaviour for a state with ambitions of being "Great". She told me that when father had first gone to America, the American President, Teddy Roosevelt, had wanted to have a canal built through Colombia linking the Atlantic to the Pacific Ocean. But there had been a disagreement over the price America would pay Colombia. Then one morning, an American warship arrived off the coast of Colombia, and the following day a coup took place, seizing part of the country. Teddy Roosevelt had created a new American controlled state – Panama – where a canal would be built at America's price.

"That's how major powers behave", mother said. "America throws her weight around in the Americas. Britain is a law unto herself in her empire. France and Holland do the same in their empires. And Japan is trying to be like them. We are the only Asian state strong enough to control our own trade tariffs, and now we want our own empire." Of course, she told me much more than that. But, in a nutshell, that was her story.

Apparently, the boys had been taught much of this in school, but in a different way. The morality of Japan copying the worst ways of the West hadn't been considered. In my home it was at the heart of our discussions. Our attitude was, "What right had Japan to impose an unequal treaty on Korea, when we hadn't wanted one imposed on us; what right did our militarists have to go to war with China, and to annex Korea and Taiwan, and to control their trade and tariffs, when we hadn't wanted similar things done to us? Creating an Empire sounds grand, but what right did we have to subject other peoples to Japanese control? If it was wrong for it to be done to us, it must be wrong for Japan to do it to others." Those were our family attitudes.

In school, I felt like an outsider. And it didn't help that I wasn't fully fluent in the language. In America I hadn't needed to speak Japanese. We hadn't even had contact with Japanese communities there. But I eventually formed a friendship with another outsider, Toshio Segowa. He was a small, lightly built boy, who was constantly bullied by the dominant boys in the class. I'd seen him once being beaten up. While he was taking the punishment, he'd managed to shout, "Yukio, your mum is watching you". In response, Yukio, who was twice the size of Toshio, answered with a pummelling of even heavier punches. I learnt later, that Yukio's mother had recently died.

It was Toshio who initiated our friendship. He asked me one day as I was leaving school, "May I walk with you?"

I was pleased and was about to ask him about the bullying, when he said, "You bow too low to the teacher and for too long". Then he quickly added, "Please don't think I'm criticising you".

I didn't know what to say.

"I do the same", he said. "I put too much into my bow."

I didn't know what to make of him. "Why do you do it?" I asked.

"I didn't realise I did, until I saw you. I think its because I pretend. I told my father about you. I told him you were born in America, and he wants me to be friendly."

"Your father's kind."

"You're right. What was it like in America? Father said you wouldn't like Japanese schools ..."

Toshio was talkative. Information poured from him. Much of it about his family. Weeks later, after we had become friends, he confessed that he'd been so nervous talking to the glamorous boy from America that he'd blurted out whatever had come into his head. I considered myself lucky that he'd done so, because I had discovered straight away that he, like me, was disenchanted with much of life in Japan. Like Fukuzawa, his disenchantment came from a purely Japanese experience.

Toshio's grandfather had been wounded and taken prisoner fighting the Russians in Manchuria. As being taken alive by the enemy was considered dishonourable, he'd killed himself. His death, according to the official code of honour, had restored his honour. Toshio's father hadn't seen it that way, and he had grown to manhood hating official Japan that had put so little value on the life of his father. And he had made sure that Toshio had grown up without a feeling of subservience to the Emperor and the State.

When I asked Toshio why he was bullied, he ignored the question and said, "Father's come out of prison. He's taken Tenko".

I didn't want to ask why he had been in prison and I had no idea what "Tenko" was. So I asked, "What's 'Tenko'?"

"Father's a writer. They locked him up because of something he wrote. 'Tenko' is when you're a Communist and you accept the Emperor and they let you out. You don't have to renounce all your views. They just let you out. You go home. Father said it wasn't hard taking Tenko. They did him a favour. He'd already come to realise that the Communists had their own Emperor and he's against emperors of any kind. He just wanted to get out of prison."

Eventually I met Toshio's father. It was when he bought our car. Father's American company had shut down, and he'd lost his job. Perhaps because it was another turning point in my life, I can clearly remember the two fathers sitting and talking together and can recall the gist of their conversation:

"I never thought such a thing could happen in America."

"It's the scale of the thing. It's such a shock."

"What will you do?"

"I'd like to go back, but America's full of engineers looking for work. I've made connections here."

"Our industries are already cramped. We're kept out of so many markets."

"I know."

"It plays into the hands of the militarists."

"That's right. They frighten me. Everything's going their way."

"Yes. They're the power now. The Emperor can't do a lot."

"You've got *contacts*. How far do you think the army can go?"

Mr Segowa answered quietly, "The Emperor would like the army to be restrained. When Prime Minister Inukai was assassinated, he was making overtures to China. And he was preparing an Imperial rescript restraining the army ... then Bang! The Emperor got the message. End of rescript. The politicians are terrified. They're afraid, that if they protest ..." Mr Segowa ran a finger across his throat.

"The army seems to think that China's there for the taking ..."

I hoped they'd forgotten about the car. But eventually they went out to look at it. Father had me explain how the car worked, and Toshio and his father were impressed. I couldn't see why. Father always had me with him when he worked on the car. He talked to me about everything he was interested in.

That was father. His world was my world. I'd watched mesmerised, while he fiddled with watches and showed me how they worked. He explained atoms and the Periodic Table and molecules and talked about physics. He started me on a life long fascination with cosmology when he told me how, when astronomers had first tried to measure the distance to the stars, they had looked at the night sky from opposite ends of the earth's orbit around the sun. They'd intended to measure the changes of position of various stars and calculate how far they where from earth. But to their astonishment, from the two positions a few hundred million miles apart, most of the star map hadn't altered. This meant that the stars weren't just distant, but unimaginably remote.

That was father. The car was mine as well as his, and when Mr Segowa bought it, I felt the loss. But I knew we would need the money if father was going to be without a job for long. It turned out he had undervalued himself. Mitsubishi weren't going to be put off from hiring engineering know-how, by a little thing like a world slump and they sought father out. They were developing their engineering complex at Nagasaki and wanted him there. So we moved to Nagasaki.

We had a huge surprise when we received the news from my brother, Juniichi, that he had started work for a New York newspaper and would be writing on Asia. He told us his research took up much of his time, so we started sending him articles and books we thought would help. Then we received a letter from him, telling us he didn't need them any more, because he was going to China. He didn't spell it out, but we realised he would be covering what had become a Japanese invasion.

I felt excited for him. And afraid. China was in a state of upheaval. Japanese officers had assassinated the Manchurian Warlord, Chang Tso-lin and tried to hide their crime. Then, they used the killing as a pretext to occupy the whole of Manchuria and the bordering provinces of China. It was blatant gangsterism. China was in chaos. Chiang Kia-shek had been fighting China's own Warlords with Communist help, until he had suddenly massacred Communist supporters in Shanghai and afterwards destroyed Communists wherever he found them. It had seemed the Communists were finished. Then somehow they had become strong again, and Chiang Kia-shek was attacking *them,* rather than the invading Japanese army. Juniichi would be amongst all this.

News from Takiko was very different. She'd married Stewart, one of the young engineers from father's old company. She'd had a baby girl, and was expecting a second baby, when her husband had lost his job. She'd written saying they were managing well, but father sent money anyway. Then, after Franklin Roosevelt was elected, she sent us a series of euphoric letters saying: "The spirit of America has changed; this man, who has been crippled by polio, is giving hope to millions; he is enacting all kinds of legislation and all kinds of schemes, getting people back to work."

A letter from Takiko was the highlight of my week. Her descriptions of America had me longing to go back. She wrote that it was huge irony, a lesson to be learned, that just when America was supposed to be least able to afford it, the Government was achieving so much, building thousands of schools and houses and miles of new roads, using men who had been unemployed. And those men were buying again. A local closed-down shoe factory had re-opened because people were buying shoes, and a nearby bakery was taking on workers because they were selling more bread. And her husband, Stewart, had landed what was to be the job of his life.

Within weeks of Roosevelt becoming President, he had taken steps to start the vast project, which was to become known as the Tennessee Valley Authority. Fortuitously, he had chosen Arthur Morgan, the engineer who had been the Principal of Stewart's old college, to lead it. Stewart must have impressed his old Head in some way, because he was invited to join Morgan's team.

Takiko told me that the Tennessee Valley project had long been in the imagination of Roosevelt and others. It was intended to control hundreds of miles of the Tennessee River, where it ran through various states, sometimes flooding disastrously. It was also intended to bring electric power to a region deep in poverty and do much else. Takiko sent me a newspaper cutting, reporting Roosevelt telling reporters that the aim of the Tennessee Valley Authority, was to reclaim human beings.

Hoover, the President before Roosevelt, had refused to distribute surplus wheat to the unemployed and had even sent the army, with fixed bayonets, against unemployed war veterans who had been demanding money owed to them. Roosevelt wasn't like that. When the veterans marched on Washington a second time, he provided them with three meals a day, and sent army doctors and dentists to see to those who needed attention. He didn't give them their money, but, Takiko wrote, he offered the veterans work in the Civilian Conservation Corps, which most happily took.

As I read Takiko's cuttings and learnt that the Tennessee Valley scheme and the treatment of the veterans were part of a great humane project called the New Deal, which obviously made economic sense, I realised that something different was happening in America. An extraordinarily compassionate individual had become the leader of a powerful country. I made up my mind to go back to America when the depression ended.

Against father's wishes, I started work at Mitsubishi rather than going into higher education. I wanted to learn a practical skill. I thought by doing so I would be more likely to find work in America. Once there, I could study while working. That was my naive dream.

I received a warning of what was really to come, when my old school friend Toshio, on leave from China, visited us. He'd been called into the army along with many of the boys from my old school in Tokyo. Because I was working on bombsights at

Mitsubishi, I had been left alone. Toshio brought the usual tales of bullying and thuggery by more senior soldiers, which was part of army life. But as soon as we were alone, he also gave me horrifying accounts of murder.

He told me that, along with other "rookie" soldiers, he had been forced to bayonet a Chinese prisoner. While he was telling me, he became emotional. He didn't cry. He was sufficiently Japanese not to do that. But there were tears in his eyes.

I interrupted him, "They *forced* you to do it?"

He looked ghastly, "Don't judge me", he pleaded. "The prisoners were going to die whatever I did. If I'd thought I'd just get a beating, I would have refused. One recruit wrote a 'disloyal' letter home. He died from the beating the other soldiers gave him ..."

Previously, if I had known of someone who had killed a helpless prisoner, I would have refused even to be in his company. But here was *my* friend, sitting in *my* house, telling me that he had done such a thing.

Then he was saying, "But I've saved lives. The army treats the whole Chinese population as the enemy, and that's what they've become. How could they ever be *our* friends? I try to make amends. I let prisoners go. I save them whenever I can."

Then for the first time, from Toshio, I heard about the use of poison gas and other atrocities. Looking at this small pathetic figure, I found it hard to blame him for what he'd done. He'd been dragged against his will into an army that was engaged in large-scale brutality. He *had* done the bayoneting, but was stricken by the experience and was struggling to remain the moral person he had been before. That was the important thing to me. I assured him that I couldn't pass judgement on him, because I had never been put in the position he'd been in. Then I decided to move the conversation on.

"Toshio. Remember the February Coup? The would-be coup. Did you hear what the Emperor did?"

He looked grateful, "Yes. He ordered the officers responsible to be shot immediately, without honour, and all kinds of other officers were dismissed. I understand what you're trying to tell me. The Emperor is really on our side. He's against the militarists. Yes, it looks that way. The trouble is, to defeat one army faction he needed the support of another. And now they're in control, and *they* are running things in China." Toshio knew more than I did.

To take his mind off China, I brought out Takiko's letters. They were packed with news from America. I left them with him, while I went to prepare refreshments. When I returned he was reading one of them. He looked up, "Father will be interested in these. This one. Can I copy it?"

I took the letter from him. In my replies to Takiko, I'd asked her questions about Roosevelt's New Deal. Sometimes she had taken them as criticisms. This letter was a reply to one of my "crit icisms". She'd written that one of the workers whom Stewart had taken on had suddenly become very ill. A doctor had diagnosed silicosis: he had only a short time to live.

Stewart hadn't known that the man, not long before, had worked on an infamous job, cutting a tunnel near a place called Gauley Bridge. The contracting company hadn't used extractor fans or issued the men with protective masks, so they had to work in a cloud of silicon dust. Since then, hundreds of them had died, and the survivors couldn't get work without lying about their past. Takiko had written that *that* company and others like it, were the reasons recent changes in the law favourable to trade unions were needed.

Toshio's request gave me an idea. "How is your father?"

"He's fine. He's a respectable journalist now." Toshio tapped his forehead, "But he's still the same inside".

"Why would he be interested in the letters?"

"He writes about America. It's part of his job. He gets invited to the American Embassy. Functions. Things like that. And he gets material from the Government and analyses it for them. He likes to know what ordinary Americans think. He'd love to read these letters."

"I could come to Tokyo. I'd bring the letters."

Toshio's face lit-up, "Come back with me. Dad'll fall over when you walk in."

His father didn't fall over. But he did welcome me and he took the letters, promising to return them before I left. Before that happened, however, enchantment entered my life. One of Toshio's cousins was being drafted into the Army. The usual family celebration was taking place, and I went along with Toshio.

Toshio's cousin's home was in a cul-de-sac behind a Christian church. As we walked around the corner of the church, we saw two girls running and hiding in the garden. They thought we hadn't seen them, but when Toshio called, they came out of hiding. One of them was Toshio's cousin, Shidzue. The other was her friend, Kiku. From the first words we exchanged, I was attracted to Kiku, and as the afternoon passed, I realised I was in love and took Toshio aside and asked him about Kiku.

He told me there had been a marriage arranged between Kiku and Kozo Shimizu, one of the boys from our old school. But he'd been killed in China. Officially he had died bravely, fighting for the Emperor. But Toshio had been in the same unit and knew the truth. A grenade he was carrying exploded. That sort of thing wasn't supposed to happen, so Kozo was turned into a hero.

When Toshio realised how interested I was in Kiku, he warned me, "You'll have to move quickly. Remember Kozo's friend, The Prof, I think Kiku's father is considering *him*."

"The Prof!" My heart sank. The Prof had been a strange boy who, apart from his friendship with Kozo, had been in a world of his own. He had been a scholarly boy, and his father was a high-up civil servant, so I thought that to Kiku's father, he would probably seem a good choice.

The thought that I might be too late spoilt the rest of my weekend. I asked Toshio to quietly let Kiku know how I felt. I had decided to act quickly and tell my parents about my feelings for Kiku as soon as I returned to Nagasaki.

Although I was preoccupied with thoughts of Kiku, I did manage what I hoped was reasonable conversation with Toshio's father. He'd liked Takiko's letters and said they had helped him to understand why ordinary American's still loved President Roosevelt.

I asked him, "*Shouldn't* they love President Roosevelt?"

He nodded, "They should prefer him to what went before. He's put millions of Americans back in work. But that leaves millions unaffected. His mind is less shackled than President Hoover's was, but he's intellectually orthodox."

That was too much for me, "Orthodox! Roosevelt?"

"He's an extraordinary personality, I know."

"But 'orthodox', 'shackled'?"

He stopped and looked at me for a moment. Then he continued, "Most people are ruled by the governing ideas of the time and the place they live in. Take Japan ..." He paused. Then he pulled a face, "No. Let's stick with America. In America, the governing idea, or what was the governing idea, is less straight-forward than here. There, the idea of individual liberty was hijacked to mean liberty for Business. That meant Government was supposed to keep out of the business of Business. It became an ideology, a mental straitjacket, and President Hoover was locked into it. The system collapsing! Millions unemployed! Mass destitution! Yet Hoover was paralysed by the ruling ideology.

"Then along came Roosevelt. What was it he said? 'We have had no plague of locusts. We have plenty within the sight of need.' He was going to use his power as President to bring need and plenty together. And he seemed to have the will to do it. The trouble is he's still affected by the old ideology. He's been advised that there will be dire financial consequences if Government acts to get all those millions back to work. As if leaving millions in depression isn't dire ..."

"Pardon me Mr Segowa, but you make it sound so easy."

"To move that many men, to get the economy going and produce things that are needed, valuable things that would lift America, would require more dollars than Roosevelt is prepared to pledge. But it can be done; some congressmen have worked out the cost ... Americans think Roosevelt has broken with the old thinking, and most love him for it. But all *he's* done is loosen the ideological straitjacket."

I wasn't mature enough to listen. I only wanted to hear favourable things about Roosevelt. So I asked, "What about Roosevelt's Good Neighbour policy. He's pledged not to intervene in the affairs of weaker countries."

"That's different, it's what the world needs ..." Although it was a private conversation, he lowered his voice.

I needn't have worried about The Prof. Kiku wasn't interested in him, and she was sufficiently modern to let her father know that she liked me very much me. And so we began our friendship and were so certain of our feelings and wanting to be together we decided to go ahead with our marriage.

But I did the most stubbornly foolish thing. I asked to be taken off bombsight work. Father tried to talk me out of it. He warned me that I might be called up for service in China. But to me it was a simple matter: now that I knew the truth about China, I shouldn't be doing military work. I would deal with the future when it came.

And it came. The call-up papers arrived while we were deciding on the date for the wedding, so everything was rushed. I had such a short time with my lovely Kiku. Then I left her with my parents. I didn't think even then, I'd been foolish. My simple code was that some things were out of my hands and others weren't. Also, in a way, I wanted to go to China. I'd rather not have gone as a soldier. But if that was the only way to see for myself what was happening, I'd have to put up with it. I had evolved a simple philosophy that I hoped would get me through whatever happened. It helped me to leave Kiku: it was that these things were all part of being Japanese, and I would just have to be Japanese and do the best I could.

My greatest fear was that, like Toshio, I would be ordered to kill a prisoner, but I was determined not to do it. I put in for officer training. I had plans. Toshio's father had told me that, during the Russian war, General Nogi had set very high standards for his army in Korea and had punished soldiers who mistreated civilians. And I knew that both General Nogi and Admiral Togo had treated Russian prisoners with consideration. I also knew that the Meiji Emperor, whose memory was revered, had issued a rescript to the army ordering soldiers to have a sense of right and wrong and to behave honourably. He'd actually said, that if soldiers neglected valour and acted with violence, the world would look on them as wild beasts. I planned, if I became a platoon commander, to talk to my men about this and to say that we should be true to our honourable tradition. General Nogi had been our Emperor's tutor and I would try to get over to my platoon that our Emperor would want us to follow both the Meiji Emperor and General Nogi's example.

I actually tried my powers of persuasion sooner than I'd intended. I was sent for training as a Platoon Commander as soon as I arrived in China.

On the first day, I thought I was seeing things when, on walking into the canteen, there was a soldier who looked exactly like The Prof eating at one of the tables. I took my meal and sat down opposite him and discovered it *was* The Prof, and he was on the same course. I'd never seen him as part of the herd, and thought that if anyone would be receptive to my appeal, it would be him.

But he cut short my peroration with an agreeable nod and, "You're right. But let's live in the present."

"What's different about the present?"

He laughed, "You're kidding me. Things change. There's the army for a start. The army wasn't supposed to be involved in politics once. But where would our country be now without the army? We'd be like the Chinese. Slaves."

So The Prof was an army supporter. I'd always imagined that behind his other-worldliness, there was an elevated mind. But after all, he hadn't thought beyond official Japan.

What I dreaded happening, happened. At the end of the

course each of us was expected to behead a Chinese prisoner. I'd been detailed once, to march a prisoner to a field on the edge of the camp. We were told he was a captured guerrilla. But I knew that he was just as likely to be a non-combatant. He was tall and thin and was so battered, I felt like crying for him. It was then that I realised the magnitude of my mistake in letting myself be called-up.

I thought the prisoner was going to be shot, but when we arrived, Second Lieutenant Nomura was waiting, and I guessed what was about to happen. This officer was known to behead prisoners for the sheer pleasure of it. A hole was being dug while we waited, and the prisoner was made to kneel right at the edge. Then the officer pulled his sword out.

The standard issue "Showa" swords buckled when they were used. But this horrible man had a sword that was a centuries-old product of craftsmanship, and it kept its shape even after constant use. He poured some water on the blade and swished it through the air to get it off. Then with a second movement he beheaded the prisoner.

I didn't follow the movement through. I shut my eyes just in time not to see the sickening sight. When I opened them, the prisoner and his head was already down in the hole. The officer tried to clean the blade with a single wipe, but there was something stuck to it. After he'd rubbed it off, he turned to us and slid his sword back into its sheath. His posture proudly told us, "That's how it's done".

This was the man I would have to face when I refused to do the same. I hadn't seen him in action before, but I knew him already as a typical professional officer who breathed the "superiority" of the Japanese nation, especially the military. He was incapable of stepping outside of his role as a cog in the military machine. He lived to establish his country as a world power, by winning an empire. He regarded non-Japanese with contempt. That other people in Asia might have rights was beyond his comprehension. For him, outside of the Japanese nation there was no morality. I knew I would find no way into his mind by expressing sympathy for his Chinese victims. But I wondered if I could shake him by using my argument on the Meiji Emperor's rescript and my wanting to be loyal to General Nogi and Admiral Togo's example.

The awful day I'd dreaded eventually came, and I found it hard to think clearly. I didn't know what was going to happen to me for disobeying an order. My mind ran over all kinds of possibilities including, fancifully, my own decapitation, but I knew that to be a truly honourable person, I shouldn't flinch even from that. I thought I might be sent on a suicide mission. Strangely, I found that thought bearable.

We were led into a field where the Second Lieutenant and some senior officers were waiting. A group of emaciated prisoners were under guard. I tried not to look at them. It was obvious from the faces of the other cadets that most of them felt as sick as I did. We were made to watch, as the Second Lieutenant demonstrated on a prisoner what we had to do. I didn't close my eyes this time. I wanted to be a witness, however nauseating it was. And it *was* nauseating. The officer raised his sword, and a split-second later the man's head was off, and blood spurted out from where it had been. Then the body collapsed slowly into the pit. Each soldier in turn had to go forward to produce the same result. Some cadets had to be forced forward and some botched the job, leaving their victim wounded but alive. Then they had to strike again and again, until the head was off and there was blood all over the place. I felt I was living in some barbaric age. And I was. The Prof's name was called and he went forward without hesitation and did what was required. Unlike most, he was able to go smartly back to his place.

Then it was my turn. By then I had realised that this was no place to make a speech. So I decided to walk out and feign collapse. It was the limit of my courage. If I had to, later, away from this scene, I would put my argument. But as I approached *my* prisoner, he was suddenly on his feet. His blindfold had come down and he stood facing me. He was in an impossible situation, and there was no way he could survive. I put my hand on the hilt of my sword, "Run", I urged him. I couldn't think of anything better. He looked at me with such hate, and at that moment, facing this man who was about to die, I found my courage. Thought and action were coming together in my brain. The words were forming in my head, "Is this what General Nogi would have wanted …" I was about to turn to the Second Lieutenant in anger. The consequences for me wouldn't matter.

"Cut him down", screamed the officer. Simultaneously the prisoner kicked me hard on the knee. Despite his plight he knew what he was doing. Then I was on the floor and he was running surrounded by sword-swinging cadets. They went on longer than was needed.

The Prof didn't join in the butchering, and he was already beside me when the angry officer arrived. "I knew him at school", he told the officer. "He was sickly. He couldn't stand blood ..."

That day left me with an indelible memory of the man who faced me briefly and bravely tried to fight back, before being cut down. His example had sparked me to the point of an action that would almost certainly have cost me my life. I don't think it's unnatural that I'm glad I survived. Yet, although I couldn't have saved him, a part of me regrets that I wasn't able to make my stand and have him see me do it before he died.

And that day, more than any other, turned my dreams into nightmares. The reality was horrific, but somehow the dreams have been worse. When I wake-up, I feel I have been released from something like the Christian hell, although time has lessened their intensity.

My leg was out of action, and for the moment I was of no use to an infantry unit. Luckily, I was considered inadequate rather than rebellious. My Platoon Commander ambitions were finished, and when I recovered I was to be sent to wherever I was needed as an ordinary soldier.

A rumour was about that one of the doctors treating us wounded soldiers, was also part of a special unit conducting "research" on prisoners, and when this doctor told me there was a non-combatant job that would suit me, I very quickly became a "loyal" soldier who wanted to fight for the Emperor.

So I found myself, before I was properly fit, part of a big offensive towards the city of Nanking: the alternative would have been far worse. I was transported by truck to join my new Unit on the road to Nanking. The men I joined were veterans who had taken part in the assault on Shanghai. They had expected a quick victory, but the ferocious Chinese defence had meant they had had to fight right through the summer and autumn. From the way they looked at me, I don't think they were impressed.

I assured my new Platoon Commander that I wouldn't be a liability. I told him my leg wasn't so bad and I would be able to fulfil my duty to the Emperor. But as I really knew, my knee wasn't up to it. I didn't care about damage. I knew I had to be seen to make the effort. So I forced myself to continue until I fell down and couldn't get up again and was left behind.

The medic had cut away my trouser leg and left me sitting by the side of the road with a grotesquely large knee and fat lower leg. I must have had a high temperature, because I enjoyed sitting in the cold. Sitting with a damaged knee in the winter chill, knowing I was out of it, I was content. It seemed the whole army was walking past. Some gave themselves away as rookies, shouting things like, "Poor bugger, you'll miss the fight with the Chinks".

"I'll catch up", I'd sometimes shout back.

The next day I set off on my pretend pursuit of my Unit. Also, I'd become very cold and was looking for somewhere indoors where I could warm up. Sometimes passing soldiers offered their help, but I "bravely" refused. I did accept hospitality, however, at the first village I came to. The people had fled and the new occupants, fellow soldiers, found me a comfortable corner in a warm room and let me share their meal.

"We're leaving now", I was told when they were moving out. They didn't expect me to go with them. I relaxed after that, and stayed for a few days.

The next village I came to was no place to stay. For some reason the villagers hadn't fled and had paid the price for their misjudgement. Their bodies were strewn around. There'd been no battle. Few had been killed by gunfire. They'd been clubbed and slashed and stabbed, and some of the men had been beheaded.

Could the men I'd marched with, or those who had called sympathetically to me, or those who had looked after me in that last village, have done this? Had any of *them* been capable of *this*?

After that, I left the road. I wanted to get away from the army. Thankfully, the land was hilly, and when I looked back, the village was out of sight. I needed shelter and a place to think, and when I came upon an empty village, I decided to stay as long as my rations lasted. There was one house taller and finer than the rest, and I made for that. But the army had been there before me. Right in front of the house were five bodies, a man and a woman and three children in a large pool of blood, all with their heads off.

My first reaction was to get away. But the hilly ups and downs had taken their toll, and I was almost finished. I remembered a Chinese phrase I'd been taught, so I shouted it repeatedly, "I am your friend. I am your friend. I am your friend." Then it struck me, who would believe it. I felt uneasy about the bodies, but I needed to lie down.

I was in a state of semi-sleep, when I became aware of something lightly touching my face. I peeped, hardly opening my eyes. A tiny girl, little more than a baby, was standing by the bed with her hand on my mouth. As I thought, "How can I avoid frightening her", she climbed on to the bed beside me. I was warm and she was cold. Keeping my eyes closed, I put my arms around her. I'm sure that I was the only human being she had seen in days and that was why she came to me. Perhaps I was in the bed she was used to climbing into to be with her parents.

For the next week, the baby became the centre of my existence, as I fed and cleaned and entertained her and kept her warm, while we slowly made our way, to what I believed would be the safety of Nanking. I had in my pocket, photographs of her family. One of them was of her. On the back was written *in English*, "Rainbow, July 1937". Rainbow had belonged to an educated family.

As we approached the city, occasionally we heard gunfire. Not the kind of sporadic or mixed firing, you might hear from a gun battle, but sudden intense firing, going on for minutes before tailing off. It was murder. I didn't need to see to know. But I did almost see some of it eventually. We were resting near the river, just over the brow of a hill. I'd scattered grain where the ground was level, and some doves had landed and were pecking it up. I was enjoying watching Rainbow comically running about after them, when from somewhere I heard a voice. It sounded like a military command.

I crawled and looked carefully over the top of the hill. Hundreds of Chinese men were standing on the bank of the river, guarded by our soldiers. I picked up our baggage and we were on our way before the firing started. We kept away from the river after that, but we still occasionally heard protracted gunfire.

When we reached the outskirts of Nanking there was no sign of live Chinese civilians. Only bodies. And there was debris. Not the debris of war. Outside of undamaged houses, was the debris of looting and vandalism. The only living, were Japanese soldiers and sometimes marching with them, Chinese prisoners.

No one bothered me until the commander of one group of prisoners walked out to block my path. It was The Prof. Before I could talk, he turned and shouted a command, halting his column. Then he took my elbow and walked me away to the side, "You need medical attention".

"I've a baby here", I told him. "I've got to get her to safety." He pulled the top of the blanket back and looked. Rainbow looked back, unafraid. Then he bowed, *to me*, a common soldier. It was the most unexpected and inappropriate thing he could have done.

"I'll get her to safety", he said, and to my surprise added, "You're a true soldier".

He sent his column off, and we went into the nearest house to wait for the return of his men. I had mixed emotions. I was grateful to The Prof, but I knew what his soldiers had gone off to do.

The Prof was genuinely concerned for Rainbow. He made an effort to let her know that she was in friendly company. When we'd fed her and she was asleep, I asked him about the fate of his prisoners, and he answered, "We haven't got enough food to feed them, but if we let them go they'll fight us again. We're under orders. We don't like it, but what choice do we have?" He left unsaid what was probably happening right at that moment.

"You *could* let them go", I answered. I should have argued further, but I felt giddy from the constant pain in my leg and my overwhelming concern was for Rainbow.

The Prof looked uncomfortable, "What you've seen outside, all that killing. My men had no part in it. There's no justification for it." Then he said, "Remember *that day?*"

I knew the day he was talking about.

"You refused to draw your sword. I understood what was in your mind. No one else did. Remember when you talked to me in the canteen? I never forgot it. And when you left your sword in its sheath, I knew why. I told one or two of the others. I was careful who I spoke to. They were impressed. Until then, I'd had one aim … remember Kozo Shimizu?"

"Yes, your friend. He died last year."

"He died *in battle*", he corrected me. "I was determined to be worthy of his memory and do whatever was required of me as a soldier. Then, when you left your sword in its sheath, I realised that your courage was greater than mine … when I became Platoon Commander I talked to my men the way you talked to me that day in the canteen. I was lucky; I had raw recruits. Anyhow, they're not natural killers, and they appreciated my little talk. It lifted a weight off their shoulders. Believe me, my men aren't responsible for any of the sights you'll see around Nanking."

After telling him how relieved I was, I said, "There's something I think you would want to know. It's about Kozo."

He looked puzzled, "Tell me".

"He didn't die in battle. Toshio told me that a grenade he was carrying exploded. It was an accident."

"Why didn't Toshio tell me …?"

I waited while the news sank in. Then The Prof sighed, "Kozo was always fiddling with things".

The Prof's men returned with a bus. Then, under his direction we drove across Nanking. Rainbow was awake and I faced her into the bus, so that she couldn't see the scenes outside. The soldiers responded to her, smiling and pulling faces. I was astonished that after what they had recently done, they could behave that way. And I was equally astonished at Rainbow. She showed no fear. By some freak, she must never have seen Japanese soldiers before.

Bodies were everywhere. Later, senior officers would organise mass disposal of their handiwork and try to deny what had happened. But as we drove through the streets of Nanking, the proof was all around. Sometimes, I didn't understand what I was seeing, until I realised that I was looking at females who had been victims of the sexually depraved. And there was looting: lorries were being loaded with the contents of rich residences. "It was the same in Shanghai", said The Prof, "It's all going back to Japan".

The Prof explained to me that we were taking Rainbow to the Safety Zone. It was an area that some Europeans and Americans had established, hopefully, to become a refuge for Nanking residents. Although adults were constantly being snatched in army raids, it was the safest place there was for children. It didn't sound safe to me, but it seemed to be the only place where being Chinese didn't bring an automatic death penalty.

Eventually we arrived at our destination, a women's college within the Safety Zone. When we arrived, a lone European woman was standing at the gate. She looked ready for a fight. But as we drew close, her face changed, "Oh, it's you", she said to The Prof.

The Prof looked pleased, "Don't worry. They're my men on the bus. And they're staying there."

"What have you got for me?"

"Miss Vautrin", I said, The Prof had briefed me, "this is Rainbow …"

And so I parted with Rainbow. I saw her only once more. That was when I discovered that I was being sent home and I tried to adopt her. From amongst the mass of refugees, Miss Vautrin had traced an aunt from Rainbow's village. I went to see her. I hadn't anticipated the effect my request would have. When Miss Vautrin translated my words, the aunt looked horrified. Her face answered, *"You want Rainbow to live in the land of murderers?"* Far worse, was that when I tried to hold Rainbow she recoiled from me and cried.

When I returned to Nagasaki, Kiku and mother and father couldn't have misinterpreted my joy at being home, especially as I had my own baby girl to return to. But I know that my behaviour was sometimes abnormal and I couldn't tell them why. I think, before our second baby was a year old, I had, to my family, returned to my old self. But my mind was still filled with images of what I'd seen in China, especially in my dreams. I never had a night that was free from nightmares. And I still thought about Rainbow and compared her situation to that of my children. And our war on China continued.

It was father who brought the news of Pearl Harbour. One evening he came home from work looking pale. "They've attacked the Americans", he said quietly. "They've bombed Pearl Harbour." I knew how much he loved America and how horrified he must have been. And he, better than most, understood how powerful America was, "I always knew the Military were stupid", he said. "America isn't China. Japan is fighting far above its weight … God, they're stupid."

Even while Japanese forces were easily conquering the West's Asian empires, father was predicting, "Wait until the Americans mobilise. Then we'll know what war is."

The tide of war did turn and, even though the Government wouldn't admit what was happening, the shortages made it obvious. We had gone to war with America and the European colonial powers, to overcome President Roosevelt's trade restrictions and get the raw materials needed to continue our seizure of China. Yet, we were even shorter than before of the raw materials of war, which told us that Japan was no longer a power at sea. And the fleets of heavy American bombers that flew over, whenever the weather was fair, told us who controlled the skies.

Yet in Nagasaki, considering we were on the losing side, life wasn't bad, as the months of war stretched into years. Despite the dire shortages and the killing that was going on elsewhere, we were able to enjoy a happy life with the children. I considered it a fluke, pure chance that we lived in a relatively peaceful place and I made the most of it and gave my children the best possible life.

There were plenty of air raid warnings, but the bombers that came by Nagasaki usually passed over. They were on their way to bomb elsewhere. Our city had only been bombed a few times and even I, who had expected the worst, became used to being safe; the Americans had more important targets than Nagasaki. The main one was Tokyo, and I went there in the summer of 1945.

We hadn't heard from Kiku's family for a while, so I travelled to Tokyo to see how they were and to offer them refuge with us in Nagasaki. But when I arrived, there was so much destruction I couldn't find familiar landmarks and became lost. It was only after talking to several people that I arrived at the ruins of the Christian church, behind which Toshio's cousin had lived and where I had first seen Kiku. Behind the shell of the church there was only knee-deep ash.

I had to think hard of how things had once been, to make my way to where Kiku had lived. I walked from the church to the remains of the cinema on the corner and turned right. Ahead of me was a fork in the road that went to either side of the area where Toshio had lived. But there were only fire-blackened remains of houses. I took the left fork and then the second road on the right, where Kiku's family-home had been. Nothing recognisable had survived. Opposite where Kiku's family had lived, a lone man was raking through the ashes with a stick. When I reached him, I pointed and asked, "Do you know what happened to ...?"

By then he had straightened up, "No one from along this road survived", he said. "Not them", he nodded towards where I had been pointing, "Not anyone. It would have been impossible."

I walked on and crossed the main road and into the street where The Prof's friend, Kozo, had once lived. There was nothing there. If I had known where The Prof's home had been, I would have gone looking for his family. But I didn't know.

"New kind of bomb dropped on Hiroshima – much damage done", was the headline of the newspaper I bought at the railway station – yes, by some miracle of human organisation, the railways were still operating. I wasn't impressed by the idea of a new American weapon. I had seen what the American's had done to Tokyo with her old weapons and couldn't imagine how anything could be more destructive. On the train I read that Hiroshima had been destroyed, apparently, by a single American bomber. I didn't believe it. I knew that no single bomber, even America's biggest, could carry enough chemistry to produce such an effect. Then I remembered: father and I had discussed the possibility of a bomb

based on nuclear fission, and I realised that if the newspaper report was true, it must have been a nuclear weapon.

I wanted to be home. If America, instead of sending a fleet of bombers to one city, could send a single bomber carrying the new weapon to every city, how long would we have to live?

The train braking and coming to a halt woke me from a deep sleep. I was disappointed; we weren't in Nagasaki. I looked out of the window, not to appreciate the countryside, but as usual to see what kind of food was being grown. I could see perhaps ten people in the field, but it wasn't the kind of crop they were tending, or supposed to be tending, that I took in. It was that they were all standing and looking in the direction of Nagasaki. A woman not far from the train beckoned me down.

In the direction of Nagasaki, was a colossal cloud. I'd never seen anything like it in nature before. As I tried to judge the distance and whether it *was* actually over Nagasaki, the driver came back announcing that the train was going no further. It was obvious that there had been a major bombing and possibly, what I had dreaded, that the new weapon had been used on Nagasaki. I continued my journey on foot.

There were other people walking along the tracks to Nagasaki, and one of them spoke to me. He was an old man whose son worked at the Mitsubishi steel works. He had heard the American plane flying over the city and seen the flash and felt the blast and heard the enormous explosion. He said that as soon as he had recovered his senses he had set out to find out if is son was still alive. I wished him luck and hurried on.

When I reached a place from where I could look down on the city, I could see that a large part of Nagasaki had either been demolished or badly damaged. From then on, despite my unreliable knee, I ran until I was nearly home and met my neighbour, Mr Komoto.

I didn't recognise him until he spoke to me, "Don't go any further, my friend", he said. Then he sat down on the road. His face was burnt and he looked as though his nose had been broken. He was obviously exhausted. "Your father", he pointed up the hill, "has gone to Urakami hospital".

"Was he on his own?"

"Kiku and your mother were with him."

"Do you know where the children are?"

He didn't look at me. He let his head hang between his knees, "I don't want to be the one to tell you".

"Mr Komoto, I've got to know what happened."

"Your children are dead."

Those four words were worse than any possible physical blow I could have received. If Mr Komoto was right, the most terrible thing that could have happened in my life had happened.

From our elevated position half way up the road to Urakami Hospital, I could see the devastation of a large part of Nagasaki. I knew that a great disaster had happened. Perhaps because of that, despite my mind and body reeling, I managed to think rationally and ask him, "They were at school ... how do you know?"

"Your father kept them home when he heard about Hiroshima. The house collapsed on them."

I took Mr Komoto by the shoulders and dragged him to the side of the road and leant him against the remnants of a wall.

"Where are the children now?"

"Your father buried them. I watched him. He pulled them out from underneath ... I couldn't see properly, but he took care. He wrapped them. And then he buried them. Then he took your mother and Kiku up to the Hospital."

My world changed for ever, I summoned all my strength and did the most difficult thing I've ever done. Although I ached to be with my children, I helped Mr Komoto up to the hospital.

The hospital building was damaged. The windows were gone, and there had been a fire. The injured were lying outside on the grass, some of them being cared for by relatives and staff. Amongst them I found mother and Kiku. Their faces were white, especially mother's. She had no eyebrows and looked like a ghost. Kiku had a wound on the side of her head and was either asleep or unconscious. Mother's breathing was laboured, "Sorry. Sorry. Sorry", she was saying. Her eyes showed her pain.

I steeled myself, "Mr Komoto told me what happened to Juniichi and little Kiku", I told her. "Now we've got to take care of you and Kiku."

That was when father returned. I saw the look of relief on his face when he saw me, but it quickly changed to one of distress. Being surrounded by so many suffering people helped me to behave as though I was strong. I held up my hands, "Father, I already know about the children. And I know what you've been through ..."

In between doing what we could for mother and Kiku, father

told me what had happened. When the bomb had exploded he had been in the company's concrete office block and hadn't been hurt. Then when he saw the outside world and the extent of the destruction, he understood straight away the enormity of what had happened.

He had to force himself to pass the burnt remnants of people lying about. He found it even harder to pass the living. Most were so badly burnt they looked beyond help. He said he was still troubled that he hadn't stopped to do *something*, but the problem had been so huge, he would never have reached home if he had stopped.

He had found Kiku unconscious in the garden and mother trying to dig Juniichi and Kiku out from under the debris of the house. He made her take a rest while he dug them out himself. Then he had to face the terrible decision of what to do with them. It seemed to him as though the world was coming to an end. He thought the Americans might already have dropped Atom bombs on Tokyo, and he might never see me again. He had mother and Kiku to take care of. But he couldn't just leave little Kiku and Juniichi where they were, so he did the only thing he could. After wrapping them in linen, he buried them. He put them where the ground was soft, amongst the sweet potatoes.

He managed to get mother and Kiku to hospital, only to find the staff had little medicine and equipment and were overwhelmed by the casualties. Then mother had collapsed.

By the evening of that first day, mother's strange whiteness had gone and she'd turned black. The same had happened to other patients who'd had the whiteness, except for Kiku. She turned light brown and regained consciousness, while mother's condition deteriorated.

When Kiku came to, she already knew that she would never see her children again. Even though father insisted that she had been unconscious the whole time, she claimed she had watched him bury them. I thought that probably she had heard our conversation while she was half-conscious and had dreamt the rest. But I don't really know.

The Emperor's message of surrender intruded into our little world. The radio reception was poor, but I did make out, "The war situation has developed not necessarily to Japan's advantage". The words were so removed from our reality. The Emperor also told us that we would have to endure the unendurable. But I knew that I had already endured the unendurable. I'd endured the deaths of both of my children. To me, the Emperor was talking the language of the Army. He was talking about enduring the "dishonour" of surrender. Ordinary soldiers had been expected to commit suicide rather than surrender. I listened, but heard no words about anyone of high office feeling obliged to commit suicide. It hadn't mattered how many individuals, from ordinary soldiers to babies, had been sacrificed during the war: war had been endurable. Yet surrender, which would bring survival and peace, was to be unendurable but not so unendurable as to prompt the Emperor to commit suicide. Hirohito did express sympathy for the victims of the war, but I dismissed the words as hypocritical.

Yet, I was to find out, the Emperor *had* been secretly trying to bring the war to an end, and President Truman had known about it. Our Government had been trying to get the Russians to act as go-betweens, not knowing of Stalin's plans to join the war against Japan. Because the Americans were deciphering Japanese messages, President Truman knew that peace was possible, so long as the Emperor was left in place.

None of this was publicly known at the time. So it seemed that America's use of nuclear weapons had forced Japan to surrender. But we now know, that even following the use of nuclear weapons, Japan didn't give up. It was only after the American Government dropped its "unconditional surrender" demand and issued a form of words indicating that the Emperor would remain in place that our Government surrendered. The Emperor was to be subject to the authority of the occupying power: to General McArthur. Something one would have expected anyway.

Not knowing any of this, I felt I didn't have the right to separate my children's deaths and the others in Hiroshima and Nagasaki, from the war's carnage of innocents. But now, knowing that they needn't have died, I consider the magnitude of the crime at Hiroshima and Nagasaki, to be comparable with the atrocity at Nanking. The perpetrators of both carried out mass killings they knew didn't have to happen.

I have never been able to blame the American airmen. They were as ignorant as I was, of the peace that was already possible. And they knew they were fighting a barbarous and intractable enemy. They flew the planes, but I never considered them responsible in the way I did the soldiers at Nanking. *They* murdered, person-to-person, and saw the result of their own handiwork. But even then, their individual barbarity can only be understood by knowing that they had had a lifetime of preparation for what they did. They had been thoroughly indoctrinated with the idea of Japanese uniqueness and superiority, and been constantly exposed to the prejudice that the Chinese were inferior and contemptible. They were raised to believe that their supreme task in life was to be loyal and obedient to their Emperor. Then finally they had been trained to think of the murder of defenceless prisoners as a brave act. I believe that any group of men, Japanese or otherwise, who'd lived this experience, would have behaved as they did, when the order for the killings made its way down through the ranks.

I now know that the decision to destroy Hiroshima and Nagasaki was taken by a single individual: President Truman. I heard years later, that his three most senior Generals, Marshall, McArthur and Eisenhower, were all against it and Admiral Leahy was against it too, but Truman went ahead anyway. And when he heard the news that the first bomb had been successfully dropped on Hiroshima, his response was, "This is the greatest thing in history".

His comment told the world that he was incapable of grasping the horror he'd unleashed. So while the Nanking killings came from the kind of ugly, deep-rooted xenophobia that has so often produced such crimes, America's "Nanking" came from a simpler circumstance: the wrong person, of severely limited imagination, in the wrong place at the wrong time. Of course, it's known now that Truman ordered the bombing in order to impress on Stalin how powerful America was.

What apparently moral leaders will do frightens me. We also know now, that British code breakers were reading our secret signals before Pearl Harbour and learnt of the planned attack, but Winston Churchill didn't let President Roosevelt know. It puzzles me that people who do such things can keep their elevated reputations after the truth has come out.

Over the weeks following surrender, mother's condition deteriorated until she died, while Kiku's improved until I was sure she would live. We had a night of rain and wind just before mother died, and all the patients and relatives were moved into the "shelter" of the windowless hospital. The next morning the air was fresh and Kiku told me she felt much better. And so did I. Unfortunately though, it didn't help mother and she died that day.

The slight difference between what Kiku and mother were doing the moment the nuclear weapon detonated, determined their different fates. They were together, hanging out washing and because Kiku was the taller, she was stretching up to the washing-line with a sheet at the moment of detonation. Mother was standing to the side and had no protection from the searing flash. And so Kiku lived, while mother died.

None of us knew that father was doomed from the moment the bomb was dropped. He had been nearer to the dropping point than mother and Kiku, and while he was hurrying home, every breath he had taken had drawn in radioactive substances. After mother died, he started to feel weak and had bloody diarrhoea. The same had already happened to others in our hospital community who seemed completely healthy, but had suddenly deteriorated and died.

Father stopped eating and took only water. He told me he knew his insides were irreparably damaged but he didn't care. "I remember what you told me before you went to China", he said. "Going to war was part of being Japanese. You couldn't escape it. Well, I feel very much the way you did then. *This* is part of being Japanese. How could there not be a savage response to our savagery." Then he paused, *"But adults killing children ...?* When you were a child I tried to show you how wonderfully creative we humans are; I don't feel that way anymore and I'm glad to be going."

Father, I think, because he wanted to give me hope, did say some positive things before he died. But I know he died in a state of pessimism about human nature and about the future

Shortly before Kiku and I left the hospital, a typhoon struck. The wind and the rain battered Nagasaki day and night for several days. Afterwards, there was no mistaking that the air felt clean and healthy. American scientists had calculated that no one would be able to live where the bomb had exploded for seventy-five years. Yet when they came with their instruments, they found Nagasaki cleansed of the radioactive poisons that had killed father. It was as though the Gods had deliberately unleashed the elements and made it possible for us to start life afresh. I soon discovered that the Americans were doing something similar for Japan.

Our Government's propaganda had led to widespread fear of

what Japan would suffer during an American occupation. There *was* one large insensitive act, probably the work of President Truman, which appeared to justify the apprehension. Flying from the battleship Missouri where the surrender was signed, was the flag Commander Perry had flown on his intimidating Black Ships visit in 1853. Our conquerors were reminding us of the original humiliation that had started Japan along a path that led to imperial conquest.

But after that, everything was benevolent. The Americans helped to feed us and to begin a life free of military domination. And General MacArthur imposed a more modern Constitution. It was a world away from the nightmare our militarists would have created for the vanquished, had the roles been reversed.

Kiku and I returned to live in our air raid shelter, while I prepared to build a new house. We laid a mound over where father had buried Juniichi and little Kiku. I had intended to add mother and father's ashes to the soil, but the container was blown away during the typhoon. It didn't have a fixed lid, and I guess the ashes would have been scattered far beyond Nagasaki and it made me sad. I had hoped that the flowers we would grow on the hill would, in a way, unite our family again.

One evening, a sunburned, healthy looking man, carrying suitcases came into our garden. We were sitting beside the air raid shelter, and he walked right up to us. "Can I stay with you", he asked?

I started to think, "Who would want to stay here? Why is he smiling like that?" Then I realised who he was and stood up, "Is it really you?" I asked my brother.

Knowing that Juniichi had reported the war from Asia for many years, I had sent a letter to his New York newspaper as soon as postal communication resumed. They sent it back to Tokyo, where he was covering the Occupation. By coincidence, my letter reached him just as he was about to come to Nagasaki to look for us.

It was to be the first of numerous visits from Juniichi over the following two years. He lifted us from our minimal existence. I'm a little ashamed to recall, that on that first visit, I didn't think I could feel any happier until Juniichi opened his suitcases and I saw that they were full of American rations.

But he brought us much more than food. He informed us about the world we had been cut off from and inadvertently about himself. He was no pampered American. He slept on the ground, on an army groundsheet, outside our shelter. He'd been reporting the war mostly from China and was used to sleeping in the open.

After we'd finished talking about our family, Juniichi looked at me mischievously, "Your friend Toshio was asking about you".

"Toshio! When did you meet Toshio?"

"It was a few years ago. In northern China."

I looked at Kiku, "See what a good brother I have. All this food and now he tells me Toshio's alive."

"He was alive then", Juniichi warned me. "He'd gone over to the Chinese. He was with the Communist Army. Whenever I came across Japanese who were fighting on the Chinese side, I always talked to them. Toshio figured me out as your brother very quickly. He'd been sickened by his army's behaviour. And so had I. But I'd only seen their handiwork. *He* was on the side that was doing it. So he deserted."

I was thrilled to hear what Toshio had done. The idea had crossed my mind while I was in the army that I might have to desert. And I was a little in awe of my old friend Toshio: *he had acted* to end the impossible situation he was in.

"It's amazing", Juniichi continued. "The Communists see Japanese soldiers as fellow victims of Japanese militarism."

"I wonder what's happened to him?"

"Don't expect to see him again. He's found a cause: China: Chinese communism, rather. It's understandable. Of all the forces in China, the Communists were the most humane and they cared most for the ordinary farmer. They were the best fighters too."

"I wonder how he'd have felt if he'd been here when you Americans came. Americans are impressive too."

"We've got to be. Japan is ripe for Communism."

"Whatever the reason, I don't think you can know what it's like to be utterly defeated and then to receive the conqueror's largesse, or to feel better because a foreign General is running your country. I think even Toshio would have been impressed by MacArthur."

"I'm sure you're right, MacArthur *is* impressive, and so is Mao Tse-tung. I've been lucky enough to interview them both."

Kiku and I looked at each other: *tell us more.*

"McArthur doesn't behave like you or I. He thinks he's real special and when you first meet him you think, "This guys phoney". Then when he answers your questions, you realise he's got no need to put on an act. I came away convinced he'd be our next President. Mao Tse-Tung is totally different. He doesn't have any of MacArthur's *self* about him. You think you're interviewing an easy-going guy. But as he talks, you realise you're listening to someone with massive self-belief. And he's deep … he *knows* where he's going. He's completely his own man. He's more impressive than MacArthur."

"I thought MacArthur was his own man?"

Juniichi laughed, "He overdoes it. A friend of mine flew in from Okinawa with the Press Corps on MacArthur's plane. He'd seen a copy of a leaked Government document listing the reforms McArthur had been instructed to carry out. It was the result of a study Roosevelt had commissioned. Anyway, to my friend's amusement, MacArthur made a performance of getting to his feet and between long puffs of his pipe, dictating the reforms to his stenographer: adult suffrage, Trade Union rights, women's rights … a whole series of measures. Everyone on the plane was impressed, except my friend. He knew where it came from. But it worked. Word has got around about how the Great Man casually dictated a whole new constitution for the defeated country."

Juniichi's visit nourished our minds as well as our bodies. Being a member of the press corps, he was a unique source of information. During the day, I would take him around Nagasaki and tell him what I knew, and introduce him to people who would tell him more. Then of an evening, we would go back to the shelter and talk. He let us know he was worried, "The war might be over for now, but there's trouble brewing. I've been all over Asia. Everything's stirred up. European rule won't be tolerated again. In Vietnam, I could hardly believe what I was seeing. The British had suppressed the Vietnamese Provisional Government and rearmed the Japanese Army. Japanese soldiers were out on the streets keeping order, while the British waited for the French army to arrive. It was as though the Atlantic Charter had never existed."

We'd never heard of the Atlantic Charter before, so he explained, "It's a declaration of national rights put together by Roosevelt and Churchill: the right of nations to choose their own Governments, for instance. Churchill put his name to it, because he was trying to bring Roosevelt into the war. But after America came in, he didn't hide the truth that *his* war with Japan was about saving the British Empire. He told the British Parliament that the Atlantic Charter didn't apply to India. He even wanted to bring the French and the Dutch back to their empires. Roosevelt lookcd on Churchill as a nineteenth century Imperialist, but now he's dead, Churchill's got his way.

"Just before I left Vietnam, I asked the British Commander how he could reconcile the fight to free France from the Germans, with seizing Vietnam for the French. He pretended he couldn't see the connection. Then I asked him what he'd been fighting the war for, and he started rattling off the terrible things the Germans and Japanese had done. So I told him that one of the first atrocities I'd seen in Asia, was when the French Air Force bombed a column of protesting Vietnamese farmers.

"That changed him. He admitted he didn't like what he was doing. He said he'd had orders from London. But he offered to arrange an interview with the French commander when he arrivcd. It's a pity that I had to fly out. I'd love to have asked how far the French would go to deny the Vietnamese *their* independence. I'd have warned him that in China I'd seen a people who'd had *everything* done to them, get up and fight back. And I'd have asked him if he was prepared to behave as badly as the Germans did in France?"

Juniichi was worried about Korea too. While he was in Korea, in the south, the commanding American General refused to recognise the Korean Provisional Government and imposed a curfew. And if that wasn't enough to cause trouble, the Americans flew in their own man, Syngman Rhee and put him in charge.

Kiku and I had been thinking about adopting war orphans, but Juniichi's stories brought back father's bleak dying-vision of the future and we changed our minds. We didn't want to go through another war with children. It was a negative decision and we regretted it later, because war didn't come to Japan.

But there *were* Asian wars. What Juniichi had witnessed in Vietnam and Korea, were the first steps towards hugely destructive wars, and while we in Japan prospered, the Vietnamese suffered. They suffered far more under the French, than the French had suffered under Nazi rule. And later, when the Americans arrived, the way they used their tremendous firepower, made it even worse. They even sprayed forests, where people lived, with poisonous chemicals. And in Korea, when the American Air Force destroyed North Korean towns and cities, they bombed civilians who had lived through years of Japanese Occupation.

Any lingering desire I'd had to return to America had long gone, and apart from my work, I retreated into domesticity with

Kiku. She coached me until I shared her love of music and litera-
ture, while I won her to my fascination with science. We led as
rich a life as is possible without children.

Kiku has finally succumbed to the affects of atomic radiation.
Thankfully, she lived an almost normal lifespan.

Over the years my nights have been filled with dreams. I don't
know if it is normal to have so many dreams, or if how much you
dream depends on your experiences. The dreams I love, are
about little Kiku and Juniichi. I dream about them being much
older than they were, sometimes as adults, talking to me. When I
wake up I wonder if how they appeared in my dream, is how they
would have looked had they lived.

But I have other dreams. And amongst the dreams that have
spoilt my nights has been one about Kiku. I dream that she died
in Nagasaki in 1945 and I've lived my life without her. In my
dream, even though I know she's dead, I go looking for her in the
garden where she hid from me on the day we met. There, I meet
the father of her friend, Toshio's uncle and he tells me that she's
alive somewhere, but doesn't know where. I go looking for her
again, and as I wander old familiar streets and fail to find her, my
feeling of loss becomes so intense I wake up and for a brief
moment, really believe my nightmare that I've lived my life
without Kiku.

Coincidentally, shortly after Kiku died, I received an invitation
from my brother and sister to visit them in America *and* a letter
from Toshio asking me to go and stay for a while with him and
his family in China. It's what I need. The preparation is occupying my mind.

And I'm remembering that I began life as an American, and
I'm wondering how I'll feel when I get there. My brother-in-law
Stewart, is in ill health, so my sister, Takiko, will be taking me, with
Juniichi I hope, along the Tennessee River, showing me Franklin
Roosevelt's great work. I know that the Tennessee Valley project
was never completed. Anti New Dealers, who thought
Governments shouldn't do such things, stifled its development.
But I hear there's still plenty to marvel at. Visiting America is going
back to a long-lost love, a deep-down, half-remembered time.

After America, I'll be staying with Toshio in China and visiting
more recent emotions. I was delighted, when the corrupt
murderer, Chiang Kia-shek, was utterly defeated by Mao's revolu-

tionary army. And then I watched disappointed, as the new regime introduced thought control and persecution and ruined lives, while Mao shrank from brilliant revolutionary to lunatic Emperor, whose insane campaigns spoilt a brilliant beginning. And over the years I've wondered what had become of Toshio ...

9

Bilal

I AM VERY young. I live in a grey brick building. My world is made up of similar buildings spread out in all directions. If I was to go far enough along the passageways and roads, I know I would come to the edge of the camp. Beyond that, there is a hostile and dangerous world. But I've never been so far. All of my life I have lived in this camp with my sister Feriyan and grandmother and mother and father. We don't belong here. Our real home is in Palestine. I can pick father's village out on the map, but I can't say the name and when I try to everyone laughs.

Father's house was a fine house and his father had land. I want to go back and do the things that my father used to do. I want to help with the animals and play in the olive groves and collect eggs from under the hens and hide amongst the orange trees, the way my father did when he was a boy.

Many years ago, when mother and father were children, something terrible happened. People came from a place called Europe with guns and bombs and chased them from their homes and moved into their houses as though they were their own. And they took over their land and their animals and harvested their crops. They even attacked our holy places. Father's own father and other men from our village, who had tried to stop them, were captured and never seen again.

Although grandmother is my mother's mother, she has often told me the story of how my father's family were marched many miles in the summer heat away from their homes, without water or food. There were little children on the march and old people too and mothers carrying babies. They were taken to the border of Palestine and forced into another country. Some found it too much and died on the way, others were shot by the soldiers. In the new country there was little food. Many fell ill and even more people died.

Mother has a photo of herself with her older sister, Feriyan, whom *my* sister is named after and her father and mother. It was taken when mother was a girl. They're standing in a garden with their house in the background where they once lived in the city of Jaffa. Not long after the picture was taken, they were thrown out of the house and her sister and father were both dead. I know that something awful happened to mother's sister, but grandmother said it was only for grown-ups to know.

Grandmother sometimes gives me a key to hold and points at the door in the photo. "It's the key to your door", she says each time. "It belongs to you and Feriyan."

She sometimes takes papers from her box. "These show that the house belongs to us", she says. "It's still our house." Then she kisses me, "It's ours and someday you'll go back".

Almost everyone from Jaffa was chased out and the invaders took their homes for themselves; no one was allowed to return. But what was even worse was that the invaders sent planes after them. It didn't happen straight away, but later they dropped bombs and fired guns and rockets. Sometimes after a bombing when everyone was out digging in the rubble, the planes would return and catch them in the open. Or a bomb hidden under the rubble would go off. I wonder why they hate us so much that they do such things to us. Grandmother told me *they* once suffered terribly at the hands of a man called Hitler. I wonder if Hitler treated them as badly as they treat us.

Time has passed. The first year I can remember is 1982. I can't remember being aware of years before then. What happened in 1982 made me grow up quickly, even though I was young. Father's brother, Uncle Abass, came from America to stay with us. He brought me jeans and trainers and a baseball cap and a wonderful book called *Animals of the World*. And he brought Feriyan yellow and blue flowered dresses and a book about America. He brought nice things to eat and a radio and books for mother and father and clothes and chocolates and special tablets for grandmother. It was the most exciting time I'd ever had. He even said we might be able to go to live in America.

One evening, grandmother took her papers from her box and showed them to Uncle Abass. She said it was wrong for us to have to live the way we did. And it would be wrong even to go to America, while we had homes and land in Palestine. She asked

Uncle Abass if more could be done to let Americans know what had happened to us.

"I've talked myself hoarse in America", Uncle Abass told her. "And I've written letters. I've given talks. I've told people about what happened to us. I've shown *my* family's land titles. Some Americans do support us and some of them are from Jewish families. They're good people and they're my friends. Some of them have written books about what Israel did to us. *They* understand what happened. But America is a big country. There are millions of Americans. All most of them know about us, or think they know, is that we're the people who attack Israel.

"If someone injures me in America, or steals from me, I have recourse to law. If a fraction of what was done to you in Palestine, was done to me in America, I'd go to law and make myself a millionaire. And those who did it would be in jail. In this part of the world, if you're a Palestinian, there's no law to protect you. If there was you wouldn't be *here*."

"I know there's no law for us." Grandmother was very angry, "I know about the Americans and it's about time the American's knew the truth about us ..."

Soon after Uncle Abass left, everything changed. Grandmother became very ill. While she was ill, every day she talked to me and to Feriyan about her life. She said she was glad it would soon be over, but now it was *our time*. She said she'd watched us grow from babies and was pleased with us and she wouldn't have us different in any way. She said when we grow up, we must remember what she had told us about the difference between right and wrong, because our enemies didn't know and we must be better than they are. She said that things would never be easy, but right was on our side and one day we would be able to return to Palestine. She said she was more certain of that than she had been about anything in her life.

After grandmother died, father was given a teaching post at Ein El-Hilwe refugee camp, many miles to the south. And Uncle Abass sent father enough money to buy a car. I can still remember my mixture of excitement and sadness and mother holding me down, as I tried to stand to look out of the car window when we drove away from the camp. I had never seen such wide streets before, or so many people, or so much traffic. But we quickly left it all behind and drove through a green land of hills and trees and fields and villages. For the first time I saw goats and cows out in the open, and once I even saw a magnificent horse galloping across a field, but it was quickly out of sight. And for the first time I saw the Mediterranean, and it was very close. Father stopped the car, and we all got out. I could hear the low roar of the breakers as they came ashore and feel the sea wind, with its raw, strong smell. Large white birds soared above, calling as they went.

Later, as we drove south, I looked, hoping to catch a glimpse of the sea again. That's all I can remember before I woke up in the car alone. The car door was open and I climbed out and saw Feriyan standing staring. She turned to me, "We're here. We're not far from the sea."

Ein El-Hilwe camp wasn't locked up inside a city like the old camp. There was plenty of space, and we had a garden. Father was going to get chickens and build a shed for them to live in and there were other things we planned to do.

But we had only been there for a few days, when one afternoon, just as mother was breaking chocolate for us, we heard the sound of far-off explosions. She stopped and listened for a few moments. Then suddenly instead of distant sounds, there was an explosion from somewhere nearby, quickly followed by another one.

Mother ran from the room and came back carrying a blanket. She spread it out and put the chocolate and food from the cupboard into it. Then she gave it to Feriyan to carry. She picked up the heavy bag she'd kept under the table, "Hurry", she urged us, "We'll have to find a shelter".

I remember running from the room following Feriyan and realising I had left uncle Abass's book behind. Other people were running past. A woman picked me up and ran behind mother. Feriyan raced ahead.

I remember the deafening sound. Even though we were below ground, it shook the shelter. I was very scared, but I must have fallen asleep because I remember waking and seeing a man with a black face talking to mother. He bent over me and put his hand on my head and kissed me. It was father. I must have fallen asleep again. I woke up being carried out of the shelter by mother.

Outside, where there had been homes, there was rubble and people lying on the ground. I remember being put into the back of the car. I knew we were trying to escape being caught by a terrible enemy and that those we were leaving behind would be either killed or caught. I find it hard to recall the days that followed. I remember bouncing along in the dark, with mother asleep beside me, while Feriyan held me tight. We didn't travel by the coast road, the way we had come. That way, father said, we would have no chance of escaping the enemy warplanes. We went inland along mountain roads, sometimes passing villages of large, impressive houses. I wondered what kind of people lived in them.

I don't recall arriving in Beirut, but I do remember that the enemy followed us there. And I remember being in a basement full of frightened people. The loudness of the explosions made me shake. I remember being inside a tent with mother and Feriyan and then going outside and seeing lots of other tents. I'll never forget when the guns fired on us in our tents. I could see mother screaming but couldn't hear the sound. She grabbed me and ran and managed to get us into the basement of a building. Feriyan wasn't with us.

Afterwards, when we came out of the basement and returned to where the tents had been, there were dead people lying around in all kinds of strange positions. And there was blood everywhere and bits of people's bodies. Mother took me to the hospital to try to find Feriyan. It was full of people. Some were running carrying stretchers. Others were lying on the floor soaked in blood. And I saw something I couldn't understand: a baby burning in a bucket of water.

We went to different hospitals, but we never found Feriyan.

There was a ceasefire. The all-powerful Americans had finally told our enemy to stop and the guns and the bombs had stopped.

I was in a queue with mother. We were waiting for food. Suddenly I was being lifted into the air and kissed. It was father. Then father was holding mother and kissing her. He held us both, "I've prayed I'd find you. I've prayed and prayed. And I've found you. Where's Feriyan? Call Feriyan."

Mother stood with her head against father, her arms hanging by her side. She was crying.

"Where's Feriyan?"

"She's ..." Mother stopped and she was crying again.

Then father was crying too.

I didn't like the look of the boat. It was going to take father away. Some men were passing. One stopped and shook father's hand and talked to him for a while. Then father picked me up, and the man explained to me what father had already told me: that after the men had left, we would be safe. The Americans had promised that after the men had gone Israel would leave us in peace. Then the man asked me what I wanted to be when I grew up.

I couldn't answer. So he said, "Perhaps you'll be a teacher like your father. I'm sure you'll be as brave as he is."

It was only later that I found out that he had been the senior officer organising the defence of West Beirut during the Israeli bombardment. He had once been a Jordanian soldier but had joined the Palestinian cause after his King had ordered the army to fire into the refugee camps in Jordan.

After father had gone, mother and I shared a room with a woman and her baby in Sabra refugee camp. At first the baby cried a lot but gradually the crying stopped, and then I noticed her watching me and smiling. And I discovered it was easy to make her laugh. Then I saw the affect the baby had on mother and on anyone who came into the room: they relaxed and laughed. But we missed father.

Then one morning we were suddenly woken by a loud whoosh. It sounded like the start of an enormous explosion. Then it was gone. I knew the sound. It was an Israeli warplane flying low across the camp. And there were the sounds of other planes nearby. Everyone was awake. I could see from their faces, especially the baby's, that we all knew our time of peace was over.

Strangely, there was no bombing. But there was another sound. And it was growing louder. It was the sound of tanks, and they were firing as they came. And there was machine gun fire. It continued all morning. And it came closer.

I was listening to the guns, only half aware that mother was arguing with the baby's mother. She was trying to persuade her not to go out. Then I heard the baby's mother say, "No. I've got to go. I've got to get food." She laid the baby on the bed and made sure she was comfortable. Then she walked to the door. But when she opened it, the baby started to cry hysterically. Mother picked her up and I tried to comfort her, but it didn't work.

The baby's mother came back, "I'll have to take her with me", she said. The baby sobbed and choked while her mother hugged her and waited for her to stop. Then she opened the door and stood looking out, "They're watching us", she said.

"Who?" mother asked.

"The Israelis, through binoculars. They're outside the camp, up in the flats. I can see them." Then she left.

We waited all day, but they never came back.

There was noise right through that night and the room was

continually being lit up as the Israelis fired flares above the camp, to the sound of screams and shouts and gunfire. By morning, we could hear the shooting close by.

"We've got to get out", mother wrapped me in a coat and carried me out of the house, but she fell over. As we got up, I could see along the alley. There were people on the ground and men were hitting them. Mother pulled me around the corner and we ran up the alleys behind the house. Then all of a sudden amongst the bodies we saw *our* mother and baby. I looked away quickly, but it was too late. I'd seen the dark red blood where the baby's neck was cut. I felt my stomach turn. The baby looked like a large damaged doll that had been thrown away, and I tried to think of her that way and not as the baby who had been my friend. We passed other bodies. Terrible things had been done to them.

We stopped short, within sight of the camp entrance. There were soldiers barring our way. Mother gripped my hand, "Israelis", she whispered.

They were blocking our only way of escape. Two boys were running away from them. They'd been turned back.

Mother picked me up. Her face was white and I could feel her shaking. She took a step and collapsed. I could see the terrible Israelis watching us and started to cry hysterically. I knew I was crying just like the baby had cried before she died.

"Don't cry. Don't cry." Mother was kneeling in front of me gripping my shoulders. I understood. This wasn't a time for crying. I made myself stop; there was shooting nearby.

"The hospital. We'll go to the camp hospital." Mother held my hand, and we made our way, creeping around houses and running across alleyways. I noticed for the first time, that the bodies were covered in flies, and whenever we stopped the flies landed on us and then flew off when we ran.

There were many people at the hospital. They were standing outside, guarded by soldiers of some kind. Mother stopped and stood still. There were doctors and nurses in a group to one side. *The Little Doctor, Swee, was amongst them.* She was talking angrily to the soldiers. Even though I was very young, I could see that everyone, except for the little doctor, was in a state of terror.

Mother wasn't moving. She just stood looking. No one had seen us yet. I pulled her hand and we quickly hid behind a building and made our way home.

In front of the doorway was the body of the old man who lived next door. He had come in each day and watched me playing with the baby. Our little "home" had been ransacked and our bed was on its side against the wall. Mother put me between the bed and the wall and covered me with bedclothes and explained carefully to me, "I'll be sitting on the floor. If you hear anything, don't move. Don't make a sound whatever happens. Even if soldiers come into the room and there's shooting, stay there. People will come eventually and you'll be safe."

I knew that mother was preparing to sacrifice herself for me and quietly cried.

"Shhh, shhh", mother softly warned me and I stopped. From somewhere came the sound of machine-gun fire. It went on and on. I thought of the people at the hospital.

We waited and waited and mother occasionally whispered, "It'll be okay".

And it happened. Outside there were voices talking in English. "Journalists!" Mother wasn't whispering anymore. She pulled the bedclothes off me and we went outside.

A big man was leaning against the wall being sick. A smaller man, wearing glasses, was standing staring at the bodies. He was obviously shocked. He started to swear. Then the big man said angrily, "This is what I pay my taxes for". Mother "explained" later, that he was an American.

The enemy was in control, and it wasn't safe to go out. Palestinians were being picked up and "disappeared". But after the Israelis left Beirut, things improved and father managed to get back to us. He said he would never leave us again. Some men who came back never found their families.

After 1982 life was harder. But we Palestinians have learnt to live with whatever happens. I know that anytime we might be attacked and any of us be killed. Every home I've been into has photos of family members who have been killed. But Palestinians haven't always been on the receiving end. There was Damour.

One afternoon in the alley, I was listening to a group of older boys talking about Damour. Before I was born, the Christian Phalange, another enemy of ours, had massacred many Palestinans in the Tel el Zataar refugee camp, following a terrible siege. The Phalange had also killed many Lebanese Muslims. In retaliation, Muslims, including Palestinians, had killed hundreds of Lebanese Christians in the town of Damour.

In the alley, one of the older boys, Omar, was talking about

Damour. He was saying that it was right to pay back the enemy in kind: let them know what it was like to be on the receiving end. It seemed to make sense to me. But mother came running out of the house, "Omar, do you realise what you're saying? Were the mothers and children of Damour at Tel el Zataar? Did *they* do the killing? Do you really think Palestinians should do such things? How can *we* of all people ...?"

While she was scolding Omar, the familiar whoosh of an Israeli warplane drowned her out. Then it was gone. *Could it be an air raid?* As we dispersed, mother told my friends, "Samir will talk to you in school tomorrow".

I would like to have been with the older boys when father spoke to them. I was proud that people listened to him. I don't know if it was because he was older than the other fathers, or because he never lost his temper, or perhaps because he was a teacher?

But that night father did talk to me and to Said. Said had come to live with us. During the Israeli invasion, his brother had been with father at Kalde, where we fought and defeated the Israelis. Afterwards, Israeli gunboats shelled them and Said's brother was killed. Father knew that his dead friend had only one surviving relative, his younger brother, Said. So he sought him out and brought him to live with us.

Father poured each of us a cup of coffee before saying, "Mother told me what Omar said today. Omar has been through a lot. So have you both. And only God knows what the future holds for you. I'll tell you now what I'll be telling Omar and his friends in school tomorrow, and I want you both always to remember it. Whatever happens, don't let yourself be driven mad. Don't rejoice over other's misfortunes. When you're older, don't even think of taking part in anything like what happened at Damour. Doesn't it break our hearts when it happens to us? Isn't it a calamity? Why shouldn't it be a calamity when it happens to others? Imagine, another Omar, another Said, another Bilal." Father looked at me, "Another Feriyan. All dead."

"And how do you think Damour appeared to the world? Doesn't Abass tells us all the time that the Americans see Palestinians only as terrorists. Father nodded, "I know. What's done to us doesn't matter. But if *we* murder, besides committing an unforgivable sin, we make things worse. Then we make all Palestinians victims."

Father stopped and thought before he continued, "I know that we *have* to fight. That is the reality of our lives. But that doesn't mean we shouldn't be moral in everything we do. Don't you think the Israelis disgrace themselves the way they behave? Isn't their blood lust obvious? They break agreements that have given them peace so that they can go to war. And then they act like innocents when someone fights back. Our best hope is their behaviour. It might be our only hope, because no one listens to us. It won't be quick. They get away with so much. But however bad things become, our behaviour must be better than theirs."

After President Assad, the Syrian Dictator, became displeased with our leaders in 1985, AMAL, the Shia militia, attacked our camps. At first I was horrified to see people being killed again. And I was shocked because father had told me what good allies the Shias were and how bravely they had fought the Israelis at Khalde. But something inside me was always prepared for the worst. *And father was home.* When I saw our defenders carrying weapons and ammunition and hurrying to the edge of the camp, I didn't feel the fear I had felt in 1982. AMAL were attacking from just outside the camp and could be fought and stopped. The Israelis had done most of their killing from a distance, using powerful American weapons. They had been able to collapse whole apartment blocks and even kill people who were hiding in basements.

Father had fought the Israelis at Khalde, soldier to soldier, the way wars should be fought. And stopped them. The camp defenders did the same when AMAL attacked us, and our new enemy was glad to have a ceasefire.

The shortage of men meant that women and older boys had done much of the fighting, but following the ceasefire the men started to come back. Then, when it became known that the Syrian leader was supplying AMAL with artillery and tanks for a new attack, even more men came back. They were aware of what had happened the last time the Dictator fell out with our leaders and sent the Phalange against us at Tel el Zataar.

When AMAL attacked the second time, it came as no surprise; they had been bulldozing sand into great piles outside the camp. They used the sand-piles to protect the tanks that fired on us. There was machine-gun and sniper fire too. Anyone who left cover was fired at, regardless of age and many were hit. Every building in the camp was damaged, but the hospital seemed to be the main target, and its top floors were wrecked. Being under constant fire became normal.

Then one morning, we heard the boom of heavy guns from the mountains. Our allies, the Druze, had joined the fight. Very quickly the AMAL fire: the artillery, the tanks, and the machine guns and rifles, stopped. Our attackers were themselves under fire from greater weapons than their own. But soon the great guns in the mountains went quiet. The Syrian Dictator had intervened and AMAL's assault was allowed to continue.

Then the marvellous news came. The Druze and other friendly militias were driving AMAL from Beirut. It would have been only a matter of time before the camps were relieved, but the Syrian Dictator sent his army to save AMAL. And then the siege continued, but with a difference. Perhaps shamed by their role, AMAL fired only occasionally. And they allowed camp women out to buy food. But they terrorized them and stole from them and prevented them from taking medicines back into the camp. And sometimes they fired on them. Dozens of our women were shot before the Syrian army arrived and took the place of the killers.

My main sensation during the siege wasn't fear. It was hunger and cold. Everyone was starving and people fainted regularly. I had a pain in my stomach that never left me and I was always cold. But I knew that everyone felt the same as I did. And I knew that there were people who endured the siege voluntarily: the foreign nurses and doctors who treated the wounded and saved many Palestinian lives. Knowing that we weren't alone and that *they* were with us, helped me to believe we would survive.

Towards the end of the siege the wounded and the sick, who should have lived, didn't have the strength to recover and were dying, despite the efforts of our foreign friends. But the siege ended without a massacre.

The siege had hardly finished when father was asked again to go and teach in the south. We all wanted to go; we couldn't be sure that President Assad wouldn't suddenly turn against us again. We would feel safer away from Beirut.

The scenery along the coastal road is as breathtaking as it was in 1982. There are still signs of the holocaust that swept over it then: bombed houses that haven't been rebuilt, the occasional rusty remnant of a burnt out car and sometimes we drive over a repaired bomb crater.

We come to an AMAL roadblock. A militiaman sees father's blue Palestinian identity card and orders us out. But when father produces his travel permit he lets us through. "God be with you", he calls as we drive off.

A little later there's a fine view of the Mediterranean and we stop to eat. Out to sea there is a boat. Suddenly there's a flash from the boat. "Get down", father shouts. We don't need telling. We knew immediately that we've seen an Israeli war-ship in action. Seconds later, we hear a dull, echoing, boom. After a while we stand up. The gunboat is still there. There's an occasional silent flash, followed by the boom.

"It must be hitting something down the coast", mother says.

Father nods, "It's probably supporting a raiding party. We'll wait here and see what happens."

Nothing happens, and eventually the gunboat leaves.

Father has been driving for some time now. Slowly. We are approaching a bridge. A roadblock. Soldiers. Lebanese Army soldiers. There's a burning car beyond the bridge and an ambulance. A soldier lets us through. "Be careful", he warns father before we move away.

We've driven for a while. Ahead is another roadblock. As we draw close, father whispers, "Israelis. It's too late to turn back."

The windscreen shatters. Said has been sitting in the front seat next to father. Blood from his head sprays the inside of the car as he's hit. The Israelis are surrounding us. A soldier opens the door and pulls Said out by his ankles. He's still alive, gurgling as he hits the ground.

"Said!" As father jumps out he's pushed against the side of the car. Seconds later a soldier is holding father's blue identity card and pistol in the air, "Terrorists!"

He's kicked father in the stomach and pushed him back inside the car and slammed the door shut. The soldiers are backing away. One is aiming what looks like a rocket launcher. Father is trying to say something to the soldiers, and mother is praying and pushing me down between the seats. There's an overwhelming brightness …

10

Miriam

I'VE ALWAYS KNOWN that I have two fathers. One is my natural father, Sam. For most of my childhood I had only vague memories of him: his black hair, his hobbling around on walking sticks and his books: car-board boxes full of them. Sam left while I was still a baby.

My other father, Gideon, brought me up and I love him as though he was my natural father.

I live in an unusual country where Jews have come together from all over the world, many of them from old Europe. I've been told that in some parts of old Europe Jews suffered daily humiliation. For simply walking along the street minding their own business, they could be called, "Dirty Jew", and have to cross the street to avoid trouble. And sometimes, Jewish communities were attacked and people were killed. There was no point in Jews asking, "What's your grievance? What have we done?" They were Jews. So they were victims.

And there was the Holocaust!

Hitler was an extreme nationalist who didn't want Jews in Germany. Eventually, after years of terrorising them and scheming to have them expelled, he literally murdered millions. He had them rounded up and killed simply because they were Jews.

My father, Gideon, originally came from America and mother from Yemen, so they escaped the Holocaust. But some older Israeli Jews are survivors of the Holocaust. Freda, who was our neighbour when I was a child, sometimes talked about the old days in Germany. She once said to me, "Imagine all the school bullies growing up and still being bullies, but having the authorities on their side and picking on *you*. Imagine the worst school bully, gone mad, becoming the national leader and controlling the police and army. That was life for us in Germany."

I'm lucky that I've grown up where Jews aren't humiliated or exterminated. But even here there are attacks on us. Once when I was small and heard that a group of schoolchildren had been killed, I had nightmares. I remember waking up in hysterics, after dreaming there were terrorists in the house.

Over the years, many times, I have heard the terrorists who attack us being compared to Hitler. And it has been said, many times, that they want to continue the Holocaust. But I've learnt the truth.

My parents once drove me to see the Other People. Up in the hills there were Arab "villages": shantytowns built of scrap. We kept our distance. But when we saw the first one, mother said, "That's an unrecognised village. It's not supplied with electricity or water, and they aren't allowed to build houses. If they do, they'll be pulled down."

Then we went to somewhere called the "Artists' Village". "Have a good look", mother said. "It used to be an Arab village. The people who lived here live in the shantytowns now. The land around here was their land. The people who live on it now are from Yemen, Poland, New York? I don't really know where, but before 1948 the village was Palestinian."

What I saw on that day made a big impression on me, because I'd grown up knowing that in other times and places, Jews had been outcasts. Yet here in my own country, Jews had made another people outcasts.

Mother and father took me to see other villages where Arabs lived. Although they were better by far, than those I'd seen earlier, they couldn't compare with Jewish towns and villages, with their paved roads and wide, well lit streets and libraries and modern schools and sewage systems. Mother told me that the parents of the children raised in Arab villages didn't receive the child allowance that Jewish mothers received. Yet they were supposed to be citizens of our country and they paid the same taxes as Jews.

It was what seemed to me an innocent incident in school that led my parents to show me the Arab side of life in Israel. Our teacher had been talking about the different experiences that had helped to make our country a unique place. She asked the class to name the countries of origin of Israeli citizens. After the children had named various countries, I said, "Palestine".

The teacher answered, "Yes, very good. There were Jews in Palestine before ..."

But I answered, "No, I'm talking about Christians and Muslims". Most of the class laughed.

"No, no", the teacher said, "we're talking about Jews".

The following day, mother stopped the teacher outside the classroom and told her that she had been wrong to talk only about Jews as citizens of our country. To my horror, the teacher was annoyed and responded, "Haven't you noticed, we're a Jewish nation?"

"What about citizens who aren't Jews?"

The teacher answered, "If you're not happy with my teaching, go and see the Minister".

Mother said she would give me a "proper education". The following weekend, she and father took me to see the Other People.

There was another disagreeable aspect of life in Israel. It was the settling of the conquered territories by religious zealots. As far as I could make out, the zealots believed God had given the land to the Jews. So regardless of who legally owned land in modern times, in what had once been biblical Israel, any Jews who chose to could seize it, with violence if necessary.

I agreed with my parents that it was ludicrous for anyone to say that they have a right to particular land because of who they believe lived there in antiquity, even in the unlikely case of someone being able to show that a direct ancestor had once lived at some location. There has been a great movement of peoples since the time of ancient Israel and the world would be in chaos if others thought the way our zealots think. It's certainly ludicrous to believe that we can seize the land of others and live in peace. But peace isn't a priority for them, or for our Government. Land seizure is. And General Dayan started it.

Before the war of 1967 was over, General Dayan ordered the removal of the Palestinian community, which had lived opposite the Wailing Wall since mediaeval times. They were told to get out and their homes were bulldozed. They lost almost all they owned.

If they had been an ancient Jewish community, General Dayan would have treasured them. He'd have commissioned scholars to record their history, their buildings and any old writings and artefacts they might have. I have come to understand that what General Dayan did, symbolises everything Israel has done to the Palestinians. They have always had to give way before the greater right of the Jewish people. And there are always with further encroachments to come. Palestinians haven't been able to ask, "What's your grievance? What have we done?" They were Palestinians. *That* made them victims.

But the religious settlers are even more frightening than Dayan was. It's not just that they have gone far beyond General Dayan's original plans for settlements. It is that they believe there is a God who especially favours Jews and sanctions what they do. They're so insular. I could never accept their way of thinking. Especially their idea that God favours them so much, that they have the right to take other people's property and even deny them equal recognition as human beings. I could never accept that there is a God who sanctions *that*. I doubt it ever enters their heads that there might be a universal God who will one day call them to account for their behaviour.

The settlers have held my horrified interest since I spent a weekend on the West Bank with relatives of my friend and name-sake, Miriam. At first I hadn't wanted to accept her invitation, but mother persuaded me that it would be an experience not to be missed. It turned out to be a crash course in settler ideology, or at least one strand of it.

I happened to arrive just after a group of hyped-up settler children had returned from a rampage through an Arab market. The Arabs were under curfew and our patrolling soldiers had done nothing to stop the children doing their damage. The excited children were singing a song in praise of some "hero" who had gone on raids into neighbouring countries attacking Arabs. It was an appropriate beginning to my weekend's education: part of normal settler life.

Years later those children would come to mind again. It was after a settler, Baruch Goldstein, massacred twenty-nine Muslims at prayer in a mosque, Arab children amongst them. And as he killed, Goldstein himself was killed. At Goldstein's burial service, a Rabbi sent shivers up my spine, or rather my reading about it did. He said that two thousand Arabs weren't worth the fingernail of a single Jew.

After the service, the settlers erected a monument in memory of the murderer and took their children to the shrine to honour him. I still have a newspaper cutting of settler children, super-vised by adults, kissing the Goldstein shrine. It was when I first saw that picture that I thought of the rampaging children. By then they would have passed the age of military service. I wondered how *they* had behaved while "policing" the occupied territories? And the children kissing the shrine, what chance would they have of becoming decent human beings.

It wasn't things like sitting together for a meal and chatting, or humorous exchanges, or gossip, or liking someone, which coloured my weekend with the settlers. It was that I was amongst Driven people. During the first day of my visit to the settlement, Miriam showed me a map that was hanging on her aunt's living room wall. It showed an Israel that took in Lebanon and part of Egypt and extended through Kuwait to the Euphrates. When I saw it, especially after listening to the children, I found it too much to take and decided to go home. But while Miriam was still pointing at some detail of the map her cousin, Nathan, came into the room. He smiled at me, "You're looking at our future", he said. Then he walked over and kissed the map and added, "It's our destiny". Then he mumbled something. It sounded like a prayer.

He was very handsome. But, after hearing him talk, I found his good looks repulsive. I remembered mother saying that it would be an experience not to be missed. So I made myself stay.

Later in the weekend, when I asked him how we would achieve a Greater Israel, he winked and pointed at his gun, "If God wills it, we'll get there in my lifetime, and then we'll have completed our War of Independence". Over those three days I heard what could be described as a xenophobic sermon. I'd never heard Rabbis quoted so often before. And each time a Rabbi was quoted, it was meant as final proof that something was in accordance with God's will.

Father had warned me that the settlers weren't open to reason. He had advised me to listen, but not argue. I would have found it difficult to do otherwise. Everyone was so warm towards me. And they held their opinions with such certainty. I felt I would seem like a traitor if I disagreed.

I wrote down as much as I could remember of what I heard, and when I returned home, showed my notebook to mother and father. We agreed that I would never go there again.

I re-read my notes occasionally to remind me of my encounter and to reassure myself that, over that weekend, I really did hear, "Jews are chosen by God and are infinitely more holy and unique than non-Jews. We should be considered a different species. God frees us from following the codes of justice that bind ordinary nations. Israel's conquests have transferred land from Satan into the land of Israel. In Israel non-Jews must accept humiliation and servitude because God has created them inferior. The death penalty is mandatory for Arabs who throw stones at Jews. When Jews kill non-Jews it isn't murder. The killing of innocent Arabs for revenge is a Jewish virtue. Any Jew is capable of judging whether a non-Jewish child should be punished in the same way as an adult. The shedding of Jewish blood is the worst possible crime." These ugly certainties were attracting my friend, Miriam.

Soon after my stay with the zealots, I read an enlightened article, criticising the fundamentalists. It was by Israel Shahak. It might have come from a different universe. Israel Shahak is a survivor of Belsen who, when he was young, saw for himself how far extreme xenophobes can go. I've tried to think myself into his situation. I imagine he will be seared to his soul by the experience of seeing people who thought themselves unique and superior, take control of a powerful state and first persecute and then annihilate the "inferiors" around them.

While he was still young he would have witnessed the German racial "superiors" invading surrounding countries and heard their leaders justify the settling of Germans in Slavic countries, by claiming that Germanic tribes had once lived there. And he would have seen Jews stripped of their property by the Nazis.

How must he feel when, as an adult, he sees the systematic seizure of Palestinian property by fellow Jews? And when the settlers' sons join "combat" units, as they often do and are sent against Palestinians protesting the loss of their property, I can only imagine what his emotions are.

I suspect that Israel Shahak, over the years, will have heard again and again, "We must never forget the lessons of the Holocaust", from individuals who refuse to draw any moral lesson from the Holocaust and have no compassion for the dispossessed Palestinians. It wouldn't surprise me if Israel Shahak has sometimes felt despair. However he has felt, I am grateful to him for not giving up and for continuing to explain.

I think I have come to understand why our national leaders value the religious settlers so much: it is because they can't morally or lawfully defend what they do and find refuge in a religious defence, which they don't actually make themselves. The very existence of the settlers does it for them: their "God-given-right" to the land of Israel, is emotionally accepted in Christian America and helps them continue to oust Palestinians from their land.

I was disappointed to realise that while I was tortured by the knowledge of so much wrong, many others seemed indifferent to it. Yet I found an individual who shared my concern. One evening, in an idle moment, I took Dov Yermiya's *War Diary* from beside mother's bed and lay down and read it through. It was almost too much for me to bear. Part of me didn't want to know and another part had to. In *War Diary,* I learnt that in 1982 in Lebanon, not far from where I lived, our army and air force shattered the lives of everyone in their path. Amongst the destruction, Dov recalled the smell of rotting bodies from a bombed Palestinian hospital. He related how a ship bringing supplies for the many victims of our actions, was turned away by senior officers and how his own efforts to bring relief were not appreciated by the same officers.

Mistreatment of prisoners was normal. He told of a bound and blindfolded male Red Cross nurse being beaten with club and rifle butt and then left exposed for five successive days to the sun and the night cold before being released and of a similarly bound and blindfolded prisoner being repeatedly kicked in the face by an Israeli soldier. But that was only a small part of what he witnessed. He wrote of freed prisoners staggering and falling as they tried to walk home. And while these things were happening, he heard Israeli radio claiming that our Army was providing assistance to the victims of the invasion.

I was relieved to read though that there were other soldiers who shared Dov Yermiya's feelings and that he was able to get sympathetic Israelis to provide some relief for south Lebanon.

After his book was published, Dov Yermiya was "retired" from army reserve service. And he was prevented from returning to Lebanon to continue the badly needed relief work. The dismissal of the "disloyal" Dov Yermiya helped me to understand that the words "loyal" and "disloyal" can be misleading. The world "loyal" can be used to describe those who condone evil and "disloyal" can be a brand stamped on a thoroughly decent individual.

The extent to which I felt distress over my country's behaviour probably made me an unusual fifteen year-old. Dov Yermiya's experience in 1982 was confined to south Lebanon and I felt I had to know more. Then I read a review of a book by Dr Swee, the tiny doctor, who ran a medical charity to care for the many wounded Palestinians. It was about her experience in Beirut during the 1982 invasion. I felt I must have it. She had been doing medical work in the refugee camps of Lebanon during the invasion. The review told of how all of the Palestinian hospitals, except one, were bombed by our Air Force and of how that one hospital had been saved by letting it be known that there were Israelis being treated there. And she wrote of how, when our army arrived, medical staff, doctors and nurses, were arrested despite the many wounded who needed treatment. And she told of the slaughter of civilians.

I wanted to read Dr Swee's story, so I asked for her book for my sixteenth birthday. My parents couldn't get it. Instead they bought me *Pity the Nation*, by a British journalist, Robert Fisk. I had no idea when I received it that reading it would result in my going to America soon afterwards.

Early in the book, Robert Fisk recalled seeing in Lebanon what he described as "a place of destitution" and being told that it was where Palestinians lived. The book gives an account of our attacks on villages, refugee camps, apartment blocks and civilian traffic, and of massive destruction, out of all proportion to any damage ever done to Israel. He risked his life travelling around Lebanon during our invasion, recording horribly unforgettable scenes of the results of our military rampage: cellars full of mangled people tangled together in death; babies burning, even though they were submerged in water, victims of phosphorous bombs. In Sabra-Chatilla refugee camps he saw heaps of mutilated bodies blocking alleyways; Syrian soldiers promised safe passage if they left Beirut, but slaughtered from the air when they reached the open highway; carbonised bodies of Syrian soldiers who earlier he had seen alive: victims of our air power. Ein Helweh refugee camp destroyed with most of its population still inside; Palestinian refugees *in tents* in Sanaya Park, massacred by our tanks and artillery and when the fighting was over, a brutal occupation.

And I learnt from his book, that until the invasion, our Government had had an understanding with the Palestinians in south Lebanon that there would be no cross-border attacks on civilians by either side. The Palestinians had honoured it, but our forces broke the understanding. So the reason given for the invasion: to bring peace to Galilee was a lie.

I couldn't stop talking about what I'd read. I wanted my fellow Israelis to wake up to the extent of the crime. I knew there had been a huge, angry demonstration in Israel after the Sabra-Chatilla massacre. Although the Christian Militia did the killing, they were transported to the camps and went into action on Israeli orders and our soldiers fired flares across the camp to help them do their work. It was Israeli soldiers surrounding the camp, who turned back refugees who were trying to escape the massacre. Everything possible seems to have been done to facilitate the work of the killers. Our Prime Minister, Begin, knew that the massacre was taking place, but rather than order action to halt it, commented, "Its just Arabs killing Arabs". And afterwards, the guilty militia continued to work closely with our forces. And there was more killing.

There *was* a Commission of Inquiry into Sabra-Chatilla. But, however horrific, the massacre was only a small part of the carnage. That the inquiry was restricted to one tiny part of the invasion and that no one was brought to trial for either Sabra-Chatilla, or the rest of the killing, disgusted me. I can recall numerous times over the years hearing our leaders make impassioned promises to punish killers when the victims were Israeli Jews. But when Jews, or our allies, are the perpetrators, there isn't the same response. Then the passion is directed against the "disloyalty" of someone like Dov Yermiya. That was how I was thinking, even before I had finished Robert Fisk's book.

"Miriam", mother appeared uncomfortable. "Sam has asked if you would like to stay with him during the holidays?" I looked at her trying to understand what she was saying. "Sam, your father. I spoke to him on the phone earlier ..."

While she talked I had to adjust my thinking as I learnt that a father I barely remembered had spoken to mother regularly by phone from America. She explained that when she had re-married, Sam had agreed to stay out of our lives. But he had wanted to be kept up-to-date on how I was. And eventually, soon after my sixteenth birthday, when mother had told him about the book I was reading, he said he wanted to meet me.

The noise was overwhelming as the sheer power of the engines sent the plane hurtling along the runway. We climbed at what seemed an impossible angle. I was on my way to meet Sam. Mother had told me that he had been wounded in the Yom Kippur war of 1973 and left Israel not long after recovering his health. She said she hadn't been willing to go with him; whatever its faults, Israel was her home.

Gideon had been Sam's friend. He accompanied mother when she saw Sam off on his way to America and after Sam left, he called to see her occasionally. It was only after it became obvious that Sam wasn't coming back and another man was seeing mother that Gideon proposed to her. He told mother that he had always loved her, but would never have admitted it if Sam had stayed; he would never have betrayed his friend. But when he thought he was going to lose her, as well as Sam, he plucked up the courage to ask her. He almost didn't.

Mother said that for her, at first, it had been a hard decision. She was quite taken with the other man. He was a talented guitarist with a beautiful voice. He was such a perfectionist that to produce the sound he wanted, he even made his own guitars. But when she thought about him as my new father, beyond his music, he didn't have any of Sam's, or Gideon's, broad-mindedness. He even admired people like Dayan and Rabin and Sharon. She hadn't wanted me to have such a father. And she'd always liked Gideon. So she married him and never regretted it.

Meeting my father wasn't easy. He saw me first. While I was wondering which of the men in the crowd standing waiting, was Sam, he walked up to me, a total stranger, full of emotion. I guess he must have realised how uncomfortable he made me feel, because he quickly composed himself. Sam drove us through the New York traffic, pointing out the sights and talking about the city and by the time we arrived at his apartment I felt relaxed in his company.

The back room of Sam's flat was lined with shelves full of books and papers and videotapes and there was a large table with two computer terminals and a television on it. Under the table was my one remembered link with Sam: cardboard boxes full of books. On the walls were framed photographs of old Palestine: villages, which Sam said no longer existed. His main room was full of chairs and small tables. This was the room, Sam told me, where he met with like-minded friends. Hanging on the wall was a photo of Sam and mother and myself when I was a baby and one of me at school when I was eight years old.

Sam said I could look around the flat while he cooked our meal. But before he had finished, I went into the kitchen and told him I remembered him going around on crutches and asked how he had been wounded.

"Our own side did it", he said. Then in bits and pieces, as he prepared the meal, he told me how it happened. He had been concussed by a shell blast and was left lying on a stretcher. When he tried to talk to some passing soldiers, they thought he was an Egyptian. "So many attacked me", he said, "It saved my life. They were falling over each other to get at me. One of the medics dropped a hand grenade down a waste hole and the soldiers thought they'd come under fire. That medic and an emergency helicopter saved me. But I had broken bones. It was months before I could walk properly again.

"When I recovered, I became treasurer of a kibbutz. It was a convalescence job. The settlement was wonderfully designed: an avenue of trees leading to an airy dining hall. But I couldn't enjoy it. I knew about the village that had been bulldozed to build that place. Then, one night, we celebrated the 25th anniversary of the settlement. Everyone was dancing and singing. But ... I stood back. All I could think all night was, 'Have you no feelings. Have you no human sensitivities'.

"Then as if to rub salt in my wounds, some army 'boys' came over to talk to me. They knew I'd been invalided out of the army. They thought I was some kind of hero. They told me about their latest raid into Lebanon. One said, 'We weren't dealing with human beings; we shoot first, and ask questions afterwards'. Another said, 'We were dealing with animals'.

"I tried to reason with them, but I didn't succeed. I felt totally out of place. The next day, I decided I couldn't go on living in that atmosphere. I had to get away. Your mother begged me to stay and I begged her to come with me. She said I could fight for my beliefs inside the country. She might have been right. But I'd had enough.

"Believe me, I loved you both and I've tried to understand since how I could have left you. The only answer I've been able to come up with is that I was traumatised. I don't think I was capable of behaving differently ... I couldn't take anymore. I loved you so much and wanted you to follow. But then your mother took up with Gideon."

"About you now. I hear you've passed your exams ..."

It would have been a thrill to be in America, whatever the circumstances. To be walking through the streets of New York with Sam was a dream. After the long conciliation of the night before, I wanted to be with him. To talk. To listen.

During the evening, Sam had told me about his work trying to publicise the Palestinian cause in America. He said, "I tell people about the old European nationalist parties. It's the quickest route to understanding Israel. I've a friend, Ben. I've learnt a lot from him. He was born in Austria. He lived there way back. He had to go underground; the Gestapo were after him. I've tried to get him to write about it, but he's a bugger, he loves talking, but he won't pick up a pen. I'd like you to meet him tomorrow. We'll get him talking ..."

We were on our way to meet Ben.

At the back of the restaurant, a head turned. It was Ben. His eyes were so alive. He stood up when we reached his table, "So you're Miriam". He took my hand, "This is a very special moment", he said. But after that, he talked to me as though I was a little girl. Considering his age perhaps, to him, I was. It was a disappointment. But when I told him about my weekend on the religious settlement, his attitude changed. He listened, and when I had finished he said, "Some things never change. But it was simpler when I was young."

Then he told me that when he had been my age, the First World War had just ended. "I was too young to go to war", he said, "But my neighbour, Franz, was older. He was a loyal Austrian and he volunteered. He was sent to fight on the Russian front. He'd been my protector." He smiled, "Franz was some street fighter. I've seen anti-Semites cross the street when they saw him coming.

"When the war ended and he came back from Russia, he was completely changed. He was talking like a Bolshevik ... he'd been taken prisoner and was won over by the Bolsheviks. They'd opposed the war and they managed to convince him that ordinary Russians and Austrians and shouldn't be enemies: the rulers were the enemies and they should be overthrown.

"Then when the civil war started in Russia and there was foreign intervention against the Bolsheviks, Franz went back. I didn't see him for a couple of years. It seemed a long time then. When he came home again, he was different. He looked old and tired and didn't say very much.

"But gradually he came around and told me that when he'd got back to Russia, the country was already ruined by four years of war. But what he saw while he was there was collapse from ruin to something far worse. There wasn't enough food to feed the country and there was mass starvation. Yet the Bolsheviks had to find the resources to turn the back foreign armies, as well as fight a civil war.

"Franz told me that as he advanced and retreated across Russia with the Red Army, there was famine and typhoid and social collapse. The Bolsheviks had to bring in rule by decree to hold the country together. They sent armed men out to the farms to seize food so that they could feed the cities.

"Numerous times when Franz was in retreat with the Red Army

and defeat seemed certain, reinforcements arrived and defeat turned into victory. Usually the saviours were civilians without military training from nearby cities, or from mines or factories. He said he had seen with his own eyes many of the people who had made the Revolution being killed.

"Franz said that by the time the civil war ended, there was rule from above: by Commissar. It wasn't what he had fought for. He said that although the Bolsheviks appeared to have won, really they had lost. Churchill and the other interventionists had known what they were doing. They had destroyed so much, they destroyed the Revolution.

"'That's how The Powers behave', Franz said. 'They destroy rather than deal with people who do things differently'."

I asked, "What happened to Franz?"

"Franz lived for years after that. And he recovered. Thank God! A lot of people looked up to Franz. There was a film. I went to see it with him. We saw it a number of times: 'All Quiet On The Western Front'. It showed the destruction of a generation of young men in the trenches. After we'd seen it, we were convinced there would be no more war. We thought that whole nations would rise up rather than go to war again.

"But every country had its extreme nationalists. And *they* weren't repulsed by the idea of bloodshed and war, and they only cared about their own kind. We thought it would be impossible for people like them to come out on top. But I was wrong. They came to power in Germany.

"Unfortunately, we Jews had the same type of nationalists. They wanted us all to decamp and go to Palestine and take the place over. The 'great' Weizmann said that there were too many Jews in Germany. He was agreeing with Nazi propaganda. All he cared about was getting the Jews to Palestine.

"Franz never lived to see what that led to. He died in Spain. We went there to fight the Fascists ... I've got something to show you." Ben took an old piece of paper from his wallet, unfolded it and handed it to me. On it was typed:

October 1917

For the Red Guard
That stood before the Winter Palace
That frozen night,
Young men and women

Vividly living their dream,
The hours hung.
Then time raced on.

Some survived
The killing years of civil war,
Their beauty spent,
And monsters ruled the land.
And youths' dream died.

I read it. Then I looked at Ben for the significance of what he had shown me.

"That's what Franz died for. He wrote it. It was published in a dissident journal in Spain. Stalin's agents were in Spain, and they had a lot of power. They assumed the verse was directed at Stalin. And they were right.

"Franz had been in his element in Spain. There were a lot of like-minded people. I heard him, numerous times, explaining how Stalin had turned the Bolshevik's emergency measures into the normal method of rule. The Communists saw him as a threat. A few days after that poem appeared, Franz was arrested and shot. That's how the Communists behaved in Spain. I was shattered. I'd thought Franz was indestructible ... I got out of Spain while I could. They weren't pleasant times.

"Franz's half-brother, Kurt, came home from Palestine for the memorial service. He updated me on Palestine. Farmers were being evicted after landlords had sold the land for Jewish settlement, and there were shantytowns full of landless farmers. The more extreme settlers were planting bombs in Palestinian areas. The Palestinians were in revolt, and the British Army was slowly crushing them.

"The most ominous thing was that the British had created a military force of Jewish settlers. It was very aggressive. Kurt wouldn't have anything to do with it. He belonged to Mapam: it was a kind of political party. It was supposed to believe in Jewish/Arab brotherhood. But most Mapam members joined the new force. Kurt told me how some of them were taken on a night attack on an Arab village. They killed five villagers and took four prisoners. Afterwards, the British officer in charge questioned the prisoners, but they wouldn't cooperate. So the officer ordered a young Jew to shoot a prisoner. He shot him and the other prisoners cooperated.

"Shooting prisoners didn't seem to affect an officer's career. The British officer became a famous General not long afterwards: General Wingate. He had a lot to answer for. His second-in-command that night was Moshe Dayan. As you know he became Israel's top General.

"After listening to Franz's brother I decided to visit Palestine. But while I was preparing to go, Hitler sent his army into Austria. That changed everything. I didn't see Palestine until after the war.

"It was a terrible time. The Nazis believed other races had to step aside to accommodate the claims of the German people. Entire peoples were denied human rights. When victims fought back, the Nazis went crazy. The lives of German soldiers were so precious. They retaliated with collective punishment. Villages were destroyed. Civilians were killed. Countless people had their lives wrecked.

"After liberation I worked for the United Nations helping refugees ... the scale of the problem: there were millions of displaced people all over Europe. Being a Jew, I was allocated to Jews. My family had gone to England before the war and I was never caught, so I got off lightly. But most survivors had really gone through it.

"President Roosevelt sent General Hurley to talk to the Jewish refugees who'd escaped to Palestine and he reported back that most of them didn't want to settle there. And later, General Morgan, who ran the resettlement camps, sent Roosevelt a similar report saying that if they were allowed to choose, most Jews wouldn't go to Palestine. So Roosevelt put forward the ideal solution: the Jewish refugees would be offered homes in America and Canada and Britain and various other Western countries, but not Palestine. The plan was killed off by the people who would soon become the Israeli Lobby. *They* had political muscle and they wanted the refugees to have no choice but to go to Palestine. Then after Roosevelt died, the same people made a lot of noise about the poor refugees who had been left in camps in Europe.

"Atlee, the new British Prime Minister, had a plan that was similar to Roosevelt's. But President Truman was more concerned with American/Jewish votes. That was as far as he could think, and he had the refugees shipped to Palestine.

"That's how I came to go to Palestine. The refugees had nowhere else to go and I wanted to be with them.

"When I arrived, the United Nations was getting ready to partition the country. Ben Gurion, the Jewish leader, had accepted partition, but the Palestinian's hadn't. They couldn't see why they should give up more than half of their country to a minority of immigrants. It was unfair, but at last it looked as though there was going to be a limit to the amount of land the settlers would get.

"Then I visited Kurt. He told me that Ben Gurion was a trickster. He'd been at a conference where the Jewish leader had made it clear that he was accepting partition *only* as a step towards a larger Jewish State. He was preparing a military offensive to drive the Palestinians out.

"I found it hard to believe. I'd seen the terrible results of the war in Europe. And there'd been no greater victim than the Jews. Yet here, before my eyes, a Jewish leader was preparing to start it all over again in Palestine. He didn't seem capable of learning anything from the past?

"Anyway, the offensive was launched. The massacre at Deir Yassin, the Palestinian village, was part of the offensive. The massacre took place April 9th 1948, more than a month before the Arab armies became involved. By then, a flood of refugees was fleeing before the Jewish armies. Haifa fell shortly after the Deir Yassin killing, then Jaffa and many other places: all before a single Arab soldier became involved. *They* came in as soon as the British left."

I found it hard to accept everything Ben said, because I had been taught in school that on the first day of its existence, May 15th 1948 – everyone knew the date – the new, innocent, state of Israel had been invaded by hate-filled Arab armies and it was this invasion that had caused so many Palestinians to become refugees. I had never before heard the official account contradicted, not even by mother.

In the week that followed, I read in Sam's library and discovered that the sequence of events was as Ben claimed. And I found that the Jewish armies had actually invaded the half of Palestine that the United Nations had decided was to form a Palestinian state and got away with it. The books I read weren't by Arabs. They were by Americans, mostly and British writers. One was by Margaret Arakie, a senior United Nations official in 1948. Another was by a loyal Israeli citizen, Simha Flapan, born on a Kibbutz, who had lived all of his life in Palestine. After reading his book, which was based on official state documents, I realised that the reason the truth hadn't entered the public consciousness, was simply that the public hadn't heard the truth, at least not the whole truth.

They had certainly been told about the Arab threats to invade the Jewish state. But the reason for the threats wasn't included in Israel's official history. According to our History, Israel was the innocent victim.

As I read, it occurred to me that there had actually been two wars in 1948. The first was still kept in the shadows. In that war, well-organised Jewish armies had vastly outnumbered the armed Palestinians and their supporters, who numbered a few thousand. In the second war, when Arab armies came to the aid of the fleeing Palestinians, they confronted an Israeli army that was much larger than themselves. The honest book by my fellow Israeli Jew, Simha Flapan, showed this to be the truth.

I also learnt, that Count Bernadotte, the deputy head of the Swedish Red Cross, who had saved many Jews from death during Hitler's war, had been murdered by Jewish gunmen. The United Nations had sent him to Palestine to mediate the dispute, and because he was trying to get Israel's leaders to allow the Palestinian refugees to return to their homes, he was murdered. The compassion that had moved him to act to save Jews wasn't appreciated when it was applied to others. It cost him his life.

When I sent a post card to my school friend Miriam, I realised that our friendship couldn't last. And I knew that when I returned home I wouldn't be able to simply go about my old life and keep quiet about my new knowledge. I would want everyone to know why Israel was hated by Arabs: we had chased out the people who had lived on our land before us.

There had been a heat wave in New York, and it was pleasant to be inside air-conditioned buildings learning. But I had absorbed so much and the heat wave seemed to be ending. It was time to be out and about looking at America. But Sam and his friends were relentless. It was a weekend, Saturday afternoon and he was having a meeting in his apartment. I wanted to be elsewhere.

An American-Palestinian friend of Sam's, Abass, was supposed to have been there to give a talk, but he had left for Lebanon to try to find a brother he had lost touch with. At short notice, Robert, a Black ex-sailor, agreed to stand in for him and talk about what seemed to me to be fantasy: "Why Israel Deliberately Attacked the American Navy". I couldn't take it seriously. Yet the talk was to shake me.

After Sam had introduced Robert and his wife, Kat, Robert

stood up, "Thank you", he said. "I hope that Abass's problem is sorted out. Kat and I would certainly like to be here when he gives his talk." Then he sat down again and looked through his notes before continuing, "Abass and I have something in common. His people are 'unimportant'. I know about that kind of thing. And we have something else in common: we have both been bombed by Israel's Air Force. It might have been normal for him, growing up in Lebanon. For me, it was the most abnormal, shocking and unexpected thing I ever experienced. Before I tell you what it did to me, let me tell you about the attack.

"In June 1967, I was one of the crew of the U.S. Navy ship, *Liberty*. We were a spy ship. We were listening in on the radio traffic of the latest Middle East war. We had the ability from where we were off Israel's coast to eavesdrop battlefield commands. And on June 7th we began to get a lot of attention from Israeli reconnaissance planes. The men on deck waived. We were delighted to see our 'friends'.

"But we were astonished when sometime later, fighters and fighter-bombers – *without markings* – attacked us. They came in firing their rockets and cannon and then they dropped bombs on us. And they *napalmed* the decks. Then torpedo boats came in and one got us. We didn't sink, but the torpedo killed twenty-five of the crew. They even machine-gunned the lifeboats on the decks: it was hardly Geneva Convention stuff.

"After that, two huge Israeli SA-321 troop-carrying helicopters came in. We could see the commandos through the doors ready for action. But as they were about to land, they broke off and left. We found out later that they withdrew at the same time as American carrier planes were being sent to defend us.

"When the attack was over, we had a hundred and seventy casualties. Thirty-four of them were dead. We had no rudder, no power and there were hundreds of holes in the ship. I've no doubt that if those commandos had landed, they'd have sunk us and left no survivors.

"Our 'friends' in Israel claimed that they thought they were attacking an Egyptian ship. But their reconnaissance planes had repeatedly checked us out and we were flying the American flag and we had our large identification number on both sides. And if we had been an Egyptian vessel, they wouldn't have bothered to hide *their* identification markings. When they tried to jam our radio signals, they did it on American frequencies, not Egyptian! And, by the way, they actually managed to block five of our six radio frequencies and that proved that they knew who we were. We got our Help call out on the remaining one. That saved us.

"Until that day, I'd loved my work. I was immersed in it: electronics, computers, the Navy, my country. I never questioned what I did.

"But I lost dear friends in that attack. I'd helped clean up the mess and carry them and put them with the other dead and I was angry and I'm still angry. I expected President Johnson to do something. But nothing happened. The Joint Chiefs of Staff did order an attack on the Israeli torpedo-boat base, but Johnson stopped it. So the sickoes who'd ordered it didn't pay any price for what they'd done, and Johnson carried on letting them have anything they wanted: dollars, the latest fighter bombers, cluster bombs, *anything* … I couldn't live with *that*. It blew my mind, and I quit the Navy."

He turned to his wife, "With Kat's help, I managed to pull myself together. And I found that I had a new focus … you might say a new obsession: I had to find out why Israel tried to sink the Liberty. It wasn't easy. It's hard in America if you're investigating Israel. But I did discover that hours before we were attacked, there was an Intelligence report warning that Israel was considering sinking the *Liberty*." Robert shook his head, "*How many Americans would believe it?*

"When I started my research, I was naive. Do you remember the emotional state of America at the start of the 1967 war? Israel was, 'in danger of annihilation', 'surrounded by a ring of steel'. 'Her very existence was hanging by a thread.' I believed it. And I believed it for a time after I left the Navy. I'd heard General Dayan saying just before the war that he would use diplomacy to defuse the situation. And I'd heard just after that, that Israel was being attacked … *that was what Israel actually announced to the world.*

"By the time Israeli generals admitted that Israel hadn't been in danger, I'd already discovered as much for myself. Thank God for our freedom of information laws. I've looked through US state archives and found some very revealing documents, which should be put before the American public. They show where the '67 war came from.

"In March 1948, President Truman was given a Joint Chiefs of Staff intelligence report that Jewish leaders planned to take over all of Palestine and expand into surrounding Arab countries. Six years later, the American Consul General in Jerusalem was reporting that Israel was belligerent and spoiling for a fight, but that Syria refused to respond. In 1964, the Consul General was saying that Israel's neighbours weren't prepared for the fighting required to resist Israel's encroachments.

"This is part of history. I didn't uncover it. It's just that it hasn't received a lot of publicity.

"All Jewish leaders didn't agree with this aggression and when Israel's Prime Minister wanted to invade Egypt in 1955, Moshe Sharrett managed to stop him. But when Moshe Sharrett became Prime Minister and he started talks with Egypt, Ben Gurion organised a bombing campaign in Egypt and the talks broke down. As we know the invasion went ahead in 1956 and President Eisenhower forced Israel to withdraw.

"On the Liberty, we were blissfully unaware of most of this. But we had top-of-the-range radio surveillance. We were able to listen in on battlefield communications. What we picked up would reveal whether the devastating attacks on Arab forces were defensive or in pursuit of conquest. That was the reason for the attack on the Liberty: to stop us finding out exactly what was going on.

"By the way, on the day the *Liberty* was attacked, Johny Concho was due to be shown onboard. It's a film about a spoilt brat who thinks he can do anything … within days of the attack, the Israeli army was bulldozing Arab villages near Jerusalem. The *Liberty* probably picked up the instructions to do it …"

Robert gave us the names of those villages. I wrote them down for my friend Miriam: "Beit Nuba, Imwas, Yalu, Beit Marsam, Beit Awa, Habla and Jifliq".

Robert continued, "That was something else that was new to me: the lot of the Palestinians, but when I learnt what was happening, *I understood*. Any Black American would. The Palestinians are now in the position that the American Negro was once in: the utter underdog, without protection because of who they are, their appeals for justice falling on deaf ears."

I wondered how Miriam would have responded to what Robert told us next: following the 1967 war, during the War of Attrition that was fought *inside Egypt*, whenever Egyptian forces attacked our army, we retaliated against civilian targets and by 1969 our artillery and Air Force had created half a million refugees. I was certain that if it had happened the other way around, if the Egyptian army and Air Force had created half a million Israeli refugees, Miriam and every other Israeli Jew would have been in shock and considered it a great crime.

"I thought I'd learnt *everything* from the *Liberty*", Robert continued. "But when our Government helped General Pinochet overthrow an elected government in Chile in 1973, wow, that really made me sit up. At one time Chile and Pinochet wouldn't have bothered me. But I had developed the habit of looking into things. And I happened to know my military history and I knew that America had fought the Second World War for higher purposes. It wasn't supposed to lead to supporting a Pinochet.

"And it struck me that America had declined since WW2. President Roosevelt had been worshiped for his high standards ... for setting up the United Nations ... for wanting a peaceful world.

"I'm afraid that the world I once thought I lived in, doesn't exist. Everything's crooked. The real world is where an American President helps Pinochet to become a dictator. The real world is where an attack on the American Navy, if it's by Israel, goes unpunished and where the result of our investigation is kept from the public.

"Our politicians feel they have to go along with Israel; guess which lobby keeps a record on how they vote; guess who has the power to end their careers. The politicians are always moralising about someone, but never Israel. And when someone else criticises Israel ... that's when the crap flies. The more telling the criticism, the more crap. *This is the world we live in.*"

I was so attentive to Robert's talk, that I didn't notice there was a young man in the room who – he told me when I got to know him – could hardly take his eyes off me. The one time I did look at him was when Robert was talking about the Israeli lobby and I noticed a head nodding in agreement. I had no idea that the vigorously nodding head belonged to my future husband, Jonathan. Jon had been in agreement because his own father was a loyal foot soldier of 'The Lobby'. As far back as Jon could remember, his father had been writing angry letters to the Press, protesting against anything he saw as criticism of Israel and threatening to take his business elsewhere.

During his law studies, Jon had met Sam's friend, Abass and through him had learnt about the dark side of Israel. He delayed talking to his father about his new knowledge until he had figured out what he thought was the best approach.

Then he told his father about an SS officer who, knowing he was going to die at Stalingrad, had written to his wife of his regret that he would no longer be a part of the wonderful National Socialist experiment. Jon said to his father that for the officer to feel that way, he must have been able to forget, or at least not care about, the Nazi's many victims. His father had agreed. Then Jon asked, "What about Israel's victims?"

Jon told me that his father went "bananas". Jon quickly decided that he had tried the wrong approach and apologised. But he thought about it and went back to his father and said, "Look dad, let's reverse the situation. Put Jews in the place of the Palestinians and Palestinians in the place of Jews and ask, 'Is what happened still right?'" His father had answered, "You can't compare the two. It's our land. The Arabs have no right to it. There's plenty of space for them elsewhere."

Jon answered, "That's almost exactly what Heydrich, the SS Chief, said about the Slavs after the Germans took over Czechoslovakia". His father went "bananas" again, but Jon decided to stick to his guns. It was the start of a rift between Jon and his father.

I felt good being with Sam and his friends. I was overjoyed to know there was a group of Americans working for the cause that was so close to my heart. But I knew that Palestine was a difficult cause in America. And I knew that Sam's group was a tiny, very tiny part of America. *And* there was immovable Israel.

I spent my last evening in New York in the company of Sam and Ben and Jon. At the end of the evening, Ben said to me, "It took me a long time to realise that the world wouldn't change much for the better in my lifetime. The most important thing for me now, is to know that each generation has its Franzs and Sams and Miriams. Can you imagine what it would be like if only the victims fought injustice? There'd be no hope. The human race would be up a blind alley. No one knows when they're your age, what they might live through. But what you can know is that the Franzs and the Sams *and the Miriams,* will be sorely needed. So while you're young, know your own value and never forget it ..."

I flew home reluctantly. Sam had asked me to stay, and I was tempted. Apart from my feelings for Sam and for Ben and my new friendship with Jon, I had been inspired by their little group and would love to have joined them. America was the one country whose sheer power could force justice for the Palestinians. But, even though I knew that the little group had contacts across America, I couldn't see them breaking through America's blindness to Israel's wicked behaviour. So I was returning to Israel, even though I knew that my own country was as obdurate as

America. Dissidents at home were more in the public eye and there were more of them. So I would try to find a comparable group there.

Idris was aware that Miriam was on a plane returning to America. He knew that Jon had followed her to Israel and they had eventually married and had children. And he was aware of the great frustration that Miriam felt from her years in Israel … Jon and I can see no sign of genuine peace. There is supposed to be a "peace process", but how can peace be possible while Palestinians continue to have their land taken. Right through the "peace talks" Israel has been expanding her settlements and, to anyone with eyes to see, has proved that she doesn't really want peace. Despite the "ceasefire" she continued her house demolitions and her killing of ordinary Palestinians. *And,* more recently, Israel has been using her new "security wall" to separate tens of thousands of Palestinians from their land.

None of this was considered to be an outrageous breach of the cease-fire by the American "mediator". It didn't even appear to have registered as a minor breach. Palestinians were expected to remain passive whatever was done to them. And when some Palestinians responded with suicide bombings, the 'mediator' blamed the Palestinian side for breaking the 'cease-fire'. Yasser Arafat, who wasn't responsible for the bombings was made persona non grata in America, while Israel's leaders, who *were* responsible for Israel's violence, were accepted as America's 'friends'.

I find it incredible that American leaders, who stand in front of television cameras talking about freedom and international law and the obligation to obey UN resolutions, can be so blatantly one-sided. Their support for Israel is unconditional and absolute. Israel can do *anything* and keep their support.

Bur we've had our victories, Jon and I. Once we and other dissidents helped defeat a settler land-grab. We joined the villagers of el Khader in resisting a takeover of five hundred dunans of their land. The army removed us and allowed the armed settlers to uproot el Khader's newly planted olive trees. But for some reason, el Khader attracted international attention and the encroachment was stopped.

But the seizures continued elsewhere. Jon and I went to visit a family in a village that was overlooked by a settlement built on their land. We apologised to the family for what had been done to them and told them we hated our Government as much as they must do. But we found that this family was reluctant to join in our criticism. Superficially, they seemed reconciled to living with the greater power of the Jewish community. We wondered what it was that made them different from other Palestinians we had met and if they were really telling us the truth. Possibly they saw Israeli Jews as heavily armed psychotics who had to be appeased.

Possibly the Palestinian negotiators at the peace talks held a similar view. While they talked, the deliberate encroachment that was cutting up their land and splitting it into ghettoes was continuing. The viable Palestine they were supposed to be aiming for was being made impossible by "facts". Yet they talked. And there was little to be gained from the talks, apart from self-administered municipal services and trying to manage in separated enclaves surrounded by, psychotics? *How could any people, anywhere, accept what Israel expected the Palestinians to accept?*

To Jon and I, that is the problem. Nations aren't treated equally and American support for Israel has no connection to right or wrong. It's tribal. American politicians manage to bypass moral considerations and consider only *who* has done what to *whom.* If someone they don't like causes injury, it's terrible. But if Israel causes the injury, it's different and at the United Nations, American Governments have protected Israel's illegal activities.

By taking the trouble to look at what actually happened – as Jon and I have done – anyone can see that Israel's wars have been wars of aggression and that, even in 1973, when Egypt and Syria started the fighting, they had the limited aim of getting back the parts of their territory which Israel was occupying. Yet, in spite of its aggressive ways, Israel gets massive military aid from America.

One instructive contrast in the treatment of Jews and Palestinians has been the attitude towards compensation for injury. The lapse of time since the Nazi era, rightly, hasn't diminished the right to compensation to Jews for the harm done to them, including their loss of property and billions of dollars of compensation has been paid by Germany. There has even been payment for psychological damage. Even though it happened more recently, the suffering and losses of the Palestinians haven't been recognised as equally worthy of redress.

It's something Jon is looking into. He's been burning the midnight oil working out what is the clear legal right of Palestinians for restitution for the whole range of abuse they have suffered. He has finished the first part of his study and he says that, under international law, the Palestinians have the indisputable right to go home: they were the victims of *planned* dispossession.

It isn't entirely new to me. I've understood that that was roughly the case since my first visit to America. But this is different. Jon has been telling me that Return is an absolute legal right and that it is only American influence that makes the demand sound unreasonable. He is going to fight for the right of Return and I know he won't let go. He also says that Israel ignored the UN terms of Partition that protected the human rights *of the Arabs who stayed in Israel* and that *they* had most of their property taken from them.

He's looking at 1967 when a whole lot of new refugees were created and at other illegal expulsions and property seizures and house destruction over the years. He has a mass of evidence.

Jon and I can't accept that an exclusively Jewish State has any more of a place in the modern world than an exclusively Muslim state, or than an exclusively Aryan state had in 1930's Europe. Jon says that any representative of the Israeli Government could be shamed before an international court, if they could be taken there.

Jon and I are sure – we have talked to many Palestinian Arabs – that if Israel discards its obsession with a Jewish *State*, with its inevitable denial of the rights of non-Jews and recognises the rule of law, reconciliation will be possible, but that if this doesn't happen and the wrongs aren't put right, Israeli Jews, as well as Arabs, will be dying violently for generations. And with the advance of science, who knows what horrors might come about.

I have heard many times during my life, public figures passionately proclaiming, "We must never forget the Holocaust". But the same individuals apply different standards to 1948 and 1967: they conveniently "forget", or distort, what took place *then*.

I've also heard on many occasions someone asking about the Holocaust, "How could it have happened? How could it have been *allowed* to happen?" When I have the chance, I answer, "The Holocaust didn't suddenly happen. It grew. It started with a desire to have a Germany without Jews. Look around you. We are a nation of immigrants. Not many miles from our borders are refugee camps full of the people who used to live here. They weren't wanted. While they've been trying to get back, our Government has been bringing replacements from the corners of the earth." If I get that far, I end with, "Look inside yourself".

If we had thought there was the chance of a just peace, Jon and

I would have stayed with our children in Israel. But we know that in the absence of sanctions that hurt, Israel's leaders will never face up to the wrong they have done, still less agree to a just settlement. And we know that peace without justice isn't possible. So we aren't willing to expose our children to a violence that will never end, or to a national psychosis that discounts the harm done to others and blames violent responses to our violence on an anti-Semitic desire to kill Jews. We don't want our children to grow up in such an unhealthy place as Israel.

So Jon and I and our children, Franz and Miriam, are on our way to New York. There will no Ben for them to meet. Sadly he is gone. But Sam has told me that others have come along who share his beliefs, but haven't had his kind of experiences. I hope it stays that way.

We'll squeeze into Sam's place until we find a suitable home. I have few illusions about America. Jon even less. But we will do what we can. We will particularly try to get through to young Jews. We hope that amongst them there will be many prepared to face up to the reality that is Israel. After all, Jon braved the leap …

11

The Parting

IDRIS GRADUALLY BECAME aware of his body. Light. Floating. Huge. He raised his head with an effort and looked. Everything was normal. He let his head fall back and lay appreciating the restful room. Then he remembered the night before. The meal. The restaurant. The long conversation with Ian. And then those dreams. Except that they hadn't been dreams. They'd been real. *They* had been real people, and he had more than known them: he had been each one of those real people for a time. They were still all there in his head. He knew that if he wanted he would be able to recall any of the night's experiences, but he preferred to relax. He lay for a while longer and then got up.

Ian was standing by the open door of the "caravan" looking out. When he heard Idris, he turned around, "Have something to eat. You'll feel better ..."

The ground was wet, but the sky was clear and the sun was shining. They were on a real walk and walking in silence. Idris knew that Ian was leaving it to him to start the conversation. From his night's "dreams" he recalled some words, "the world's interminable violence". Those words captured a large part of the lesson he knew Ian was trying to impress upon him.

They came to a bridge that spanned a swollen stream and stopped to watch the fast flowing water. Ian sat on the low wall and looked at Idris, "We haven't got long left together, Idris. Later, when we get back, if you want to, we'll continue what we started last night ...?"

"I do want to!"

"You'll 'live' the experiences of many people and then you'll absorb hundreds of books on your world's history, science, philosophy, economics and much else. You'll absorb it all in your sleep. And when you wake up you'll have a far greater understanding ..."

"I do want to continue."

"When you wake up you won't remember, immediately, anything you've learnt. You'll 'remember' Ian from Edinburgh whose company you enjoyed. You'll 'remember' enlightening conversations you had with him ... you will have taken in huge amounts of information at speed, and you'll be a very fast reader ... you'll have all the new information in your head, and it will eventually show. Is there anything you'd like to ask?"

Idris wanted to say, "Please let me remember everything?" But he knew it would be hopeless. So after some thought, he answered, "I'm not surprised that worlds like mine don't last. If your world has put *all that* behind it, is it possible that we can do the same?"

"It might be possible. We want you to. We'd love you to become our partner and share our science. But we daren't risk it yet."

"You'd share your science ... with us?"

"We'd like to. Like all humans, for much of the time your race is admirable and you've achieved great things. And each of our races has aptitudes the other doesn't have. But we won't share with tribalists. It'd be too risky. Yet we'd love to share. In many ways we'd be suitable partners. For a start you're so close to us in development."

"I thought you were far ahead?"

"Only two thousand years ago, we were at about your level of development. On a cosmic time scale, that's closer than neck and neck. But scientifically we're far ahead of you; your science is closer to the ancient Babylonians than it is to us. But it's still an astonishing coincidence that we are so close to each other. Yet if you compare the way we live, we're far apart. We're not compatible. So for now, we're limiting ourselves to briefly contacting chosen individuals from around your world, and that might remain the limit of our communication. That's why we don't want you to remember what really happened this weekend.

"We don't know yet whether *our* longer survival is simply due to our creating a more altruistic culture, or if it's because of some fundamental difference in our nature. We've a major scientific project trying to discover whether human races that self-destruct do so simply because they fail to find a more altruistic way of life or whether they have 'suicide' written in their genes. It's complicated because of the scarcity of remains and, of course, our different chemistries. But we do we have *some* genetic materials from out there. Whether or not we help you, depends on the outcome of our studies."

Ian pointed at the blue sky, "Those other races, they didn't all commit suicide. Humans exist on tiny precarious islands of life and times when life is able to flourish on our tiny islands are interludes between hugely destructive natural events. And there are so many forces that can wipe us out and inevitably they will come. *Our* major project has got to be how to survive. And we're preparing ourselves to survive every conceivable hostile event. We're even looking far ahead to the big challenge, if we're still around, when the present phase of the universe comes to an end. Some day it will happen: all of the atoms in the universe will tear apart in a cataclysmic explosion. We'll be trying to survive that. Then will come a long hostile period, when on the face of it matter, let alone life, won't be possible. Our long term goal will be to survive that."

"Do you think it's possible?"

"I don't know. I hope we've got a long, long time to work on it. It's some goal. We'll need to predict accurately the conditions of the changed universe: what'll be there, its dynamic structure and likely evolution. In the meantime we'll be learning how to survive in the most hostile conditions we can find: inside stars, neutron stars, black holes, how to survive supernovas. If we can't manage that, we don't have a chance. But it's not as impossible as you might think … we don't know if we will be able to survive. Perhaps, ultimately, no one can. But we've a great adventure ahead of us.

"I'm sure it's crossed your mind Idris, that if we've outlived our barbarism, then it's likely that others would have done so."

"I've hardly been able to think."

"Okay. From tomorrow, I promise you, you'll be able to think as you've never thought before … we've made a special search to seek out more advanced civilizations, but we've found no trace of them. Of course it wouldn't be hard for them to hide from us. To them, if they're there, we'll still be in our early infancy. But it is possible that intelligences have survived, not just for millions or hundreds of millions of years, but for billions of years. And we haven't ruled out the possibility that some have survived from previous material phases of the universe. Or even the possibility that there might be innumerable civilizations out there: layers of them separated, forever, by chasms of time … and by even greater chasms of scientific development. If the universe has existed back into infinity and if civilizations have survived from time to time, then there should be an infinite number of them. Yet how can that be possible? Unless there is some infinite cosmic space, an uninhabited 'America West', somewhere out there.

"What we do know is that over time, if we last long enough, we'll encounter other emerging human races. We're sure that any who survive on their own will have moved beyond barbarism and won't be a problem. The problem will come if we help the wrong races. That's why we need to understand what we're doing. The future cosmos will produce an abundance of new life and it would be wrong for us to stifle it with colonists from the past, with barbarians ..."

As they walked, Idris felt as though he was in a dream, and when they got back to the "caravan" he went straight to the green room. Even though it was still afternoon, he lay on the bed and went asleep ...

Familiar feeling. Detached. Floating. Huge body. Idris involuntarily raised his head and looked. Everything was normal. It was over. But this time he couldn't remember the "dreams". The first time, he had kept a vivid memory of the people he had "been". He tried to remember something of those who must have filled his sleeping mind only a short time before. Nothing. Ian had told him that while he was asleep he would absorb many books. He tried to, but couldn't remember a thing about them.

In the main compartment, there was food on the table, and Ian was sitting waiting. Idris made his way over and sat down.

Ian looked pleased, "You'll feel normal again soon. Take your time over your refreshment."

"I don't feel like eating. I'm worried. If your study finds against us, you'll give up on us. Is that right?"

Ian looked uncomfortable. "I'm glad you're being direct. How do I answer? We are hoping that we don't have to give up on you. If we find that you are simply locked into a barbaric culture, we can help. But, if it turns out that your race is dominated by a terminal gene, we'll stand back. Yet even then, we see ourselves as midwives helping civilization to emerge, if it's here. And there is civilization on this planet. It's inside individuals: people like you. There is huge variation amongst individuals here. And if it turns out that tribalism prevails, were considering a possibility: people who will be given the chance to live on, and ..."

"But surely civilization is inside every human being?"

"But so is tribalism and it depends on which prevails. Aquiros wasn't entirely right in thinking that love alone underlay human intelligence and that tribal violence came from a culture that distorted human nature. There was much truth in Auiros's beliefs. But the capacity for group violence and the thinking that goes with it was essential for human survival. Human thought has been tribal for a very long time. It served tribal ends and its been shaped by that. And much of human history has been of 'in' groups and 'out' groups, with the powerful 'in' groups predating vulnerable 'out' groups. But in the age of high technology barbarism, surviving depends upon Aquiros's solution of adopting a universal morality, which means the whole of the human race becoming the 'in' group. Most human intelligences never made that leap and paid the price. It's a pity because they were on the threshold ..."

"Of immortality?"

"No. 'Immortality' isn't a serious word in our vocabulary. This moment, you and I together ... the time will inevitably come when it will have receded millions of years into the past and eventually, billions of years and just as inevitably, countless billions of years. And so it will go on. For various reasons, we wouldn't even consider the likelihood of individuals living down all those years. And *all* human races, if they haven't developed the science to defend themselves, will eventually fall to one of nature's violent eruptions. During *our* climb to civilization we were lucky: there was no super-volcano, asteroid, comet, supernova, or any other of nature's outbursts great enough to finish us. Other races weren't so lucky.

"If a civilization *is* lucky and manages to develop its science in time and deals with the various threats, it could go on and on through aeons of time ... *we* have systems, now, that can protect us from some of the hazards out there, but we'd be helpless in the face of others, although it is unlikely that we would be completely wiped out. We have stations and probes dispersed across the local group of galaxies. 'Immortality' doesn't enter into our calculations, but 'survival' does, and we've mobilised all our human resources to try to survive whatever we might face.

"*We* are a race of scientists. We have more than thirty billion scientists, our entire population, except for a few eccentrics. We are committed to ..."

"*Thirty billion scientists?*"

"Including our children. Like you, way back when we had only a few scientists, we had *our* 'Newtons' and 'Einsteins'. Now, we have millions of 'Newtons' and 'Einsteins' and some who rise even higher. Many thousands of scientific 'papers' are published every day. Some of them contain major advances ..."

"How could anyone follow it all?"

"We don't have to. It's held in what *you* might call a 'computer'. We call it 'Aquiros'. It holds the accumulated knowledge of our race. We have continuous mental access to it and when I consider a problem I automatically use it. It becomes an extension of my mind."

"But isn't Aquiros at home, far away?"

"Distance isn't a problem. Through science, we've overcome many old constraints and we aren't limited by the speed of light anymore. We have almost instant communication wherever we go. Every one of our stations has a duplicate of 'Aquiros' and it's up-to-date. It carries a record of our entire culture. It holds everything we've learnt about your culture and others ... it gave *you* a course of further education. It reads changing local conditions and keeps us informed of likely events across huge regions of space. Aquiros aids us in our quest to survive.

"It's sad, but your race is barely thinking about survival. You waste your human assets. Instead of treasuring and developing every mind, you use your science to be able to destroy. Every day on your planet, valuable people succumb to violence and neglect.

"When I was talking about failed human races throwing away the chance to be in our position: that's what I meant. Instead of using their intelligence to survive, they were turned in on themselves destroying.

"They could have been in our position. We certainly aren't immortal, but we understand the chemistry of life and we know why living things age and die. It isn't difficult science, and overcoming ageing isn't a problem for us. To us, it's become almost a mundane fact of our lives that we live on. We have given ourselves time, and we are making the most of it.

"But life is seldom without problems. We've solved the problem of ageing, but if we reproduce at the old rate, we'll eventually swamp life everywhere. Unthinking reproduction would conflict with part of our basic philosophy: respect for other life. Some of our finest thinkers are arguing: 'Yes, we need to cut back, but future generations have a right to be born. So, rather than cutting back *too severely* on children, lets limit our lifespan, or be stored on Aquiros and take a long break from life'. We should have the ability to do that before long …"

For Idris, it had come to an end too quickly. While he had been listening to Ian, he hadn't noticed that the craft was moving. Yet it had moved, and his time with Ian was over, and they were standing outside the "caravan" shaking hands, "There's a road at the foot of the hill Idris. There's a pleasant surprise waiting for you …"

"If I really try, might I be able to remember?"

"I'm afraid not Idris … but you'll be quite a scholar."

As he walked down the steep slope Idris looked back and what he saw, or thought he saw, caused him to stumble and fall. Somehow he came to a stop and looked back again. He'd tumbled quite a distance, but could just see the top of the rock that, for a disorientated moment, had appeared to be a giant moth looking down at him.

He realised he hadn't swapped addresses with Ian. How could he have forgotten that? It was too late now. Ian would be on his way back to Edinburgh.

When he reached the foot of the hill, by the side of the road, a group of people were boarding a mini bus. As he started to cross the road, someone called, "Idris".

He stopped and looked. "Idris". A girl came out from the crowd. It was Jeanette. "We're just leaving for Liverpool. There's room on the bus for you …"

————◄○►————

12

Sources

WHILE I WAS correcting the above story, I turned on the TV and saw a man wearing a "T shirt" that read something like, "Jews for peace in the Middle East". He was talking about the harassment of Palestinians at roadblocks and the "daily" house demolitions in Gaza. He said that the European Union's trade privileges for Israel couldn't be allowed to continue while such things where happening. *He* is amongst the people to whom this book is dedicated.

Listening to him reminded me of the note I have from a BBC Radio 4 report of March 2002, quoting an Israeli newspaper, that of the twenty-four pregnant Palestinian women kept waiting at Israeli roadblocks, the babies of six had died. Since then there has been a report of twins dying after their expectant mother was kept waiting for hours at a roadblock. Listening to him talking about "trade privileges for Israel", was also a reminder of how Israel's leaders, in spite all of the horrors they have unleashed, in pursuit of a continuing, decades long ethnic cleansing exercise, have been treated as civilized people and Israel itself indulged. Such indulges are predicated on a denial of the real history of Israel.

Palestine/Israel takes what might be seen as a disproportionately large and too detailed, part of this book, because that conflict is so close to the heart of present world conflict and Western policy is based on myths, rather than what actually happened. The huge unresolved injustice involved and the persistence of the denial has ignited Muslim anger and we are in for permanent conflict if it isn't put right. That we humans are capable of such denial demonstrates the size of the obstacle within ourselves we need to face.

A civilized future?

All of us alive today are survivors. We are the offspring, or the descendants, of people who have had to fight for their lives. Millions who have lived before us, some recently, as they tried to live their lives, have been engulfed by violence. They will have seen their families destroyed around them and perhaps died themselves. I have tried in this book not to over-use the words "tribal" and "tribalism". But those words do describe the condition that we need to think ourselves out of: the condition that desensitises us to the suffering of other groups while considering our own suffering to be special. If we are to have a civilized future, rather than a continuation of our violent past, we have to make this break.

Perhaps intelligences comparable to ours do evolve regularly across the cosmos. Perhaps because of an inherent self-destructiveness, or because we live in a dangerous universe, or both, none ultimately survive. But it is possible that we are being watched by intelligences vastly more advanced than we are. If so, there is no indication that they see any reason why they should communicate with us. We are on our own and have to make the effort ourselves to achieve true civilization.

Sources for this book

I have based *The Midwife Mission* mostly upon the events recorded in the books listed in the Bibliography, even in the detail where I could. No doubt some of the authors would not appreciate the use I have made of their work.

Roosevelt, Churchill and Truman

When I started writing *The Midwife Mission,* I had no intention of even mentioning Roosevelt or Churchill or Truman. I would be dealing with ordinary people, swallowed by world events, rather than leaders. But I found in the introduction to *The Flight of Icarus* a government prisoner, an ex-member of the Greek Resistance, complaining to the author that Churchill was the cause of his troubles. When I read that it hit me: identifiable individuals make decisions that shape world events and affect us all. So sometimes for accuracy's sake rather than write, "Britain did *this*", or "America did *that*", I have named the leader behind a decision. That is why Franklin Roosevelt, Winston Churchill and Harry Truman, are a presence in this book. They and Stalin were the key figures at the end of WW2 who had the power to shape the post-war world. But the one leader amongst them whose vision went beyond the grasping, grubby pursuit of power, Franklin Roosevelt, died and the world continued in its old ways. I make no apology for, in later pages, counter-posing Franklin Roosevelt's inspired and humanising leadership with what passes for the "world leadership" of President Bush.

Franklin Roosevelt's greatness, I believe, lay less in his partic-ular deeds, than in his wide moral vision which enabled him to step beyond narrow tribal loyalties and try to represent the inter-ests of humanity, rather than one state, or one class or group within a state. His ascendancy in world leadership gave him the potential to create a kinder post-WW2 world than we have actu-ally had. Unfortunately Franklin Roosevelt died before peace came and Harry Truman took Winston Churchill's baton rather than Roosevelt's. And the peaceful example Roosevelt had planned to set for the world never came. So today we live in Churchill and Truman's world, not Franklin Roosevelt's. The shell of Roosevelt's UN is still there. But its purpose and authority have been undermined, in a similar way to which the League of Nations was undermined, by powerful states engaging in selfish pursuits outside international law.

Churchill, Truman and Stalin bequeathed to the world the Cesare Borgia/Billy Liar School of inter-state relations. It isn't that human affairs haven't always been run according to its prac-tises. They have. It is that Roosevelt held up for the world to see, a better way of doing things. But it wasn't taken up.

Idris's story

A friend who read this story thought it was biased towards the IRA. I can't see it. I am not pro IRA. I believe that, apart from the times when Northern Ireland's Catholics have needed defending from violence, Republican violence was criminal and too often murderous and sickening and with heartbreaking consequences. I believe that after 1922, when the Dail voted for the settlement negotiated by the Michael Collins/Arthur Griffith delegation, violence directed towards winning a united Ireland was the stuff of unrealistic dreams.

But I do recognise that over the years of the peace process, those with most influence over the IRA, most visibly Gerry Adams and Martin McGuinness, have been sincerely striving for peace. Obviously, they haven't been alone. Prominently, the SDLP's John Hume and Protestant ex-paramilitaries, such as Gusty Spence and David Irvine of the PUP and Gary McMichael of the UDP, have been heart and soul in favour of peace, as has the cross-faith Alliance Party. *They* want no more of "us" and "them" and have been patiently trying to bring the communities of Northern Ireland into a relationship of mutual respect.

What my friend thought was bias was, I admit, my seeing too many Protestants, especially politicians and especially Ian Paisley and the DUP, entrenched in old tribal attitudes and reluctant to make peace with the traditional enemy, or unable to grasp that to seek peace, rather than tribal victory, parties to such a protracted conflict need to meet with their opponents as they are *and* honestly acknowledge whatever harm they themselves have done, rather than continually pointing the finger of blame at the other side.

The most heartfelt apology since the ceasefire *has* come from Protestants. One could hardly improve on the words of sorrow, "abject and true remorse", spoken by Gusty Spence in the company of other ex-paramilitary leaders, turned peaceniks. Such genuine contrition heals wound and dissolves barriers. A similar apology from the IRA, for their civilian victims and from mainstream Protestant politicians (now including Ian Paisley's DUP) for their, or their predecessor's role in igniting the troubles, would be a major message of reassurance for both communities.

Over the years, wrongs were committed by all sides: we knew of the IRA murders: the soldier taken prisoner and shot, the Catholic mother executed after attending to a wounded British soldier, the children blown up in Warrington and the other murderous bombings. We knew about the continuous Protestant violence against Catholics and that Protestant paramilitary "soldiers" main murder victims were Catholic non-combatants. And we knew about the world of the security forces: their one-sided dirty war and involvement in murder. And we knew of Ian Paisley's speeches – although he wasn't alone in this – which inflamed feelings and, I believe, played a significant part in sparking and prolonging the Troubles.

All sides could have put forward preconditions to their opponents, which would have become major obstacles to a peace settlement. But it has been the Protestant politicians demanding IRA de-commissioning – followed by the British Government – who have delayed permanent peace by years. I would have thought that if peace were the genuine aim, all parties would have treasured the life-saving cease-fire and talked to achieve a final political settlement and understood that to demand the other side's disarmament while *they* suffered violence and while your own community's paramilitaries had weapons, would jeopardise the peace.

I would have thought that, rather than backing one side's demands, a British Government seeking peace would have insisted on a timetable for mutual disarmament and mutual ending of unlawful activities. But the focus of pressure has been on the IRA, it seems to me, because the British Government has, along with the Protestant politicians, seen the IRA as a tribal enemy to be defeated.

This one-sidedness is part of a pattern: despite the first terrorist attacks of the Troubles having come from Protestant paramilitaries and a re-born, violent IRA having been sparked by violence against both civil rights marchers and Catholic communities and despite the Protestant paramilitaries long series of murders of Catholic civilians, the IRA has been held up as the incomparable villain.

The apparent execution of fellow Catholic, Robert McCarthy, over a pub difference, is a reminder of how low the paramilitaries can go. But such a murder should have been a jolt to the foot-draggers to get on with a settlement that will end any justification for the continued existence of violent organisations. Getting on with the peace process shouldn't be treated as a concession to the IRA. It is a basic need of the people of Northern Ireland.

The lop-sidedness intensified the difficulty Gerry Adams and Martin MacGuiness have had in taking their dissidents with them. An IRA decommissioning in what could be interpreted as dangerous or humiliating circumstances could increase the influence of unreformed gun-and-bomb nationalists. During the years of the *ceasefire*, there have been constant attacks on Catholics, some with intent to kill: pipe bombs into the homes of sleeping Catholic families and sometimes petrol bombs, physical attacks and attempts to "get" prominent Catholics *and their families*, occasional arson against churches and sometimes murder. It far exceeds violence against Protestants. And just as this book is almost ready for printing, mobs, denied their "right" to march through a Catholic area, have rioted burning cars, erecting barricades and throwing bombs, while Protestant paramilitaries fired on the police and army.

However much the riot might have bothered the DUP, at the time of writing, it hasn't prompted them to recognise that, in the face of the continuing threat to Catholic communities, the IRA's decision to disarm is risky and deserves the help of Protestant leaders.

This is my bias: not pro-IRA, but seeing Ian Paisley and his DUP so entrenched in their one-sidedness they are making it difficult for the IRA to achieve disarmament and take all of their followers with them. Catholics are facing a far less violent, but similar, Protestant obduracy to that which ignited the Troubles back in 1968 and 1969. And Protestant peaceniks, as then, find it hard to counter the "betrayal" rhetoric, which resonates with ingrained Protestant mythology.

(The under-aged drinker, Idris, in St Cecelia's, is pure invention. It is a law-abiding club.)

Thanasis' story

In *Inside Hitler's Greece* the author wrote that as late as the 1960s, Greece's prisons still held hundreds of men and women whose only crime had been to fight the Germans. While Resistance members languished in prison, Security Battalionists who had worked for the Nazis enjoyed a career in the state security services. In 1967, one of them led a military coup and became Greek Dictator.

Keeping myths alive is the role of the tribal writer and, although a number of the books listed in the Bibliography carry the fiction that the Communists tried to seize power in wartime Greece and afterwards, they are all well worth reading for the information they hold. I have tried to show what really happened, rather than follow the fictional accounts that were first put out as justification for Churchill and Truman's interventions and which are lazily, or deliberately, repeated, ad infinitum, by commentators.

Truman's involvement in Greece was a turning point for America and the world. When he was finding it difficult to win support for intervention he was advised by Senator Vandenberg to "scare hell" out of Congress and the American people. He did and, besides winning their support, helped create the atmosphere in which MacArthyism flourished and the Cold War had lift-off.

Other post-war Presidents were to follow Truman's lead of overseas intervention/domestic deception, most famously President Johnson in his Vietnam escalation: he told Congress and America, that there had been an unprovoked attack on two US destroyers in the Gulf of Tonkin. He got his way and, in consequence, America and Vietnam were to suffer grievously. After learning of the deceit, Senator Fulbright, Chairman of the Senate Foreign Relations Committee, became a critic of the war, but tragically it took years of mounting American – and millions of Vietnamese civilian – casualties and American trauma, before most Americans wanted out of the fatal entanglement.

In 1991, after Saddam Hussein, realising he had miscalculated, let it be known that he would withdraw from Kuwait, the US Government claimed he was about to invade Saudi Arabia. As if this wasn't enough to justify war on Iraq, it was also claimed that Iraqi troops had thrown babies off incubators and stolen the incubators. Subsequently, both of these claims were found to have been false – but too late. By then the unnecessary carnage of war had already taken place, including the "turkey shoot" of the actual withdrawal from Kuwait, when many Iraqi families lost their fathers and sons.

In getting America into the present entanglement in Iraq, members of the Bush Administration have repeatedly claimed that a link existed, which didn't, between Iraq and Bin Laden and therefore the invasion of Iraq was somehow connected to 9/11. Unfortunately many Americans, busy with their own lives and loyal to their President, believed the story and supported the war. Casualties mount.

Petrona's story

I Rigoberta Menchu is a rare and invaluable book that has come from the living experience of one of the millions of third world victims of the great powers of the twentieth century. *I Rigoberta Menchu* shows Guatemalan Indians, including Rigoberta's own family, being treated in a way that utterly denied their humanness. *I Rigoberta Menchu* was crucial to this story, as was *Bitter Fruit:* the work of two Americans.

Amir's story

The events related in Amir's story happened before the seizure of the American embassy hostages and before the Iran-Iraq war and, I hope, help explain the passion with which the Iranian students shouted their anti-imperialist slogans and occupied the American embassy. But those events don't begin to explain why the Bahais and individuals like Sattareh Farman Farmaian were persecuted. The cause of that is, I think, as is much of the behaviour related in this book, to be found more in the dark side of human nature, too frequently tapped into by both religious and nationalist fundamentalists.

Lucas's story

I failed to get enough information to attempt to write a fuller account of Congolese life at the time of de-colonisation. I did consider substituting a story about the struggle to free Angola from colonial rule and the carnage and vast human suffering that followed the Nixon Government's intervention. That might have fitted in better with the rest of this book. Probably because of the role of the UN in ousting Patrice Lumumba, as well as the shock that I still feel from his murder, I settled for one man's homage to Patrice Lumumba.

The estimated scale of recent killing in the Congo, the indirect heritage of the years of corruption and waste and misgovernment of the Mobutu years, has recently been put at over *three million* dead.

Saionji's story

The myth that it was the use of nuclear weapons that brought about Japan's surrender lives on. Yet the truth has long been out. It is to be found in, amongst other sources, *Rise to Globalism.*

To me, *Atomic Diplomacy* contains an exhaustively convincing demonstration that key figures in the Truman Government including the President, with good reason, believed that they could bring about Japan's surrender without using nuclear weapons and without invasion. Yet they used these frightening new weapons. They did so, primarily because of the power they believed it would give them in facing Stalin in the post-war world. President Truman even delayed meeting Stalin at Potsdam until the atom bomb was ready for testing in the hope of first, "laying it on Japan" to demonstrate its power. At Potsdam, his new weapon successfully tested, Truman, according to Churchill, "bullied the whole meeting". But the brash diplomacy backfired, and Stalin took it out on the people of Eastern Europe.

One of the authors of *Betrayal at Pearl Harbour* was Eric Nave, the Australian naval officer who broke the Japanese secret naval code. In his book he writes that code breaking derived knowledge of the impending attack on Pearl Harbour was passed up to Churchill, where it stayed denying the Americans the chance to ambush Yamamoto's task force and avoid becoming sitting ducks at Pearl Harbour.

Bilal and Miriam's stories: the reality behind the myths

The most powerful myth of modern times, the David and Goliath myth, is that in 1948, the new, innocent, state of Israel was invaded by hate-filled Arab armies and that the out-gunned, outnumbered, gallant defenders, heroically fought back and defeated the dastardly Arabs. It was during the course of this unsought war, according to the myth and through no fault of Israel, that the Palestinians became refugees in such large numbers. Yes, this is a myth.

The truth is that Arab armies intervened to confront large Jewish forces that were driving the Palestinians from their homes. The Arab "invasion" was the only serious physical attempt, ever, to protect the Palestinians from ethnic cleansing. The Arab armies did enter what is now Israel. But at the time the area was Palestine: the part of Palestine designated by the United Nations to become the State of Palestine. For this is where most of the "invading" Arab forces went.

The myth that grew

The 1948 myth, repeated continuously in the media, is seldom challenged. I have never heard an interviewer question it. It's the same with the 1967 myth that Israel was in grave danger, "surrounded by a ring of steel", when in reality it was Israel, not in genuine danger, who initiated a war of territorial expansion, carrying out 1948's "unfinished business". I have never heard the 1967 myth publicly questioned.

And it's the same with the general myth that the tiny, "vulnerable", Jewish state has been in grave danger since 1948, rather than the truth that Israel has relentlessly used her military superiority to wage war and seize land and crush whoever has stood in her way and many who haven't, without concern for the people destroyed in their thousands, or the even greater number of lives ruined. It is this real history of Israel that makes her citizens targets for suicide bombers.

Some years ago, by chance, I met two Israelis and about ten of their English relatives in a Liverpool pub. When I tried to get them to accept that it was Israel that had initiated the 1967 war by invading Egypt, and not the other war around, I was answered with derisive laughter. It was the same when I said that in 1948, rather than having caused the Palestinians to become refugees, the Arab armies had gone to the aid of the fleeing Palestinians.

That meeting wasn't the only occasion on which I have tried to give the accurate sequence of cause and affect to committed supporters of Israel. On every occasion their answers have been a repetition of the deception given out by Israel's leaders at the time of the conflict we were discussing.

Israel's accounts of her wars have become part of the collective consciousness of Britain and America and writers and politicians have repeated them, free of contradiction – mostly. And the public has taken it in. Mostly.

The Truman precedent

In March 1948, the Truman Government was in receipt of the Joint Chiefs of Staff intelligence report on Palestine. It referred to the "fanatical concepts" of the Jewish leaders and listed "Jewish objectives" that included sovereignty over all of Palestine and expansion into part of Jordan, Lebanon and Syria and military hegemony over the entire Middle East.

So President Truman had an accurate report of the intentions of Ben Gurion and his followers. Later he complained of the unprecedented pressure he had been under from lobbyists for the Jewish state, and at the time he was so angry he instructed the presidential staff that he wasn't to see any "extremists for the Zionist cause".

Yet he did nothing to counter the false account of events in Palestine that was reaching the public ear. And when he couldn't get a UN majority for the Partition of Palestine and the creation of Israel, he held up the vote while he bribed and threatened smaller nations until he had his majority "in favour". He even refused support for British Prime Minister Atlee's plea for sanctions to force the new Israeli state to withdraw from the territory designated by the UN for the Palestinian state.

His own explanation for his behaviour was amazingly honest, "… I have to answer to hundreds of thousands of people who are anxious for the success of Zionism. I do not have hundreds of thousands of Arabs among my constituents." His attitude was based on how best he could win the approaching 1948 Presidential election. (He and Dewey, the Republican candidate, were in competition for Jewish support considered to be important for victory.)

Truman's attitude set a pattern for future presidential behaviour towards Israel, and for most of the time since then, it has been calculations of domestic political advantage, not the merits of the case, which has determined the American Government's responses to Israel's behaviour.

Except for during the Eisenhower Presidency, nothing Israel has done has been a bar to massive aid from America. Although President Bush (senior) did make the granting of ten billion dollars of credit guarantees dependent on an end to illegal settlements. But Prime Minister Shamir wouldn't budge and got his way. (I don't know whether pressure from The Lobby brought a change to Bush's policy, or whether Israel had to wait for the money until Clinton's victory over Bush, but Israel got the money.)

Shamir was an unapologetic extreme nationalist, who had played a part in the murder of Count Bernadotte, the Schindler-like saviour of Jews from the Nazis. Shamir, while Prime Minister, praised Jewish terrorists after they had blown-up Palestinian Mayors who were cooperating with Israel: he called his fellow terrorists "Good boys". That such a man was able to influence the American political system in his favour isn't surprising, considering the range of behaviours America's politicians have been prepared to put up with, from the destruction of thirteen Lebanese airlines, because a Palestinian terrorist had been carrying a Lebanese passport, to the

Sharon-led rampage through Lebanon in 1982, and from the deliberate shooting of Palestinian children (dealt with in a Save the
Children report), to the firing on medics (referred to in a UN
report).

The 1967 war: Jeremy Bowen's important *Six Days*

In a recent speech to the Knesset, Prime Minister Sharon said
that in 1967 Israel was attacked and Israelis protected their lives
with their backs to the sea. At about the same time, Israeli liberal,
David Grossman wrote that Israel hadn't wanted the 1967 war.
These claims correspond with public opinion in Israel, America
and Britain and form an indelible, never challenged, image, of
the 1967 war.

Nearer to the truth, was Ariel Sharon's jocular remark, from
1967, reported in *Six Days,* that Israel had peace: a piece of Egypt.
BBC correspondent Jeremy Bowen has recently published *Six
Days,* which shows that Israel launched the war, even though there
wasn't a genuine danger of an Arab attack. *Six Days* shows that
Nasser, the Egyptian leader, in closing the straits of Tiran and in
sending troops into Sinai, the Egyptian province bordering Israel,
was making a gesture meant to deter Israel from an intended
attack on Syria. The book makes it clear that the Egyptian Army
was in no condition to go to war with Israel.

In *Six Days* the author relates how Israel's Prime Minister,
Eshkol, asked his generals, "Will we live forever by the sword", to
no avail. Too many generals considered there was unfinished
business from the 1948 war: land to be seized and settled. But
there was an additional reason. General Sharon explained it
when he said that delay in attacking Egypt was eroding Israel's
best deterrent: Arab fear of Israel. The meaning of this was that
Israel, the regional Top Dog, must set the pace in military
confrontation. Israel had previously carried out serious military
actions against Egypt and Jordan that were greater acts of aggression and far more humiliating for those countries than Egypt's
risky, but limited, challenge was for Israel. But Israel was the Top
Dog and Egypt was getting cocky and it was a great opportunity.

Notably, the old advocate of military expansion, Ben Gurion,
was angry with General Rabin for leading Israel to war. Probably the
reason for his change of heart lay in his experience of President
Eisenhower's readiness to use sanctions to punish Israel for her

aggressions. In retirement, it might have seemed to Ben Gurion that President Truman, with his sycophantic indulgence of Israel, had been an aberration. After all, not long before he died, President Kennedy had warned Israel that his Middle East policy would be in America's interest and not Israel's and there was President Johnson's unfavourable response to Israel's 1966 attack on Jordan. But it turned out – then and later – that it was Eisenhower who was the exception. During the 1967 crisis, Johnson rushed military supplies to Israel, while blocking those to Jordan.

Six Days explains that at the end of 1966, while King Hussein had been engaged in secret talks with Israel, Israel had, without warning, launched a serious military attack into Jordan. The US Government was so concerned it supported a UN Security Council condemnation of Israel. It also airlifted urgent military aid to Jordan. Hussein, shocked by the aggression, correctly considered count down to a new war had started.

In 1967, fearing the risk of fighting Israel alone, he allied Jordan to Egypt. He obviously felt he faced Hobson's choice: be forced to fight alone against a hugely superior enemy, or join the fight alongside Egypt against a hugely superior enemy.

In the war, although Syria fired her artillery in support of Egypt, she agreed to a ceasefire before any direct confrontation with Israeli ground forces. It was after Syria's ceasefire and standing down of defensive forces that General Dayan, learning of Syria's vulnerability, sent his army into Syria.

Six Days deals with cross border violence leading up to the 1967 war and quotes General Dayan honestly saying that Israel provoked at least eighty percent of the cross border clashes with Syria. And after a delegation from thirty-one Jewish settlements lobbied the Government for war with Syria, General Rabin referred to "all the trouble" the settlers had caused and called them "arrogant bastards", and General Dayan said that the settlers were just interested in grabbing good farmland.

Six days quotes the future President Weizman admitting that in 1967 there hadn't been a danger of "extermination" and it quotes future President Herzog agreeing that Israel hadn't been in danger and General Peled making a similar acknowledgement.

Serious History now accepts that *it was* Israel that began the war by attacking Egypt. Yet at the time, Israel's broadcasts claimed it was countering an Egyptian invasion. Lurid claims led Israeli troops to believe they were fighting for the survival of their families. For example, Israel's Air Force personnel before going into action were told that the Egyptian army was moving to annihilate the Israeli people.

Perhaps this belief contributed to the savagery of the military actions; although it could only be a part of the explanation: the leaders commanding the attacks knew the truth about the opportunist war. One Israeli pilot later questioned the need for the slaughter from the air of the retreating, defeated soldiers from the shattered Egyptian Army.

Six Days tells of murder and unnecessary killings by the attacking Israelis. Twenty-eight young Palestinians captured while fighting for the Egyptian side in Gaza were summarily executed. And there were a number of other cases of murder of young men of military age, whom according to their families, had not been fighting. (The author reminds us that in 1956 the Israelis carried out a number of massacres in Gaza, killing between 500 and 700, including children.) There was also napalm bombing of fleeing civilians and serious looting of Palestinian and UN property, including medical incubators from hospitals. And the Israeli Army deployed a characteristic pacification method: A battalion of tanks crossed and re-crossed Ramallah, firing on all sides, until it fell silent.

Six Days describes hundreds of Jewish fundamentalists and soldiers, arms linked, dancing opposite the Wailing Wall on ground where an ancient Palestinian community had just had their homes and possessions bulldozed and had their lives shattered.

Six Days is, in my experience, without equal for it's accurate reporting of the war. One could glean more relevant information from *Alice in Wonderland* than from most, available, accounts of this conflict.

Unfortunately, it is domestic political calculation, not the truth about how Israel came to have control of Gaza and the West Bank, which decides America's material support of Israel's settling of stolen land. The convenient "Israel is the victim" fairy tale enables American politicians to pretend their indulgence is consistent with human decency. Supporters of this myth constantly claim that Israel has "its back to the sea". And this fairy tale extends to the 1973 war.

1973: another war, another myth

On the BBC Radio Today programme of the October 7th 2003, a correspondent, in an aside, referred to, "1973 ... when Egypt and

Syria launched a surprise attack on Israel." That kind of statement about 1973 is common.

What actually happened in 1973, was that Egyptian and Syrian forces, for a unique moment, had state-of-the-art Soviet weapons that enabled them to deal with Israel's advanced warplanes and tanks, and attacked, not Israel, but Israel's forces occupying Egyptian and Syrian territory. The occupation was in defiance of a UN Security Council resolution requiring Israel's withdrawal. But Israel's leaders had been planting Jewish settlements inside both Egypt and Syria, making clear their intent to stay. (And they are still inside Syria today.)

Some of the 1973 fighting did take place just inside Northern Israel, but the intention, and the plan, was a limited war. (There was no planned assault into Israeli territory, in the way that Israel has so often driven into Arab territory.) The war's limited aim was in support of a UN Security Council resolution. It is worth remembering that during the course of that war, the Nixon Government re-supplied Israel, in a huge airlift, to make up her material losses and prevent the limited defeat that would have obliged her to comply, at least in part, with UN wishes and with international law.

Limited defeat *then* could realistically have led to further compliance with legality and cut short the land seizures, settlement and army violence against civilians, which have fuelled so much hatred of Israel and America. President Nixon's military supplies, in the absence of Soviet re-supply to the Arabs, enabled Israeli forces, in defiance of a UN Security Council Resolution, to retake Egyptian and Syrian territory and keep the illegal settlements there.

Myths in the making

Since 1948, Israel's accounts of her wars have, with the exception of 1956 and at times 1982, become the accepted "truth" in Britain. The 1982 invasion of Lebanon is sometimes described as having been launched to stop cross-border attacks on Israel, when in truth all parties in Lebanon had complied with a UN brokered deal, which ended cross-border attacks. In 1982, Israel broke the agreement.

In my experience, Israel's pretexts for her wars have formed the bedrock policy underlying newspaper editorial commentary and radio and television interviewers' attitudes.

On 23rd January 2004, a Labour MP (whose name I missed), a supporter of Israel, referred, unchallenged, on BBC radio, to Palestinian suicide bombings starting in 1994 "while peace talks where in progress". This was supposed to mean that it was the Palestinians, not Israel, who broke the ceasefire. Is this too to become an accepted "truth"? The loyal New Labour MP ignored the reality of an Israeli-style "ceasefire": land seizures, a flood of fresh settlers on to Palestinian land, raids (in which Palestinians die) and targeted assassinations – while the Palestinians keep the peace – until some Palestinians have had enough and respond with rockets or suicide bombings. Then it is always Palestinians who have broken the "cease-fire". Ours is a Franz Kafka world.

An Israeli Government Minister did actually offer, if the Palestinians would return to negotiations, to end land seizures and only to use lethal fire in future when Israeli lives were in danger: a frank admission of past behaviour. This aspect of Israel's "ceasefires" doesn't get into the version of events the British and American public repeatedly hear. Outrageous behaviour from Israel is barely noticed. It is suicide bombers, "breaking the ceasefire", who get the headlines.

In bits and pieces, we may hear, or some of us may, depending upon which newspaper we read, that the suicide bomber had lived in a village which had much of its land taken by the recent wall and that the village's fruit, or olive trees had been bulldozed, and we hear of Palestinians being killed prior to the bombing. But none of this was as up-front as the news of the suicide bombing.

There is a dire need for the news on Israel's activities to be presented honestly. By successfully portraying itself as the victim, Israel has been able to violate, probably, every aspect if international law that was meant to protect vulnerable civilians from an occupying army. Knowledge of what was being done to the Palestinians has been hidden in the shadows during the long years of our country's tribal identification with Israel. The truth is beginning to emerge. Very slowly.

Non-book sources for Bilal and Miriam

Miriam's visit to a religious settlement was based on news reports, although the "sermon" by the young settler is based on quotes contained in *Jewish Fundamentalism,* from fundamentalist Rabbis who "inspire" the religious settlers.

Bilal's end, I put together from more than one news report on the behaviour of Israel's soldiers in Lebanon some years ago. One report was of a driver of a car, checked at a roadblock and found to have a gun on board, being kicked in the stomach. Another report was of a soldier, as a car approached a roadblock, getting down on one knee and shooting a boy in the passenger seat in the head. The soldier then pulled the boy, still alive, out of the car by the ankles. Two other reports were of cars full of people being destroyed: one was run over by an Israeli tank, the other had a rocket fired into it at close range.

The hyped-up settler children rampaging through an Arab market and later singing their song of praise for a famous murderer of Arabs, was based on a TV documentary. The two young soldiers saying, "We weren't dealing with human beings," etc, was based on what two young Israeli soldiers said in another TV documentary. At the time, I didn't realise I would be using the reports and didn't record the sources. But thousands of people beside myself would have seen them.

Miriam's visit to the Artists Village, once the home of nearby Palestinians, was based on an Observer article, of which I have lost the date.

There was a T.V. documentary on the attempted sinking of the *Liberty.* Unfortunately I didn't keep a record of its contents. But the American sailors featured in it were convinced that there had been a deliberate attack on the *Liberty,* in the knowledge that it was an American ship. The two accounts I have read of the attack were both by American writers. Both supported the view of the American sailors. The account I have mostly used is contained in Stephen Green's *Taking Sides,* (a source of much other valuable information). There *is* a whole book on the attack on the Liberty, again by an American writer, which also supports the view that the attack was deliberate. I once browsed through a copy in Liverpool's central library, but cannot recollect either the title or the author and couldn't locate it anywhere in the British library system.

I would have loved to have got my hands on the American Government report on the attack on the Liberty but, as usual in the case of investigation of Israeli wrongdoing, the results were never released to the American public – not even to the families of the dead and wounded sailors.

The attack on Miriam's father, Sam, by fellow Israeli soldiers, who mistook him for an Arab prisoner, was based on reported widespread killing of Arab prisoners during the 1973 war.

Can we humans learn from history?

The most valuable lesson we can draw from barbarous periods of history, must surely be how not to behave. The Nuremberg Tribunal identified certain Nazi practices as War Crimes. And the Fourth Geneva Convention and The Universal Declaration of Human Rights were drawn up with the benefit of the experience of Nazi behaviour. The creation of the United Nations was supposed to usher in a new world order where the rule of law would prevail. Taking the land of others, ethnic cleansing, collective punishment of communities, including house demolition, the mistreatment of prisoners and of course, wars of territorial expansion and war against civilian populations, would all be illegal under international law.

The Nazi regime had hardly fallen when the State of Israel came into being and proceeded to commit all of these crimes. The illegalities weren't technical. They have caused huge suffering to the Palestinian and other Arabs.

And they still do, primarily because of Israel's hold on American politicians. Elected Congressmen know that every time they vote on an issue, even indirectly affecting Israel, the vote is recorded and added to the record kept in pro-Israel lobbyist's files and can affect their careers. They know that Israel's lobbyists can bypass them and go straight to their constituencies. I have read of four cases of congressmen with the wrong voting record losing office after pro-Israel lobbyists moved against them. I doubt that there aren't others. The "sin" of one of them had been to alter his vote at the last moment and *support the American Government* when it wanted to sell AWACS planes to an Arab country.

This distortion of American politics by lobbyists for a foreign power is probably unique. Israel's lobbyists don't merely seek to influence America's elected representatives in how they vote on particular issues. They change the make-up of America's democratic institutions. It is an historical irony that an American Government brought the state of Israel into being by interfering with what should have been a free vote of the United Nations and now agents of Israel interfere with the free vote within the American House of Representatives and Senate.

The lobbyists and their many foot soldiers are just as rigorous in their watch over the American press. That Americans Identify with a mythical Israel isn't surprising. They have been fed fairy tales.

International Terrorism: "the main threat of our time"?

Understandably the people in the terrorist networks who were responsible for so many innocent's deaths on 9/11 and 7/7 in London and the other mass killings have been called "Psychoes", "Sickoes", "Crazies" and other names. Understandably, there are many who say that the only way to deal with them is to fight and defeat them.

Yes everything possible must be done to combat them. But there has been series of atrocities that didn't get the same attention. They began well before Muslim terrorist attacks on the West and were a contributory cause of them, and everything possible must be done to combat them too. Below are a number of quotes taken from "The Massacre", one of the chapters added to the 2001 edition of Robert Fisk's *Pity the Nation.*

"The tarmac of the UN compound was slippery with blood, with pieces of flesh and entrails. There were legs and arms, babies without heads, old men's heads without bodies ... On top of a burning tree hung two parts of a man's body ... shells had physically torn these Lebanese refugees apart, bursting in the air to cause amputation wounds, scything through arms and stomachs and legs ... this was a butcher's shop. It was so terrible, so utterly beyond comprehension ...

"... Fijian UN soldiers were walking through this slaughterhouse with black plastic bin-liners, picking up here a finger, there a baby's arm ... I kept thinking of Hieronymus Bosch's triptych of hell. A UN soldier stood amongst a sea of bodies and, without saying a word, held aloft a decapitated child.

"French UN troops had now arrived. One of them, a young soldier ... was muttering oaths as he opened a bag into which he was dropping feet, fingers, pieces of people's arms ... A United Nations official ... simply broke down, weeping uncontrollably ... Many of the Fijian soldiers were crying ...

"I started squeezing the numbers on my mobile phone ...

Above the screaming, I could just hear Steve Crawshaw's voice coming down the line from the *Independent's* office at Canary Wharf in London ..."

Below are comments, taken from *Pity the Nation,* by Israeli soldiers from the Gun battery responsible. They had previously appeared in Kol Hai'r, an Israeli weekly.

"No one spoke about it as if it was a mistake. We did our job and we are at peace with that."

"... it's war and in war these things happen ... it's just a bunch of Arabs."

Those words, "It's just a bunch of Arabs", perform a familiar role. They seek to dehumanise the victims, so as to justify, or lessen, the crime. In that context they mean, "You can do anything to Arabs".

And the excuse is so easy, "... it's war and in war these things happen", as though in war it is okay to kill the other side's civilians.

But was it war? The trigger for the claimed "war" was the death of a 14-year-old Lebanese boy, killed by a road-side bomb, which was unlikely to have been the work of anyone but the Israeli-created and controlled South Lebanese Army, or Israeli soldiers. Hizbollah responded to the bomb by firing rockets into northern Israel badly burning a woman who, of course, was totally innocent of the killing of the Lebanese boy.

In response, the Peres Government ordered an attack by artillery, warplanes and warships on the towns and villages of southern Lebanon, deliberately turning 400,000 civilians, totally innocent of the rocketing of the Israeli woman's car, into refugees fleeing on the roads north to Beirut.

The words, "its war" suggested a fight for survival. Yet Israel wasn't fighting for anything resembling survival. Lebanese civilians were fleeing for survival and Israel's armed forces were committing war crimes.

Israel's bombardment of the UN compound happened after Hizbollah fired mortars – from approximately 600 metres outside the compound – at Israeli troops, whom they had seen laying mines inside the UN zone. During the shelling, an Israeli pilot-less observation plane capable of sending back instant television pictures was seen flying overhead. It was videoed by a UN soldier. Yet, amongst the misinformation Israel put out about the massacre was a denial that the robot plane was there. Under US Government pressure on the General Secretary, the UN wouldn't acknowledge that the videotape existed and instructed its

Peacekeepers not to talk about it. But one of them delivered a copy to Robert Fisk. The Peacekeeper told Fisk that he had two children the same age as the ones he had carried, dead, at the UN compound. "This is for them", he said.

Robert Fisk told the full story in *Pity the Nation,* (2001). And shortly after the massacre, in 1996, he broke the story in *The Independent,* obliging the UN to admit the truth. The significance of the revelation was that the UN compound was shelled deliberately, and the UN did report, weakly, that it had "probably" been deliberate.

The 1996 atrocity would have affected many Muslims as much as 9/11 and the other terrorist atrocities affected the Western world. And it would have been noted that an American Government had, once again, tried to prevent the whole truth from being told about Israel.

Below is one last quote from Robert Fisk, with his permission, of an entire report from the Independent, from July 1993, three years earlier than the Qana massacre. It reports some of the results of an Israeli military blitz, which sent hundreds of thousands of innocent Lebanese civilians fleeing for survival along the roads to the north:

"A land without people. For 20 miles we drove below the Israeli gun line yesterday, through a blitzed landscape of smashed homes and bomb-cratered roads, the sky alive with the crack of Israeli shells and the howl of fighter aircraft.

Only at Sultaniyeh did a man run across the road from his house, saying: "There were 2,000 people here now just 35 of us are hiding in my home. An Israeli plane has bombed three cars down the road. They killed a woman and two children."

A minute down the road and we found the scene, a massive hole, a spray of rubble and three Mercedes cars tossed upside down on to the powdered concrete. Terrible shapes lay inside two of them, the doors running with blood. At Jouaya, the Israelis shelled a baby clean out of its cot.

We found the three-month boy in a Sidon hospital, crying silently on a huge bed, internal bleeding in its tiny head and the word "Majhul" written on its name tag. "Unidentified." All this, we are to believe, is to rid southern Lebanon of Israel's latest enemy, the pro-Iranian Hizbollah who have been fighting the occupying (and very definitely pro-American) Israeli army for just over a decade. What we saw in southern Lebanon yesterday, however, was a disgrace.

Four hundred terrified villagers – old men, women and children with a smattering of youths – hiding in the basement of the Tibnin hospital scarcely half a mile in front of the guns; Shia families crowded into United Nations bunkers; an 80-year-old woman with almost all her skin burned off by an Israeli phosphorous shell, naked and dying in a hospital ward. How much further into horror could a "war against terrorism" go?

We listened to the reports of Israel's proxy militia radio station, the ominous Voice of the South. No cars – not even the UN or the Red Cross – would be permitted on the roads, it announced. They would be treated as enemies. And at 7pm, the Israeli planes would return to bomb the villages again.

How fast we drove those roads, acknowledging the greetings of the few, courageous men and women who still stood in doorways, refusing to obey Israel's orders to leave their homes.

And the Hizbollah, the guerrillas, the resistance – the "terrorists" in Israel's all-purpose lexicon – were still there. They hovered in the alleyways of Tyre, drifted in the backstreets of Qana, in a battered Volvo, even hauled a Russian-made Katyusha launcher up to the very rear of the Irish UN battalion's Position 6-42 east of Haris and fired off three missiles towards the Israelis.

The rockets hissed over our heads. In a Tyre hospital, the local Hizbollah commander tried to explain why the "Islamic resistance" was worth so much bloodshed: "The Prophet, may his name be praised, once said that if Islam could only be saved through his death, then he wished for death." Was this what the commander really believed?

Six Hizbollah wounded had been brought into the Jebel Amal hospital in Tyre in 48 hours, but in the past four days, 185 wounded civilians arrived, 19 of whom had died, two women. In Sidon, I found the Red Cross placing two refrigerated lorries – used to carry fruit to Saudi Arabia – at each end of the city as mobile mortuaries, both packed with bodies.

There seemed no end to it. High up on the ridge line above the Litani river we could see the puff of smoke from the Israelis' American-made 155mm guns, the shells howling over us at five a minute.

In Tibnin, an Irish army corporal shouted "shelling sporadic" – an understatement. A few minutes later, the Israelis fired three artillery rounds just over the top of the Irish headquarters to land 50 metres from us as we stood in a Norwegian UN compound.

So many shells had been fired in to the centre of Tibnin that I momentarily lost my way in a village I have known for 17 years; the houses blasted down, the road cratered, the electric wires hanging forlornly over a carpet of concrete and glass.

In Qana, in Siddiqin, in a dozen villages, it was the same story, whole fields laid waste by fires. A burned land as well as a land without people. The UN claims 300,000 have fled their homes which was, so Yitzhak Rabin has told us, what he intended.

In the Hammoud hospital in Sidon, bodies had been stacked outside the mortuary for lack of space. Leila Karaki from J'baa lay with 50 per cent phosphorous burns on the second floor. "The shell came right into our room. How could I leave my house? I have no money. I have my children to feed. I have nowhere to go."

In one room, I found the unknown baby alongside Mohamed Shabayta, a three-year-old Palestinian wounded in the arm by an Israeli gun boat shell as he picked a fig from a tree near his home in the Ein Helweh camp, and a seven-year-old called Hussein Qassem who lay squirming with pain on the other side of the room. Parts of his genitals had been burned away by an Israeli phosphorous shell."

There have been many reports similar to the above article from 1993, by Robert Fisk and other journalists, many of them of smaller-scale attacks: an ambulance destroyed by an American supplied helicopter firing an American high-tech missile, a whole family killed by a similar American helicopter firing an American missile, civilian traffic attacked from the air while fleeing north, a boy with steel nails deep in his head, victim of an Israeli shell, Israeli gunboats firing on civilian traffic: all "terrorist" targets. Muslims will know that Israel's psychotic killing of innocent Arab civilians, over many years, has failed to disturb her cosy relationship with her European and American allies, and their material support.

While I was putting the above section together, an American politician, once tipped to be a member of a Kerry, Democratic, Government, said on BBC Radio, that Israel was under mortal threat of extinction. To anyone who knows the comparative military strengths of Israel and her Arab neighbours, this might seem merely an inanely inaccurate statement. But American public opinion has been shaped by the constant repetition of this kind of wildly inaccurate claim from politicians who know their words are constantly monitored in a vigilant, never-ending loyalty check, by lobbyists for Israel.

An Israeli state that really was under mortal threat of extinction from it's neighbours could hardly have been attacking the civilians of those neighbours over so many years without suffering a major military defeat. The one unique moment, in 1973, when two of those neighbours had high-tech weapons that Israel couldn't deal with and they used them to try to regain part of their national territory, it was portrayed as "yet another attack on Israel".

And contrary to these Orwellian truths, loyally accepted in America, Israel has been responsible for all of her wars. And, certainly, the Arab states haven't retaliated to Israel's relentless violence against Arab civilians, with remotely comparable violence against Israelis. That is an indication of the power of Israel.

Israeli civilians are in danger. There is no doubt about that. The suicide bombings against them are the work of a people with no military power, who see no other escape from life lived under a brutal military boot. It is American politicians, Republicans and Democrats, making it possible for Israel to do the terrible things she does that produce such desperate retaliation. Similarly, the rockets that are sometimes fired into the north of Israel by Hizbollah, the Lebanese Islamic Resistance, would never have been fired if American politicians hadn't given Israel the means to do the terrible things she has done in Lebanon.

The Leadership we have lost

At the end of WW2, when a reeling humanity was struggling to recover from the devastation of global war and wanted no more of it, President Roosevelt tried to meet the main need of his time: his plan for the creation of a global forum of states, before which conflicts would be worked out according to the principles of justice and not through brute force, won huge international support. The prime role of the United Nations was to be to avoid war, and Roosevelt specifically told a press conference that the UN's purpose would be to stop nations that sought to grab territory, or invade neighbours.

Roosevelt wasn't just trying to stop the imperialism of others. As Eleanor Roosevelt later recalled, her husband disliked America's "Big Brother" behaviour towards its neighbours and replaced it with the "Good Neighbour" policy, which barred interventions.

During WW2 Roosevelt had tried to cure Churchill of his addiction to imperial bullying, but failed. Churchill was beyond cure. He even told his Foreign Minister, Eden, that he hated the word "independence". Roosevelt would have understood that in the major countries there were a host of Churchill type politicians whose "sphere of interest" activities were accompanied by "freedom" rhetoric. He would have realised that, in trying to change their fossilised thinking, he had a mammoth task on his hands. And he wouldn't have been surprised when each of the five permanent members of UN Security Council won the right to veto UN decisions. After all, major powers are reluctant to accept restraints on their behaviour. They tell others what to do.

The world had an example of this reluctance when even after the slaughter of WW1, with whole nations mourning their losses, the League of Nations never won the leverage amongst the powerful to gain serious authority.

Even before President Wilson's League of Nations, President Taft had tried to replace armed conflict between major states by a limited system of arbitration but, despite popular support in America, failed. Yet he too was infected by "Great Power" thinking and in 1910, reflecting the dominant political culture of his time claimed that a foreign policy pursuing abstract justice could include interventions to secure US business opportunity.

And so it was that in 1935, a US General, Smedley Butler, was able to write of his 33 years service in the Marines, "I spent most of my time being a high-class muscle man for Big Business, for Wall Street and for the bankers. In short, I was a racketeer for capitalism ... Thus I helped make Mexico and especially Tampico safe for American oil interests in 1914. I helped make Haiti and Cuba a decent place for the National City Bank to collect revenues in ... I helped purify Nicaragua for the international banking house of Brown Brothers in 1909-1912. I brought light to the Dominican Republic for American sugar interests in 1916. I helped make Honduras 'right' for American fruit companies in 1903."

By 1935, when Smedley Butler's honest words were published, Franklin Roosevelt was two years into his presidency and had already captured the passionate support of most Americans for his humanising of US Government domestic policy. Similarly, by

1945 his humanising attitude to relations between nations, expressed in his post-war plans, had won him the love of the world. He, the world's most powerful leader, was going to ensure that vulnerable nations, used to receiving orders, would be respected in the post war world. In Franklin Roosevelt, leader of the major power, the world knew that it had found a very unusual politician.

It was because he was different that he dissented from both Stalin and Churchill's plans to arrange the world according to the interests of the three key WW2 victors. That the war had been a war of liberation of peoples hadn't impressed either Stalin or Churchill. Each intended to emerge from the conflict as leader of an imperial power. And, when at the Yalta Conference, Churchill thought he had heard that India must get her independence, he leapt to his feet in a rage, protesting, "Never. Never. Never". And Stalin applauded, "Bravo. Bravo": he recognised a useful example when he saw one.

Roosevelt didn't want to follow "Great Power" example. He, after the ordeal the world had been through, thought it was time to outlaw the old unequal relationships between nations, which had contributed hugely to global conflict (and, throughout history, to "civilization's" interminable warring). Roosevelt's United Nations was to put an end to all that. He even talked about putting himself forward as candidate for UN General Secretary – where his worldwide moral authority would have enhanced the new organisations standing. But sadly he died.

Speaking to Congress, in March 1945, weeks before his death, about the work of the Yalta Conference, at which the proposed UN had been discussed, Roosevelt said: "It spells – and it ought to spell – the end of the system of unilateral action, exclusive alliances and spheres of influence and balances of power and all the other expedients which have been tried for centuries and have always failed.

"We propose to substitute for all these, a universal organisation in which all peace-loving nations will finally have a chance to join.

"I am confident that the Congress and the American people will accept the results of this conference as the beginnings of a permanent structure of peace upon which we can begin to build, under God, that better world in which our children and grand-children … can live …"

Sadly, for many, it wasn't to be.

The end of the Cold War and an era: a time to relearn forgotten lessons

At the end of the cold war, with the Soviet adversary gone, a review was needed: did it make sense to continue to spend hundreds of billions of precious dollars on a military machine that had been created to face the huge standing army, navy and air force of the Soviet superpower? And what about America's long series of worldwide interventions carried out in the name of the Cold War? Were they to continue? And there was an even larger question: can we humans find a better way to live?

In answering this last question, it is worth remembering that, until recently, for decades, the two superpowers stood ready to launch, at a moments notice, a nuclear war that would have wiped out a significant part of humanity and rendered our world difficult to survive in for generations. Such was our mental state at the time that millions of us accepted the terrible risk involved. We pushed it to the fringes of our consciousness and got on with life.

But, even without the imminent danger of nuclear war, do we want to live in a weapon-filled world, where differences are so often sorted out by military action: by killing people? Is this the world we want our children to inherit? Shouldn't we be searching for a more civilized way of life? Wouldn't we prefer to live according to international law? Probably, it was Franklin Roosevelt asking himself similar questions that led to the creation of the United Nations.

If we remember that President Truman, on behalf of the nascent Israeli lobby, spectacularly undermined the UN, by subverting the free vote of the General Assembly through intimidation and bribery of small states to win the vote for partition of Palestine, we will realise that it isn't inevitable that the UN is undermined. Truman didn't have to do what he did. He could have decided to be honest and publicise the intelligence he was receiving about the Jewish leaders aggressive military intentions.

There are always pressures from interest groups and different individuals respond differently to them. Sometimes a national leader, as Truman did, pursues the narrow aims of one interest group. And, too often, as then, there are victims who are considered to be of little consequence.

In stopping the military expansion of Japan and Germany, the world had just paid a huge price in blood and suffering. Truman could have let the UN decide, according to the recent, expensively learned lessons, what was acceptable behaviour in Palestine. Eisenhower didn't approve of Truman's indulgence of Israel and certainly would have stood up to the lobbyists who determined Truman's policy towards the Jewish state.

US post-Roosevelt interventions

In three cases of US covert intervention covered in this book, in Guatemala, Lumumba's Congo and Iran, national leaders who were making human development a priority were overthrown. The US-initiated coups in Guatemala and the Congo led to corrupt dictatorships, which dropped human development in favour of corruption, torture and murder. In Iran the Shah did put oil money into human resources, but ran a corrupt administration, which wasted billions on an oppressive military state. In none of these three cases was US intervention carried out to prevent a Communist takeover.

The same is true in the vast majority of US interventions. It seems to me, there was usually a combination of motives involved: to block leaders and movements with too independent an attitude, who were too concerned with putting national resources directly into human development; to support US business interests, and the pervasive reason: to compete with Soviet influence by installing a compliant local dictator.

In the case of Greek intervention, there was a US intelligence report, which President Truman would have received, saying that the Communist leadership of the Resistance didn't have a communist programme, but was in favour of a free market Greece within the British sphere of influence. And he could hardly not have known that the Communists weren't in a majority in the Resistance, or trying to seize power but, like other ex-Resistance members, were fighting for survival and seeking negotiations.

Even in Vietnam, after WW2, the Nationalist/Communist Provisional Government based its declaration of independence on the American Declaration of Independence. And it looked up to America and appealed repeatedly for American friendship. In Vietnam, where, during the years of savage foreign intervention, there were millions of civilian casualties, a friendly US approach was most likely to have won the hearts and minds of the people. Likewise in US-admiring South Korea, after 1945, American friendship would have been more likely to win the people than the suppression of a provisional government and the heavy handed imposition of a Leader.

I believe that during WW2, in their onslaughts on Nazi Germany and militarist Japan, Britain and America crossed a moral threshold. Facing such barbarous adversaries, understandably, they demonised their enemy, or, more accurately, the enemy, by its behaviour, demonised itself. When, during the Spanish Civil War, Nazi warplanes had bombed Guernica, killing many civilians, it was seen as a war crime unique to the Nazi way of war, (yet the RAF's Bomber Harris, hardly attracting attention, had already perfected his skills at bombing civilians in Iraq.)

But both Britain (against Germany) and America (against Japan), by far surpassed Guernica in their bombing of civilians. And it was within the atmosphere created by a barbarous war that President Truman was able to use nuclear weapons on two Japanese cities.

It seems to me that Churchill, Bevin and especially Truman – with his "scare hell" deception – were able to transfer the demonising of the wartime enemy to the "Communist" enemy wherever they found them, real, imagined, or invented. American leaders, thus, were able to break international law subverting and overthrowing sovereign governments, most of which were not Communist. And where they found genuinely Communist adversaries, as in Korea and Vietnam, they inflicted huge civilian casualties, way beyond Guernica and beyond moral justification.

We have now passed the time when various Great Powers sent their armies and navies and warplanes to the less developed world "competing" for commercial advantage. And we have now passed the time when Stalinist Russia occupied Eastern Europe and vied with the United States for international influence. In the stories in *The Midwife Mission,* I tried to give examples of the human cost of those struggles. I could have given examples from the Stalinist zone of occupation. But those times are gone. Stalin's crimes are universally known.

Unfortunately – apart from seeing insufficient commitment to the fights America has fought – the individuals in power in America today don't have the capacity for genuine reflection on the lessons of recent history, or for self-criticism. Instead of responding to changed times with changed behaviour, they keep to their fixed ideological pursuits and use international terrorism, which requires very different solutions, as an excuse to carry on as before.

Are we prisoners of history?

There will always have been, I'm sure, people who have stood back horrified, at the slaughter of fellow humans in war. But placed by history in contention with others, it was beyond the power of our individual forebears to break free from the violence of their times. In modern times conscientious objectors have proliferated, but like their predecessors, they have been unable to exert serious influence.

Yet in modern times there have been influential individuals, who thought it might be possible to outlaw war and who attempted to establish international codes of behaviour by which states must abide. The most notable of these was Franklin Roosevelt, who hoped that his United Nations, equipped with the authority of international law, would be able to outlaw violent solutions to conflicts and bring fair play into relations between states.

Yet so deeply ingrained in our state cultures were selfish habits that from the earliest days, leaders of the major powers simply took their old habits into the new organisation, led by Roosevelt's successor, Harry Truman.

But since Roosevelt's time there has been no US president who has broken so completely with Roosevelt's aims than the present leader, G. Bush. He and key advisers are steeped in a world-view of conflicting national interests where violence plays its part and where, amongst the contending states, the US is Top Dog. They believe in unassailable US military dominance, and the only use they have for the UN is as an instrument of *their* power. In particular they believe they need a permanent military presence in the Middle East to guarantee their oil supplies. And, as Americans now know, had considered an invasion of Iraq even before 9/11.

G. Bush's advisers have been praised for being smart. One is the "product of advanced studies". Another is a "brilliant ideas man". Yet another is a "genius". Yet, the "product of advanced studies" belongs to the "pursuit of US interests", rather than "morality" school of foreign policy. The "brilliant ideas man" once wrote a paper that considered the pre-emptive use of chemical or nuclear weapons a possible policy option. And he was involved, with like-minded colleagues, in producing a paper, which considered that some catalysing event for American power was needed, such as a new Pearl Harbour. The "genius" is said to have provided the President with an insight: Islam finds it hard to accept its loss of imperial sovereignty; America might not win the love of the Muslims, but through military power can win their respect.

I think that Ian's explanation to Idris that human thought has traditionally served and been shaped by tribal loyalty, is a help to understanding these genuinely clever people. They are in the service of Great Power tribalism and their thinking and perhaps their empathy, is confined by their tribal loyalty. Some people are like that. But there are probably additional reasons for their attitudes, such as corporate connections, and addictive involvement with the bureaucracy of conflict.

But they *are* tribalists, and tribalists fight from the "good corner" against the "bad guys", who are the embodiment of evil. G. Bush has a facility for finding words to express this blinkered mentality, which is probably why he is their leader. When answering a journalist's question, the sense of which was whether a humiliating photo of Saddam Hussein would provoke more attacks *on Americans* in Iraq, he answered without embarrassment, "I don't think a photo inspires murders. I think they're inspired by an ideology that is so barbaric and backwards that it's hard for many in the western world to comprehend how they think". *This* from the head of a Government which has put aside the Geneva Convention in its handling of Muslim prisoners and whose war has killed tens of thousands of civilians in Iraq and whose military have used phosphorous, napalm and cluster bombs amongst a civilian population; from a President who has *done* nothing to end the US material aid which helps Israel's continuing land confiscation in the West Bank.

G. Bush's tribal blinkers were on show again when he said that the Soviet occupation of Eastern Europe was one of the greatest crimes in history. *This* from the wing of American politics, to which the US/Contra terrorist campaign in Nicaragua, which destroyed schools, health clinics, farm buildings, houses and the people in them, was okay, because it came from the "good corner" and to which the horror, which was the Vietnam war was fine because that too came from the "good corner", as did the overthrow of Guatemala's President Arbenz, the attempted assassination of Fidel Castro, the overthrow and murder of Patrice Lumumba and all the rest.

George Bush's Curriculum Vitae for the role of world leader

The Government of George Bush Jnr, with a policy of unassailable world military hegemony, has increased spending on the weapons of war. It is hostile to international agreements that might impede its freedom to act in any way it chooses: it withdrew from the anti-ballistic missile treaty; it rejects the comprehensive test ban treaty; it won't countenance an international agreement to end the menace of land mines, which, for years after conflicts have ended, still cause mutilation and death in countries far from America.

While menacing Iran, which it suspects, perhaps rightly, of having nuclear ambitions, the Bush Government, intends to develop new classes of atomic bombs. Pertinently, delegates at a recent meeting of non-nuclear states complained that the International Atomic Energy Agency was engrossed in monitoring non-nuclear nations, even though nuclear powers were failing to live up to *their* Non-Proliferation Treaty commitments to nuclear disarmament. It's, "Do what I tell you, because I am the Top Dog. I'll do whatever I like".

Although President Clinton signed the treaty agreeing to the formation of the International Criminal Court, the Bush Government claims that it has no obligation to it and refuses to send it to the Senate for ratification. *It has even pressured individual states with withdrawal of aid* if they don't accept that US citizens will not be subject to extradition by the ICC. In sharp contrast, the European Union supports the creation of the ICC as an important step in the protection of human rights. And it is direly needed as a civilizing influence on our world.

Consistent with their anti-ICC attitude, Bush and his Government refuse to honour the Geneva Convention in their treatment of Muslim prisoners, who for years have been held, without charge, without trial, outside the law, obviously presumed guilty and treated abominably, some to a degree that kills them, others to the point of suicide. Yet one Red Cross official estimated some time ago that from 70 to 90 per cent of the prisoners had been arrested because they happened to be in the wrong place at the wrong time. And some prisoners are held after being named by individuals suffering torture.

A State Department paper on the seriousness of the problem of global warming, was called by George Bush a report from the bureaucracy, and referring to the damaging carbon emissions, he said he would do nothing that would harm the US economy. He also said, "… first things first are the people who live in America".

He and his Government reject the Kyoto agreement and refuse to be part of an international action to seriously tackle the time bomb – of momentous consequence – of global warming.

George Bush: champion of democracy?

This American President's CV hardly shows a fitness for world leadership. Yet grafted on to his record is what has been called a crusade for the spread of democracy and President Bush verbally lays about him on the subject. *It has even been suggested that he is a new Franklin Roosevelt.*

A clue to understanding his, to many, anachronistic concern for democracy is to be found in his newly created office for post-conflict reconstruction, the holder of which manages teams from the US private sector in changing "the very social fabric a nation", according to the holder of the office. "Reconstruction" includes selling off state owned enterprises and creating "democratic and market oriented" states. Plans have been prepared for "reconstruction" in twenty-five targeted "post conflict" states.

These plans appear to be in operation in Iraq, where billions of dollars worth of contracts have gone to US companies. There is certainly a lot of money to be made when privatisation is treated as a corollary of democracy. Moscow, in Yeltsin's time, the centre of the biggest transfer ever from public to private, now has 33 billionaires: more than any other city in the world.

Bush's call for democracy will be welcomed by nations that have suffered years of monolithic control. It is understandable if citizens of those countries, immersed in their own problems, listening to the American President talking about, for instance, Georgian "sovereign territory" and alluding, critically, to the Russian bases on Georgian soil, don't think too much about his Government's world military ambitions, or about the US, Guatanamo, base on Cuban soil, or about the people of Diego Garcia expelled from their island home to make way for a US military base, from which American warplanes go on bombing missions.

But someone who is genuine about championing freedom and democracy leads by example. When a court decision in favour of

returning the Diego Garcians to their homes was over-ruled by
Tony Blair's Government, a genuine George Bush would have
over-ruled Tony Blair and supported the rule of law. He would
have insisted on the right of the expelled people to return home.

A genuine George Bush would have started his campaign by
withdrawing the US base from Cuban soil. He would have
explained to Americans that the base didn't have the consent of
the Cuban people and dates from times when Cuba was a
subject state, obedient to American power and that US values
didn't support such a relationship in a free and democratic
world order.

And he would be even-handed in the Middle East. Rather than
stridently insisting on only Syria withdrawing from Lebanese territory, as he has done, he would be just as insistent on Israel too
pulling back from Syria and taking its settlements with it. After all,
Syria's presence in Lebanon didn't involve planting settlers on
the neighbour's land, while Israel's occupation of part of Syria
does.

And he wouldn't ignore the real history of Israel's conflict with
Syria, confirmed in UN and US intelligence reports, of Israel's
premeditated expansion and the many aggressions in support of
that expansion (referred to by General Dayan in Jeremy Bowen's
Six Days).

And there is the UN. If the American President's campaign for
democracy were genuine, he would demonstrate it at the world
forum: there would be no more subverting of the free vote at the
UN: no more US pressure, in the form of threats and promises
over aid and trade, to force votes for US sponsored aggressive
initiatives. A genuinely democratic George Bush would renounce
such methods. They wouldn't be used, as they are, to pressure
other states to impose sanctions on Cuba. And they wouldn't have
been used, as they were, when his Government was pressuring UN
member states to support his war with Iraq.

And there is the professional and reputable, al Jazeera TV,
which has transmitted to its fifty million viewers explicit images of
civilian casualties of America's battlefield weapons: the stark
reality of war. Al Jazeera's reporters have been harassed and
detained by US forces. One was incarcerated in Guantanamo. Al
Jazeera offices were attacked by the US military in both
Afghanistan and Iraq. And now this practitioner of free reporting
is barred from Iraq. If the Bush Government's passion for democracy were real, would this be happening?

A defining attitude

The art of being phoney pervades the Bush Administration. When John Kerry spoke about the need for sensitivity in putting together an international coalition, he wasn't talking about how to wage war. Yet a member of the Bush Government responded as though he had been and treating the idea as ludicrous, he asked, "How do you fight a sensitive war?" He was talking about the war in Iraq, in which battlefield weapons were used amongst a civilian population.

This chilling Bush-camp question was contained within a public speech and, one would expect, have been prepared and scrutinised and considered. It wouldn't surprise me if it were later qualified. Yet it is revealing about the Bush Administration's way of war.

It helps explain why the Israeli military, which knows only how to use hugely disproportionate violence and make enemies, were asked for advice on the Iraq war and even brought into the training of US forces.

It helps explain how a disillusioned US marine-sergeant became so sickened after he and his fellow marines had killed "a lot of innocent civilians" at checkpoints that he spoke publicly about it on BBC Radio 4 and is now an ex-marine.

And it helps explain Falluja. The city surrendered to US forces without resistance and could have been used as an example of benign occupation. But, in Falluja, prior to the development of an insurgency, US troops shot dead sixteen demonstrators and wounded dozens. A US officer said that US fire had been directed at targets, yet the film recording the extent of US fire showed that the wide area where civilians had been killed had been sprayed with bullets. It was probably with the victims in mind that unknown individuals horribly mutilated six American civilian workers after they had been killed.

The Bush Government's military response left six hundred residents dead: hundreds of innocent people blown apart by modern weapons for the death of six Americans. The action could hardly have failed to create fresh enemies, and in Falluja the insurgency took-off.

After a delay, the residents were invited to leave, but many stayed. Then there was a fresh US assault, which destroyed 36,000 homes, 60 nurseries and schools and 65 mosques and religious sanctuaries: according to official Iraqi figures. According to reports, Falluja became practically a free fire zone and thousands were killed in a "gloves off" assault, in which phosphorous weapons were used. Thousands remain living in tents on the outskirts of the city, while an unknown number of residents can't go back, because the US authorities are barring return to anyone not actually born in Falluja.

The International Red Cross and its Arab section, the Red Crescent, are empowered by the Geneva Convention to help the victims of war. Yet, in a move reminiscent of Israel's behaviour in south Lebanon in 1982, the US military denied Red Cross relief lorries access to Falluja, thus breaking international law. (There was word at the time from mothers whose children had diarrhoea and hadn't eaten for days). Unusually for the International Red Cross, it has spoken out and condemned "the utter contempt for humanity" shown in Iraq by the US and also by its opponents.

US military power was supposed to win respect. It didn't work that way in Falluja. And for many others in Iraq, it didn't work that way.

It isn't surprising. When *we* hear of "x" number of Iraqi civilians being killed on a certain day, to us it might be a mere abstraction. But for someone in Iraq those figures represent: a mother killed in front of her children as she served them food, her face and head a bloody mess; a dead father, his insides hanging out; your toddler child, who was playing in front of the house, lying in a pool of blood, her head yards away from her body; your mother and father, who have just been talking to you, in the front seat of the car, the top of their heads gone, their blood and bits all over the inside of the car.

Thousands of Iraqi civilians have had experiences like these, and the fact that terrorists are now killing large numbers of fellow Muslims shouldn't alter the conclusions we should draw: the consequences of using warplanes and cluster bombs and depleted uranium tank rounds and helicopter gun-ships and artillery and napalm-like explosives and missiles and phosphorous weapons and machine guns and high-velocity M16s and grenades amongst civilians are so terrible it shouldn't happen, unless in support of a morally justifiable purpose *and* if the consequences of not doing so are even worse. And even then, some of those weapons should never be used.

Of course, those preconditions for war should apply to any armed conflict, civilians or no civilians. American fathers and sons, mothers and daughters, shouldn't be considered dispensable simply because they are in the armed forces. In or out of uniform, life should be treasured and not sacrificed for schemes of world dominance.

Out-of-date, dangerous relics of our past

Nationalist leaders of powerful countries in violent pursuit of global or regional power have invariably been conscience-deficient individuals, who were prepared to sacrifice the lives of their countrymen in aggressive wars and were even more callous in their attitude to target nations. Throughout history, such people have decimated peoples and sometimes, whole generations. Those in power in America today, to me, are true to type. The human losses of the cold war years don't seem to have affected them, except to instil them with a "more of the same" compulsion. In particular, neither the bloody carnage of civilians in Vietnam, nor the deaths of over 50,000 Americans there, nor the many who were left mentally scarred by the experience, nor the many of *them* who have since committed suicide, appear to have aroused in their souls any revulsion to war. They appear to be immune to moral considerations and won't let the human cost deter them from sending others to war.

It was to thwart the plans of such people that Franklin Roosevelt proposed the United Nations. And today, amongst the old major powers, it is only the United States, which keeps the assumption of the right to invade sovereign states – with a compliant British Prime Minister in tow.

Most people in our world do not believe the unconvincing explanations for the invasion of Iraq and do not accept the assumption by the Bush Government of the right to invade other countries. It is well understood that other technically advanced states don't maintain colossal arms programmes and have prospered without global military power and don't go to war to secure "a strategically vital region".

Today, Germany and Japan are the most obvious examples of having moved on from the past. They, like most nations, use diplomacy. They talk. And today, there are no Germans or Japanese dying in foreign wars. Amongst the old major powers this is left to Americans and Britons. And Americans and Britons are the prime terrorist targets.

Such a war as G. bush's war on Iraq, destructive of so many

lives, shouldn't be fought just to get control of an important oil state, or as part of a strategy for global hegemony, or as an irrelevant response to 9/11, or to demonstrate to a whole region how terrible is your power. Such a war shouldn't have been launched while weapons inspectors were still searching and failing to find alleged WMD.

The reasons given to justify the war – and therefore its consequences for soldiers and civilians – haven't survived examination. As has been repeatedly pointed out in America, there was no known involvement in 9/11 or Al Queda by the Saddam Hussein regime. And the argument that Saddam Hussein was defying the will of the international community by violating UN resolutions is a convenient excuse. And it is barefaced hypocrisy, coming as it does, from people who pamper Israel, considering that country's record of violations of UN resolutions and human rights.

One of the arguments for the invasion has been that it was to prevent state resources going to terrorists. Yet, revealingly, after victory US troops guarded the physical facilities of the oil industry and the Oil Ministry itself, neglecting virtually everything else. Equipment and explosives connected with nuclear research and many weapons, were stolen from unguarded laboratories and armouries. If that's preventing state resources from falling into terrorist hands, George Bush *is* Franklin Roosevelt.

When Kerry talked of going through the UN, the Administration answered by asking if America needed to ask before it defended itself. But the evidence does not support the claim that the Iraq war had anything to do with defending America. It suggests that Americans are dying in Iraq in pursuit of a neo-conservative scheme of conquest, which pre-dated 9/11 and which had nothing to do with combating terrorism.

Those behind the war are blind to the need for world leadership beyond the old self-seeking, violent, "Great Power" dominance, which Roosevelt wanted consigned to history. Just as President Truman failed to make use of Roosevelt's moral authority, to lead *by example*, with even-handed, lawful, world leadership, President Bush, during this temporary window of US sole-superpower ascendancy, is failing to set any example for humanity worth following. Instead we are receiving old lessons in how not to behave. And, I believe, how not to escape from the evolutionary cul-de-sac we have long been heading up

Roosevelt versus Bush

In a message to both houses of Congress in January 1945, stressing US fidelity to the United Nations, Roosevelt said, "International cooperation on which enduring peace must be based in not a one-way street. Nations, like individuals, do not always see alike or think alike, and international cooperation and progress are not helped by any nation assuming that it has a monopoly of wisdom or of virtue …" In keeping with that attitude and in opposition to Stalin and Churchill, Roosevelt repeatedly asserted, publicly, the right of *all* nations to freely choose their own Government. There was no small print to the message.

In extreme contrast, the Bush Government's "monopoly of wisdom" interference in other's affairs is a continuation of the old unequal relationships, and it delivers the neo-conservative formula, relevant or not.

In the face of a momentous change on our planet, who is relevant: George Bush or Franklin Roosevelt?

In his Inaugural speech as Governor of New York in 1928 (to extend the quote from the Thanasis story) Roosevelt said, "… our civilization cannot endure unless we, as individuals, realise our personal responsibility to and dependence on the rest of the world. For it is literally true that the 'self-supporting' man or woman has become as extinct as the man of the stone age. Without the help of thousands of others, any one of us would die, naked and starved. Consider the breakfast upon our table, the clothes upon our backs, the luxuries that make life pleasant; how may men worked in sunlit fields, in dark mines, in the fierce heat of molten metal, and among the looms and wheels of countless factories, in order to create them for our use and enjoyment."

This was Roosevelt letting New Yorkers know of his appreciation of the *whole* human community. It wasn't a passive appreciation. While he believed in American capitalism, when corporate activity threatened to hurt the community, he sided with the community. When private energy companies were being innovative, creating intermediate companies through which to charge the public more, he championed public energy production. And the public companies were innovative *in the public interest,* introducing rural electrification and lowering prices.

While still a New York State Senator in 1912, Roosevelt had acted to protect the forests. He proposed public inspection of private forests and compulsory reforestation in watershed areas. He brought in for support, Gifford Pinochet, Teddy Roosevelt's old forestry chief, who showed the senators two photographs. One was of a sixteenth century painting of a Chinese city surrounded by crops and forests. In the picture, the artist had captured signs of logging. The other photo was an up–to-date photo of the same city (now deserted) and surrounded by bare hills.

Roosevelt, talking about the photographs, said that was what would happen to NY State if individuals were allowed to do as they pleased with its natural resources to line their own pockets. When twenty-one years later he became US President, his concerns for natural America led him to create the Civilian Conservation Corps. And his Tennessee Valley Authority didn't just produce and sell electricity. Amongst its activities was reforestation.

Such concerns don't seem to trouble G. Bush. Last January the Observer reported that, in 2000, mining executives lobbied him, complaining that regulations were making it hard to get mining permits and he responded favourably: after he became President, regulations were loosened and amongst the wooded hills of the Appalachian mountains, mining companies are now creating a wasteland. They are taking the tops off mountains and dumping them in surrounding valleys, so that they can get to a thin seam of coal. Four thousand acres have been blasted and over a thousand miles of streams buried.

The Natural Resources Defense Council, an American-led environmental organization, with over a million members, has produced a report on the Bush first term, which says that his Administration had a relentless anti environment agenda and has given polluters "a free pass". The report shows that the Bush Administration is easing off on environmental regulations for corporate America. It says the Government has attempted to undermine the Clean Air Act, has tried to narrow the scope of the clean Water Act, is reversing forest protection measures for fifty eight million acres of pristine national forest and is "moving to hobble" the Endangered Species Act.

The Bush Government seem incapable of looking up from its one-dimensional pursuit of corporate interests to perceive Roosevelt's multi-dimensional human community *and its interests*. It is as though natural America is the property of corporate America and not the prime source of American life, to be husbanded and treasured by and for, all Americans.

The impact of human power

The complex web of human activity, sustaining us in our billions on this planet, depends on a healthy wider nature. And it depends upon modern science and technology being used in a considered way, their effects being so intrusive and so potentially damaging: our children have plutonium in their teeth; animals in the wild, even in apparently pristine wilderness, have man-made chemicals in their bodies; man-made, long-life substances are up amongst the benign, high altitude, protective ozone, destroying life's ancient defence against deadly ultra-violet radiation. And according to the British Government's chief scientific adviser, there is now more carbon dioxide in the atmosphere than there has been for 55 million years: enough, given time, to melt both icecaps and submerge various cities, including London, New York and New Orleans.

A huge majority of US, as well as world, scientists agree that today's rapidly changing climate is not part of a natural cycle, but is man-made. Our climate, according to some scientists, might even have been made warmer and more hospitable by human agricultural activities since early man. If so, the present global heating is part of a very long-term man-made process, which is only now turning, rapidly, to our disadvantage.

The problem is that a mass of carbon from past eras, locked underground for millions of years, has been released by human activity into the atmosphere and forests, where significant quantities of it might have been absorbed, have been destroyed; even if the forests remained as extensive as they once were, there would probably still be a serious problem. The two activities, forest destruction and carbon release, continue relentlessly.

With great complexities involved, the process isn't linear and easily predictable. A recent, surprise discovery by Cambridge scientists is that atmospheric warming is taking over from CFCs as a destroyer of our protective ozone. As I understand it, as temperatures in the lower atmosphere are rising, in the stratosphere it is getting colder. This is helping the formation of clouds within the ozone belt, and this in turn speeds up ozone-destroying chemical reactions. As a result, instead of the ozone, as had been expected, recovering its density, destruction continues, and recent meas-urements have shown that over the *whole* northern hemisphere, there is now less ozone than since measurements began and consequently greater penetration of ultra violet radiation. Unforeseen processes are at work, with an unknown rate of ozone destruction to come.

And there are the oceans: the world's water-borne biomass has even greater capacity for carbon absorption than the forests, and it too is being affected. With warming oceans and carbon absorp-tion, carbonic acid is on the increase and our seas are becoming acidic rather than slightly alkaline, affecting the survivability of water dwelling life.

American scientists are reporting that the melting Artic ice cap, over the last few years, may well have passed the point from which the winter reversal of its seasonal summer ice loss is possible, even with human intervention. The world's oceans are already warming significantly and the removal of Artic ice, which reflects solar radiation back into space, will speed up heat absorp-tion by the newly exposed waters.

Marine scientists have already warned that at some point, as water temperature rises, millions of tons of methane will be released from below the ocean floor triggering, beyond-control, runaway global heating.

An additional source of methane is the melting, vast Artic permafrost: as it melts and organic matter decays, huge quantities of this ultra potent greenhouse gas, as well as carbon, are going to be released. The process is already underway.

According to climate scientists, just two degrees rise in world temperatures will create runaway heating beyond human control.

A time for reflection

During the, perhaps, six thousand years during which the modern world has evolved, we have experienced fairly stable and usually predictable, weather patterns and seasons in which to grow our crops and raise or catch our animal food. And we have been able to build our cities and sustain ourselves in our millions. Yet those conditions have been temperature-dependent and fragile, and we are rapidly altering them and risking *everything*.

It is so easy to be become absorbed in our daily pursuits, so easy not to question the larger scheme of things. It is especially easy if you are a Western city dweller and part of a seemingly permanent metropolis, where our needs are met and our food is always there in the local supermarket. Yet we, unlike all of the other species in our world, through sheer human intelligence, can put together historical and scientific evidence and make an effort to work out what is happening to our planet and change whatever is causing the problem. Scientists, who have already done the working out, are advising us to get on with it and act. Now.

If only there wasn't the problem of lack of will to get on and do it. If only the American President wasn't part of that problem.

To digress and compare, (at the risk of repetition): in his time, Roosevelt provided the initiative in trying to create permanent international institutions through which freedom and peace would be secured. After rampantly aggressive world war, it was the central need of the time. It is true that he was a party to the Yalta agreement, which, as G. Bush has pointed out, sanctioned Stalin's occupation of its neighbouring European countries. It is also true and hardly remembered, that for the sake of cooperation in the war effort, Roosevelt eased off on his direct criticisms of Churchill's imperialism.

It is worth pointing out that none of this was wilful cooperation with imperial allies. The main concerns of the Americans at Yalta were bringing Russian forces into the war with Japan, which US generals and admirals thought was vital and winning support for the creation of the United Nations. It was well understood at Yalta that Soviet armies were poised to finally smash the Nazi armies and occupy those eastern European countries anyway. And Winston Churchill had already made a personal agreement with Stalin dividing the region: the Yalta agreement has been referred to as a formalisation of Churchill's deal with Stalin.

None of this makes Yalta right. But a post–war settlement is bound to be messy if you believe in the freedom of nations and your coalition partners are Stalin and Churchill. Roosevelt tried to counter the mess with his uncompromising public statements on the right of *all* peoples to freely choose their own Governments. *And he had his United Nations.* Still in the age of direct empire, Roosevelt was doing his best to establish important principles of freedom and law. In *The Lion and the Fox* and else-where, it is recognised that Roosevelt expected to be alive after the war to exert his personal influence on Stalin.

I digress this far, because I believe that Roosevelt's example is relevant today and the positive lessons we should learn from his life have been ignored by his successors. Neither the Yalta episode, nor others, where Roosevelt was wrongly accused for being "soft" on Stalin, can take away from him his genuine attempts to meet the central need of his time. Roosevelt rose above selfish pursuit of narrow interests, including narrow corporate interests, to champion the world's peoples, and the world's peoples responded to the genuine article. America can be proud of having produced such a leader at such a time.

Today's US President, in the face of a threat potentially even greater than Nazism, has chosen not to cooperate with Kyoto in cutting greenhouse gas emissions, it seems, in deference to a section of corporate America. He prefers to talk about developing technologies to lock up carbon out of harms way. But that is for the future. Scientists say that there are already critical quantities of the gases in the atmosphere and that a great and accelerating change is already taking place and *immediate* intervention is vital, if we are not to be too late.

Neo-conservative thinking, which is single-mindedly tribal, isn't suited to dealing with broad human problems – despite its assumption of the right to dominate other nations. The neo-conservatives have their own narrow concerns and they are likely to insert *their* pursuits, inappropriately, into dealing with any problem America, or the world, might face, as they did when they misused 9/11 to invade Iraq. Their response to global heating has shown how inappropriate is their thinking. In a British TV interview, at the time of G8, G. Bush said, defending his non-cooperation with Kyoto, that he was acting in the American interest, which considering America is on planet earth, demonstrates his Administration's inadequacy.

(Just as this book is close publication, Hurricane Katrina has hit America's southern coast. It is early days, but there are indications in reports from America that the Bush Government, despite the high probability of damaging hurricanes, had rejected requests from the experts for more to be done to protect human communities along the Louisiana coastline. President Bush's inaccurate statement, following the disaster, "I don't think anyone anticipated a breech of the levees", was, I believe, rooted in an ideological disregard of much of the human condition that lies beyond neo-conservative concerns: a state of mind that led to the failure, prior to Katrina, to attempt an organised evacuation of Louisiana and to the earlier failure to prepare to reconstitute Iraqi civil society after the dislocation of war.

Hurricane Katrina is an example and a costly warning, which shouldn't have been needed, of the awesome, large-scale devastation, which both nature and the affects of man on nature, can produce. We all knew that sea temperatures have been rising and that these higher temperatures favour hurricane creation. And we knew of the many changes taking place within the oceans and the wider world, which included an historically rapid warming of America's most northern state, Alaska and a potentially dangerous temperature increase of the waters of the Gulf of Mexico. Yet the Bush Government rejected the need to take significant action to tackle global warming and actually cut money for southern tornado defences, while using precious resources to invade Iraq.

One doesn't need a vivid imagination to realise that if the devastation in and around Louisiana were of continental proportions, the people affected wouldn't just suffer for a week while they waited for relief, but many would never receive help and millions would die. If such devastation was worldwide, most would never receive help and human populations would crash, amidst much misery. While diminishing numbers of survivors would face a grim struggle to stay alive.

Doing little to combat the larger changes to our planet, while spending billions of dollars to rebuild New Orleans, might be futile: without drastic action, well within this century, New Orleans could be drowned by rising seas. In the years ahead, warmer seas are expected to produce fiercer hurricanes and America's southern coastline can anticipate the tornado season becoming increasingly dangerous. With Texas and US oil facilities in the firing line, even the most faithful servants of America's domestic oil industry should accept the need for urgent action to halt global warming.

Previous calculation failed to predict the present acceleration of Arctic melting and ozone depletion and present levels of carbon and methane in the atmosphere. The actuality is happening far faster than predictions foretold. A modern "Franklin Roosevelt" would, I believe, assume we are in crisis and take emergency action to tackle the central problem of our time.

The missing Leadership

The Bush team came to power planning to impose their will on others and have been refusing to join with the world's nations to find solutions to world problems. They seem to think that being the dominant military power and throwing their weight around constitutes world leadership.

But it isn't only George Bush and his team who are failing to face global warming. Global warming continues, hardly checked, because it isn't being seriously tackled. There has been no decisive action: no restriction on car size or use, or on air travel and no assault on the excessive uses of energy in our society. There has been insufficient effort to draw public involvement, such as campaigns and inducements to change to non-carbon-producing power companies, or use, now viable, of household wind power-generators, or solar panels. No setting targets for local government, or encouragement of local initiatives. No *effective* trade sanctions/rewards, aimed at the forest-destroying states, to restore the forests; international bankers have even granted loans for "development" which has accelerated Brazil's forest clearances, even though there are signs of the Amazon forest drying out, and even though what happens to the Amazon affects the world's climate.

Our own Government doesn't have a good record: Britain is one of the biggest importers of wood from illegally cleared forests. And even though polluting-China, with its plans for sustainable cities and Brazil, with its development of non-carbon-accumulating power, are showing a promise of needed world leadership, their explosion of trade with each other, is actually accelerating Amazon destruction. As far as I am aware there is no worldwide scheme for planting trees, to lock up carbon, wherever it is environmentally feasible.

And there has been insufficient assurance to nations with rapidly developing economies with potentially, vast, lethal carbon emissions to come, such as China and India, that the already industrialised states will share with them responsibility for cutting greenhouse-gas emissions.

Perhaps our leaders have been reflecting past public opinion. But we, the public, need leadership. The conclusions of the scientists should be presented to us with the full authority of governments and of the United Nations.

In America there are probably many more *local* initiatives than in any other country. But America like the world lacks an effective, coordinating leadership.

A crucial need: an international science of survival

We now understand that periods when life thrives on our planet are interludes between hugely destructive natural events, when many species are destroyed. We know that our race has survived because, during our evolution, we have been lucky not to have suffered the most catastrophic of those events. Geneticist, Professor Steve Jones tells us that, if I have understood him, the relative narrowness of our shared human genes shows that we are all the descendents of a small number of survivors of some great natural catastrophe.

We know that sometime our luck will run out and we will have to deal with the large asteroid that will one day visit us, or risk extinction and the super-volcano – amongst others – under Yellowstone National Park, where the ground is rising, will erupt sometime. And there are other threats in waiting, which will affect life on earth.

Our race will someday face the problem of conquering those threats. But we will need to have anticipated each threat and developed the science to defeat it. We shouldn't assume that such things happen only in the remote past, or the remote future. It isn't being alarmist to be realistic and accept that next year is as likely as any other, to be the year during which we face such a danger. If one did come and it could, we might be too late.

And we have global heating and the destruction of the ozone layer. In the scale of their potential destructiveness, these man-made threats to life resemble the natural ones. And they are here now making their presence felt. Facing this crisis, we should recognise that we have come of age and lift our thinking to meet it – and dare I say – put our, now petty tribalism, with its wasteful, uneven morality, behind us. Instead of seeking advantage over others, instead of financing huge arms bills with which to do it, we should put aside the old rivalries and dedicate science and technology to human survival.

Without red tape, without long delay, world scientists, under the authority of Roosevelt's UN, should send delegates to an international conference, which would produce a guide to reversing the heating of our planet. As there are already sufficient long-life greenhouse gases in the air, over time, to severely harm the world human community and much of life on earth and because they are still being poured out, serious government intervention has to follow. We all have to accept alterations to our lifestyle, with all its difficulties. The alternative is likely to be forced change for many alive today, so drastic it will utterly change the way we live and eventually undermine our "civilization" and our children's ability to feed themselves: hardly the legacy we would choose to leave to them.

Either we deal with the problem and create sustainability, if it is possible, or our present "civilization" becomes unsustainable. In the latter case, wealth creation and the means of supporting civil society and, particularly science, will crash. And so will our capacity for deliberate intervention in the natural world. (And radioactive waste, from hundreds of nuclear power stations, which will remain dangerous for a million years, could become a menace.)

It is possible that the human race will become helpless in the face of changed nature, except for survivors doing what they can to survive in the absence of the old supporting networks of sophisticated society. (Is it possible that there is a clue somewhere here to why the SETI programme, which scans the cosmos for radio signals from other intelligences, has drawn a blank? Could it be that the warlords always win?)

Dealing with the immediate crisis is the priority. The necessary international effort, if it succeeds, could hardly fail to be a transforming and unifying experience. Especially if it is accepted as the beginning of a long-term programme for human survival where scientists would identify and analyse the array of threats to the human race, from asteroids to disease and hunger, and work on the means to defeat them.

Even if an immediately threatening natural event didn't come for many generations, the effort will have been worth it. We will have learned much about wider nature, and there will have been many beneficial results, not least the coordination of our national sciences for mutual benefit. And, hopefully, our colossal arms expenditure will have been diverted to the common purpose of human survival and development.

The whole world would be enthused by a leadership from America, which encouraged this degree of change, and such is American scientific ascendancy that this kind of leadership would be a major motivator for the world's scientists. Who knows, we might, within not too many generations, become a race of scientists.

In a recent speech, George Bush said, "There is no higher

calling than service in our armed forces". Hopefully, before too long, an American president will say, "There is no higher calling than service on the Programme for Human Survival and Development", or words to that effect.

The future

We humans have conflicting behaviours. We can be self-seeking, short-sighted and murderous tribalists. We can also be compassionate, inclusive and far-sighted, visionary thinkers. In earlier ages, it must often have been necessary to close tribal ranks, think tribally and fight for survival. There are victims in modern times who have had no option but to respond that way. When we see a people with inadequate weapons fighting against overwhelming odds, it is usually what we are seeing. But for developed countries dealing with the less developed world, such tribal assertion isn't appropriate. Those with huge military power can afford to be magnanimous. And, in the case of Israel and America, it is in their interest to be so. If they do, I believe, they will be surprised by the magnanimous response they will receive in return.

A different set of American leaders, acknowledging the supremacy of international law and international institutions, could lead us away from the infantile selfishness, which has characterised the Bush Administration.

Today, we need to think beyond tribal groupings and face the threats from the wider natural world and those that our own social and scientific developments have brought upon us. We face failure as a species if we squander our scientific genius on creating ever more sophisticated weapons with which to wage tribal war. We should be lifting our minds to the brilliant and challenging future we could be leaving to our children.

We now understand that the scale of the universe we live in is vast, beyond the imagination of earlier generations and the time extending ahead of our race is possibly never ending, depending upon what we choose to do during our short individual lives. I believe the time has come to move beyond the age of uneven morality and uneven treatment of peoples, when states and sometimes groups within states, fight each other and when the vulnerable, too often, live in an Orwellian world, with an Orwellian boot on their faces. The time has come for the peoples of the world to come together to use science for the common purpose of surviving together, for what could become a brilliant and fantastic future.

November, 2005

13

Bibliography

Northern Ireland

Cusak, J. and McDonald, H. *UVF,* Poolbeg, 2000.

Dillon, Martin. *Stone Cold.* Arrow, 1993.

Dillon, Martin. *The Shankill Butchers - A case study of mass murder.* Arrow, 1990.

McKay, Susan. *Northern Protestants.* Blackstaff Press, 2000.

O'Neill, Terence. *Autobiography – Prime Minister of Northern Ireland, 1963-69.* Rupert Hart Davis, 1972.

Taylor, Peter. *Loyalists.* Bloomsbury, 2000.

Taylor, Peter. *The IRA and Sinn Fein.* Bloomsbury, 1998.

Maloney and Pollak, *Paisley,* Rupert Hart Davis, 1972.

Greece

Alexander, G.M. *The Prelude to the Truman Doctrine – British policy in Greece – 1944-47.* Clarendon Press, 1982.

Andrews, K. *The Flight of Icaros.* Penguin, 1984.

Byford-Jones, W. *The Greek Trilogy.* Hutchinson, 1945.

Hondros, J.L. *Occupation and Resistance: The Greek Agony 1941-44.* Pella New York, 1983.

Iatrides, J.O. *Revolt in Athens.* Princeton University Press, 1972.

Jones, H. *A New Kind of War – America's global strategy and the Truman Doctrine.* Oxford University Press, 1989.

Mazower, Mark. *Inside Hitler's Greece.* Yale University Press – New Haven and London, 1993.

Myers, E.C.W. *The Greek Entanglement.* Hart Davis, 1955.

Sarafis, Stefanos. Major General. *ELAS: Greek Resistance Army.* Merlin Press, 1980.

Sfikas, Thanasis D. *The British Labour Government and the Greek civil War 1945-1949.* Ryburn Publishing, Keele University. 1994.

Vlavianis, H. *Greece, 1941-49 – From resistance to civil war.* MacMillan, 1992.

Woodhouse, C.M. *The Struggle for Greece, 1941-49.* MacGibbon, 1976.

Guatemala

Barry, T. *Inside Guatamala.* The Inter-Hemispheric Education Resource Center, New Mexico, 1992.

Black, G. with Jamail, M. and Chinchilla, N.S. *Garrison Guatemala.* Monthly Review Press, 1984.

Handy, J. *Gift of the Devil – A history of Guatemala.* South End Press Boston, 1984.

Melville, T. and M. *Guatemala – Another Vietnam?* Pelican, 1971.

Menchu, Rigoberta. *I Rigoberta Menchu – an Indian Woman in Guatamala.* Verso, 1984.

Painter, J. *Guatamala – False Hope, False Freedom.* Catholic Institute for International Relations and Latin American Bureau, 1987.

Schlesinger, S. and Kinzer, S. *Bitter Fruit - The untold story of the American coup in Guatemala.* Anchor Press – Doubleday, 1982.

Iran

Azadi, Sousan. *Out of Iran.* Futura, 1991.

Armstrong. Karen. *Muhammad.* Victor Gollancz, 1991.

Bakhash, Shaul. *The Reign of the Ayatollahs.* Counterpoint – Unwin Paperbacks, 1986.

Bill, J.A. and Louis, R., (editors). *Mossadeq, Iranian Nationalism and Oil.* Taurus, 1988.

Farman Farmaian, Sattareh. *Daughter of Persia.* Corgi, 1993.

Heikal, Mohamed. *The Return of the Ayatollah.* Andre Deutch, 1981.

Hiro, D. *Iran Under the Ayatollahs.* Routledge Keegan Paul, 1985.

Hunt, Paul. *Inside Iran.* Lion, 1981.

Mahmoody, Betty. *Not without my Daughter.* Corgi, 1991.

Roohizadegan, Olya. *Olya's Story.* Oneworld, 1994.

Roosevelt, Kermit. *Counter Coup.* Macgraw-hill,

Lumumba's Congo

Archer, J. *Congo – The Birth of a Nation.* Bailey Brothers, 1971.
Kansa, T. *The Rise and Fall of Patrice Lumumba.* Rex Collings, 1978.
Lumumba Speaks. Little Brown – Frederick Muller, 1972.
O'Brien, Connor Cruise. *To Katanga and Back – a UN Case History.* Universal Library, 1966.
West, R. *Brazza of the Congo.* Jonathan Cape/Victorian Book Club, 1973.

Japan

Aaron, D and Bendiner, R. (Editors). *The Strenuous Decade – A Social and Intellectual Record of the 1930s.* Anchor – Doubleday, 1970.
Akizuki, T. *Nagisaki 1945.* Quartet. 1981.
Chang, I. *The Rape of Nanking.* Penguin, 1997.
Cook, Haruko Taya and Cook, Theodore F. *Japan at War.* The New Press, 1992.
Fukuzawa, Yukichi. *The Autobiography.* Schocken Books – New York, 1972.
Harvey, R. *The Undefeated.* MacMillan, 1994.
Ienega, Saburo. *Japan's Last War.* Basil Blackwell, 1978.
Ishimoto, Baroness Shidzue. *Facing Two Ways.* Cassell, 1935.
Manchester, W. *American Caesar – Douglas MacArthur, 1880-1964.*
Mosley, Leonard. *Hirothito.* Weidenfeld and Nicolson, 1996.
Rusbridger, J. and E. Nave. *Betrayal at Pearl Harbour.* Michael O'Mara Books Limited, 1991.
Sugimoto, Etsu Inagaki. *Daughter of the Samurai.* Charles E. Tuttle, 1990.
Suyin, Han. *The Crippled Tree.* Jonathan Cape, 1965.

Palestine/Israel

Arakie, Margaret. *The Broken Sword of Justice.* Quartet Books, 1973.
Bowen, Jeremy, *Six Days,* Simon and Schuster UK Ltd, 2003.
Brenner, L. *Zionism in the Age of the Dictators.* Croom Helm, 1983.
Catton, H. *Palestine and International Law,* Butler and Tanner, 1976.
Cutting, Pauline. *Children of the Siege.* Pan, 1988.

Finkelstein, Norman G. *The Holocaust Industry – Reflections on the Exploitation of Jewish Suffering.* Verso, 2001.

Fisk, R. *Pity The Nation.* Oxford University Press, 2001.

Flapan, S. *The Birth of Israel.* Croom Helm, 1987.

Green, S. *Living by the Sword. America and Israel in the Middle East, 1996-88.* Faber and Faber, 1988. Also, *Taking Sides,* by the same author.

Hirst, D. *The Gun and the Olive Branch.* Faber and Faber, 1977.

How, R. W. *Weapons.* Abacus, 1981.

Hewit, Garth. *Towards the Dawn.* Society for Promoting Christian Knowledge, 2004.

Miller, J and Mylroie, L. *Saddam Hussein, and the crisis in the Gulf,* Times Books (US) and Random House (Canada), 1990.

Palumbo, M. *Imperial Israel.* Bloomsbury, 1992.

Palumbo, M. *The Palestinian Catastrophe.* Quartet Books, 1989.

Shahak, I. and Mezvinsky. *Jewish Fundamentalism in Israel.* Pluto Press, 1999.

Swee, Dr. Chai Ang. *From Beirut to Jerusalem – A Woman surgeon with the Palestinians.* Grafton Books, 1989.

Yermiya, Dov. *My War Dairy,* Pluto Press, 1983.

Hersh, Seymour M. *The Sampson Option.* Faber and Faber, 1993.

General

Aaron, D. and Bendiner, R. *The Strenuous decade.* Anchor – Doubleday, 1970.

Alperovitz, Gar, *Atomic Diplomacy: Hiroshima and Potsdam.* Penguin Books, 1985

Ambrose, Stephen A. *Rise to Globalism – American foreign policy since 1938.* Penguin, 1985.

Barnet, R. J. *Intervention and Revolution.* Paladin, 1972.

Bishop, Jim. *FDR's Last Year. April 1944 – April 1945.* Granada Publishing/Hart-Davies, MacGibbon, 1974.

Burns, James MacGregor. *Roosevelt: The Lion and the Fox.* Smithmark, New York, 1984.

Lamb, R. *Churchill as War Leader.* Bloomsbury, 1993.

Mann, James. *Rise of The Vulcans, The History of Bush's War Cabinet.* Viking, 2004.

Mee, Charles, L, Jr. *Meeting At Potsdam.* Dell Publishing Co., Inc. 1976.

Morgan, Ted. *FDR.* Grafton Books, 1985.

Pearce, Jenny. *Under The Eagle*. Latin American Bureau, 1982.

Rhodes, James, J. *Churchill – A study in failure, 1900-39*. Weidenfeld and Nicolson, 1990.

Ruthven, Malise. *Fundamentalism*. Oxford University Press, 2004.

Singer, Peter. *The President of Good and Evil, Taking Bush Seriously*. Granta Books, London, 2004

Stettinius, Edward R., Junior. *Roosevelt and the Russians. The Yalta Conference*. Greenwood Press, Westport, Connecticut, 1970.

14

Sources, Part Two

(The original draft of Sources, it was pointed out to me, had too much crammed into it, smothering the argument. After an initial cutting of passages, for those who might wish to read them, I have reintroduced most of them here.)

The Arab-Muslim corner

The Muslim world-view will have been largely shaped by the shabby treatment traditionally accorded to them by the more powerful West. In modern times Western armies and navies have been a regular, active, presence in their region and Western leaders have defined their borders and decided who would be their rulers. One aspect of this Western dominance has been the dispossession of the Palestinians. Many Muslims have been deeply affected by their fate.

In the time of the grandparents of today's Muslims, having been told they would be rewarded with independence, thousands of Arabs, including Palestinians, fought to defeat the Turks, only to see many fellow Arabs die at the hands of British and French forces when they tried to claim that independence. At the time, under the League of Nations Mandate, Britain's prime purpose in administering Palestine was supposed to be to benefit the native Palestinian population. But it was the ever-increasing numbers of Jewish immigrants who were ultimately to be the sole beneficiaries. An awareness of these events has become part of the consciousness of Arab-Muslims, and the injustice of the dispossession of the Palestinians has become a central unifying grievance for millions of Muslims, even beyond the Arab world.

When Hitler's armies killed civilians and destroyed their property in retaliation for guerrilla attacks, it was a war crime: this is accepted in Europe and America. Yet Muslims see it happening all the time. People who have had nothing to do with attacks on Israel's soldiers and civilians have their homes destroyed and are killed in retaliation. It happened in Jordan. It happened in Lebanon. And it happens in Palestine.

When a Muslim sees a film of a young Palestinian child screaming in terror next to the ruins of his bulldozed family home, we shouldn't be surprised if empathising Muslims, see the larger story behind the picture: billions of dollars worth of US military supplies and billions of dollars of cash aid that goes with it, telling Israel, "It's okay. Carry on. They're only Arabs." Millions of Muslims will know that today's American President, whose Christian piety is on full public display, is a devoted supporter of Israel, and millions will have heard of the large financial donations from American fundamentalist Christians to help extremist Jews settle Palestinian land. Should we be surprised if some Muslims believe that Christian morality sanctions Israel's actions.

Muslims will be more likely than we in the West to see a Palestinian "militant" assassinated by Israel as a human victim who throughout his, or her, life has been treated as less than human and so has joined an armed resistance group. They will be more likely to see Palestinian suicide bombers as tragic human beings who have been pushed and pushed and pushed until they can take no more and so end their own lives in a desperate attempt to do *something* against the occupiers of their land.

Israel's refusal to deal with Yasser Arafat because he had "blood on his hands" and President Bush's dutiful following of this policy, might have gone down well in America. But Arabs know that Ariel Sharon has an incomparably greater bloody record than the Palestinian leader had. And they will know that the PLO's record would easily survive honest comparison with Israel's record.

And Muslims will know that when negotiations take place Palestinians are expected to behave as the lowly, beaten underdog whose needs have little importance compared to those of Israel.

Like us, Muslims have their newspapers, radios and televisions. But they, unlike us, will hear clear accounts of the Palestinian side of the breakdown of negotiations: that they haven't turned their backs on a "generous offer" and that Israel was insisting on keeping them unlawfully surrounded by, often fanatical and aggressive, settlers. They are more likely to know that the reality behind the claims that Arafat had turned down the division of Jerusalem is that

Israel has designated rural areas, "part of Jerusalem" and agreed that some of these rural areas would be Palestinian.

And they are more likely to hear the details of the one-sided "ceasefire" during which Israel raided and assassinated and continued its high-speed settlement of Palestinian land. And while we will have heard of the crazed suicide bombers who broke the cease-fire, Muslims will be aware that Israel's leaders hold Palestinians in such low regard that they demand they hold their fire while losing their land and being killed.

The main grievance of Arab Muslims against America has been that, over decades, it armed and financed the dismemberment of the Palestinian nation. They will have seen Israel, without pity and with much violence, take tiny, cramped, economically unviable, Gaza, home to over a million Palestinians and settle 8,000 Israeli citizens on large tracts of the best agricultural land. In the much larger West Bank, they will have seen, with the recent wall, the takeover go beyond 50% of the total area, more than making up for the land left behind in Gaza. And in both of these areas, they will know that Israel has severely restricted Palestinian water use, while taking the lion's share of the water for the settlers and denied needed Palestinian building, while, itself, rapidly increasing building for settlers.

They will know that Jerusalem, in 1948, even after decades of Jewish immigration, was predominantly Arab and that since then Israel's policy has been to turn the area into a Jewish zone, which has involved ethnic cleansing. They will know that the Palestinians who remained in Israel after 1948 had almost all of their property taken from them. They will know that this single–minded ethnic cleansing has been repeatedly condemned by the UN, but protected and made possible by American largesse and supported enthusiastically by American fundamentalist "Christians".

That is the bare bones of the crime against the Palestinians, upon which many injustices and indignities have been laid, including constantly putting the blame on the victims. It constitutes a considerable crime.

And Muslims with know the truth: that there have been many aggressive acts against neighbouring Arab states, including war and seizure and settlement of other's sovereign territory and that in accordance with Israel's Orwellian version of events, the aggressor has been presented as the victim. That over decades, Arabs have been unable to penetrate this curtain of Orwellian "truth", which is cynically accepted by America's politicians, will have greatly increased the frustration of many Muslims.

In the West it has been repeatedly said that it is important to try to understand the mind of the terrorist, as though that mind is the prime source of anti-Western terrorism. From the Muslim point of view, what is more important is that we in the West understand the minds of Sharon and his predecessors such as Rabin, Perez, Shamir, Begin, and Ben Gurion and know their ideology and history and that we understand the minds of their American politician supporters and invaders of their region.

With little power and unable to bend America from her material support for Israel's encroachments, it has been a tiny, very tiny minority of Muslims who became so frustrated and desensitised that they decide to "hit-back" and visit on others some of the indiscriminate violence fellow Muslims have suffered. Unfortunately, when they do, it is the innocent who suffer.

That these terrorist attacks have come *after* long years of Israeli violence on civilians is, I believe, because that violence has always been a part of life. But in recent years fresh events have made an impact on young Muslims. There was the suffering of Muslims during the break-up of Yugoslavia and particularly the massacre of Muslims at Srebrenica and the horrors of Yeltsin and Putin's war on Chechnya and the wars on Afghanistan and Iraq. And there is the memory of the impressive victory in the earlier war against Russian occupation of Afghanistan.

Many Muslims will understand American anger over 9/11, but will not accept that that horror justified the horror that was then visited upon the civilians of Afghanistan and Iraq. They will also know that the invasion of Kuwait, which brought the 1991 war, was a mere skirmish compared to Israel's, unpunished, 1982 killing-rampage through Lebanon. And they will know that the horrors of Saddam Hussein's mass graves came after US presidents, Nixon and later, Bush (senior), encouraged rebellions and then left the rebels to be destroyed. And it could hardly have gone unnoticed that the American President's "hand over Bin Laden" ultimatum to Afghanistan, which didn't follow normal legal process, might well have been crafted to humiliate and be rejected and provide an excuse for war. Muslims will know that Western interference has brought much war and many deaths.

To young Muslims a fresh, historically significant, assault on fellow Muslims is underway. For a new generation, who otherwise might have been absorbed in football, cricket, music, studies and careers, Iraq, in particular, has brought it all up for re-examination, and there is an awakening taking place. As never before, they are watching world events. They have become sensitised to the flexible morality of America's leaders, rigorously applied when dealing with Muslim "foes", but bent out of sight when doing business with "friendly" oil regimes and with Israel. And as never before, when Palestinians suffer, while an American President looks the other way, young Muslims feel the pain.

Uneven standards continue in a variety of ways. A recent example has been the American President's demand that the new Palestinian authority stamp out the armed militants, while financing Israel's continued taking of Palestinian land in the West Bank, which provokes armed militancy.

Another glaring example, which can hardly fail to highlight this uneven moral culture, involves recent American and other Western, outrage over the probable involvement of Syrian officials in the murder of a Lebanese political leader and over the Iranian President's wild, self-damaging, "Israel must be wiped off the map", rhetoric. The statement from the Bush Administration that the existence of one Government's organisation of assassination within another state couldn't be tolerated, must remind Muslims of Israel's many international assassinations, which haven't provoked a similar angry response. And the outrage over the "wipe Israel off the map" rhetoric, will remind no few Muslims that Israel actually did wipe out the UN sanctioned Palestine state, just as it was in the process of being born and that successive American presidents have funded the continuing wiping out process.

Of course, not every Muslim will know of every action of Israel. But there will be quite a few who know of an event linking these examples of hypocrisy: in 1981 Israel's Mossad assassinated Naim Khader, in Belgium, after he had contacted Israeli officials for Yasser Arafat, seeking peace talks: Israel's leaders were determined to keep Palestine wiped from the map and still had much Palestinian land to seize and settle. Naim Khader paid with his life for supposing Israel might want peace.

And today, while Israel is continuing its "wiping off the map" exercise and taking land in the West Bank, young Muslims see Syria and Iran, but not Israel, on he receiving end of the West's angry ultimatums. They must wonder if Western leaders will ever understand that to end terrorism, the West must move on from its double standards.

For the vast majority who won't touch Al Qaeda, these continuing flexible standards will certainly intensify their anger. Although I wouldn't speculate how they might express that anger. But it is likely, I believe, that as young Muslims become aware of the actual facts of Palestinian history and, in particular, that the 1948 seizure of Palestine was a deliberate, planned, act of ethnic cleansing and land and property-theft, nothing less than restoration of the United Nations 1948 borders, for them, will suffice for a settlement. Possibly only the Right of Return for the refugees to their legal homeland, alongside Jews, in a non-racist state, will suffice. They would be justified and have the law on their side, in demanding either of these options for a settlement.

I believe lasting peace won't be possible without, at a minimum, the 1948 UN border being restored. But it might take more: there has been a huge amount of property taken from both Palestinian refugees and Palestinians who remained in Israel. There is much compensation owed, and there are many who are still unacceptably barred by military power from their legal homeland.

Iraq: non-compliance with UN resolutions brings sanctions, bombing and invasion. Israel: non-compliance with UN resolutions brings billions of dollars worth of military and civil aid

When Egyptians, Syrians and Palestinians heard President Bush and Prime Minister Blair preparing for war in 2003 and claiming that Saddam Hussein had for twelve years not complied with UN resolutions, many of them would have remembered 1973 when Egypt and Syria were able to take back from Israel some of their occupied national territory, in support of a UN Resolution, only to be forced back because of American government actions.

And the whole Muslim world would have remembered the fifty-plus years during which Israel has ignored many UN resolutions requiring her to end her unlawful behaviour. Below is a sample of those attempts by the UN to apply the law. (They are mostly taken from *Israel and International Law*, which gives a much fuller account of them. The book also explains illegalities from earlier years that led to the creation of Israel.)

Following the war of 1967, in June and again in July, a UN General Assembly resolution called upon Israel to allow back the

400,000 recently displaced refugees. In July 1967 and again in September 1971, the UN Security Council condemned and declared invalid the demographic changes then taking place in Jerusalem and the occupied territories. The actuality of the demographic changes was the replacement of Muslim and Christian population by Jewish, along with a corresponding seizure, or destruction, of property.

Similar UN General Assembly resolutions were passed in July 1967, December 1968, December 1971, December 1972, December 1973, November 1974 and December 1974. In September 1975 a General Assembly resolution expressed grave concern that no progress had been made towards returning the Palestinians to their homes.

The UN had made even more serious attempts following the 1948 war to get the million displaced Palestinians home. Count Bernadotte was appointed UN Mediator. But he was murdered by Jewish terrorists for his efforts to enforce the 1947 UN Partition resolution and return the refugees. The men involved in the murder were quickly let out of Israel's jails and allowed to flee the country, and no one was ever brought to trial for the crime. There was an American government investigation into Count Bernadotte's murder. *The results were never released and remain classified.*

Nazi property seizures in occupied territories during WW2 were declared at Nuremberg to have been war crimes. Yet UN resolutions that addressed Israel's property seizures have been ignored with impunity. Down the years to the present, the UN has passed many resolutions covering different aspects of Israel's illegal activities, some requiring action, which Israel has ignored.

Three times, that I am aware of, once after the 1967 war, again in 1984 and recently after an army operation that flattened a residential area of Jenin, killing residents, the UN has created a commission to investigate Israel's behaviour. On each occasion they were refused access to the relevant occupied territory. Yet there was no public fuss from an American President or from a British Prime Minister, about "flouting UN resolutions" or "ignoring the will of the international community". There was just the usual tolerance of Israel and the undisturbed flow of dollars and weapons from America and continued favourable trade arrangements with Europe. And the American Government has backed Israel in blocking the, badly needed, involvement of UN observers that would certainly have limited lawless behaviour.

The 1948 UN Partition Resolution was unjust. *It allocated only forty three per cent of Palestine to the two third Palestinian majority.* And it was hardly legal. But it *was* supposed to ensure a Palestinian state on a specific area of land. Israel's leaders have traditionally traced their legitimacy largely to that Partition Resolution. Yet they violated the same resolution by invading the Palestinian "half" of the country.

From 1948, the Ben Gurion/Moshe Dayan military faction controlled Israel. They were hyperactive, always seeking conflict and plotting to expand Israel's borders. According to *Israel and International Law,* between 1948 and 1976 (when it was published), the UN Security Council condemned Israel no less than 40 times for raids on Arab states and refugee camps. One of the raids, by a special army unit, was infamously led by, later to be, Prime Minister, Sharon, on the Jordanian village of Qibya. UN observers who arrived shortly after the raid found the houses blown up and bullet-ridden bodies near doorways. Sixty-six people had been killed – men women and children. The raid was in response to a grenade attack, by unknown individuals, which had killed a woman and two children; the Jordanian authorities had tried but failed to get Israel's co-operation in tracking the killers.

Today the man who led the Qibya raid is, with impunity, ignoring a decision of the international court and seriously in violation of the law, in building a wall deep within the West Bank, reportedly, separating 200,000 Palestinians from the land and other property they need to live something like a normal life. The wall was apparently accepted in America as having been built to protect Israel from bombers. Yet when the secret decision to confiscate all of the land and property taken by the wall was reported, there was no political storm in America, no public lectures from the American President, no language of ultimatum. Such treatment is reserved for "Bad Guys".

Rachael Corrie, Tom Hurndall and James Millar: the visible tip of a larger wrong: or how to create suicide bombers

During the Spring of 2002, within a two month period, Rachael Corrie, an American and James Millar, a Briton, were killed separately, and Tom Hurndall, also British, was mortally wounded by Israeli soldiers in Rafah refugee camp Gaza.

Rachael Corrie was protesting, standing in front of a bulldozer that was demolishing Palestinian homes, when she was killed. A companion, in a John Sweeney BBC TV documentary, relating what happened, said that, even though they were gesticulating to the bulldozer driver and pointing and screaming, the driver ran her over.

Another witness said that the driver withdrew, leaving his scoop on the ground, which would have crushed her a second time.

Rachael was found to have ribs, both shoulder blades and five vertebrae broken, arms crushed and internal bleeding. Israel closed the case, saying that the two soldiers in the bulldozer hadn't seen her and had done nothing wrong, and that she had died after stumbling on building waste, not by being hit by a bulldozer.

Less than a month later Tom Hurndall, a photographer turned protester (while in Palestine), was shot in the head as he stooped to pick up and carry a child to safety, after a soldier in a nearby Israeli watchtower had started firing shots. Israel's official explanation, shown by the same documentary to be totally false, was that Tom Hurndall, wearing military camouflage, was a gunman firing at the watchtower.

Three weeks after the shooting of Tom Hurndall, James Millar, a Television Cameraman and writer, was killed by a single shot, as he stood alongside two companions, one of them carrying a white flag. It was dark but the Armoured Personnel Carrier from which the shot was fired had night vision, and James was shining a torch on the flag when he was shot.

What had happened was that earlier the protesters James had been filming, had shouted to the army-bulldozer crew asking if a family, or families, could retrieve their furniture before demolition, but had run for cover when they were answered by gunfire. A little later in the documentary, a soldier could be heard (subtitled) shouting that he would hit them with gunfire if they didn't go inside.

They retreated into the home of a Palestinian family.

Later, when they considered their day's work done, they decided the safest course of action was to openly approach the bulldozer and ask for safe passage. So they walked towards it, James Millar shining his torch directly on to the white flag. When there was a single warning shot, they froze. But, after a thirteen seconds pause, a second shot killed James Millar.

It was implied in an Israeli Army Statement that the fatal shot had struck the victim from behind. If true, it would have exonerated the soldiers. But the shot was proved to have been fired from the front, and the bullet to be an army standard issue very-high-velocity round.

Another Israeli soldier who was shown the evidence, said on the programme, that there was no chance that it was an accident, that it looked like "he" wanted to kill him.

It should have been possible, immediately, to examine the soldiers' guns and discover who had fired the bullet. But it was two months before there was an announcement that the guns would be called in for examination and a further fortnight was to pass before that happened. Such haste. (A Palestinian who was *suspected* of killing an Israeli Jew would have his house bulldozed within hours.) An investigation was eventually promised.

The experience led Tom's father to say there was a policy of complete impunity for Israeli soldiers.

Tom's father is a lawyer and since the documentary, his pressure and publicity to a degree Palestinian families has never been able to bring to bear over the deaths of their loved ones, has borne some fruit. A soldier has been found guilty of the "manslaughter" of Tom Hurndall.

On the wider relevance of the three cases, an Israeli journalist, Gideon Levy, said that after killing 2,600 Palestinians, not even six cases had been investigated and no one brought to court. He said that many innocent Palestinians had been killed but there was a culture of hiding the truth and of lying and giving soldiers the message that if you kill a Palestinian nobody really cares. He said that nobody asks questions when you kill a Palestinian.

The killing of these three remarkably courageous young people has come under the public spotlight to a degree that has never happened for large numbers of Palestinian civilians who have been killed by Israeli soldiers. The experience of the Corrie, Millar and Hurndall families has been consistent with claims Palestinian families have been making for years, about false accounts put out by the Israeli army of the killing of their loved ones.

What happened to those three brave young protesters is the visible tip of a much larger mass of sanctioned killing and other misbehaviour, which Palestinians have experienced for much of their lives. *Imperial Israel,* the work of an American, gives a documented account of this behaviour from the beginning of the occupation.

It starts with Israeli army behaviour during the short 1956 occupation: after Eisenhower forced Israel's withdrawal, the UN found a mass grave of forty Palestinian bodies, all with their hands tied behind their backs and shot in the head. They were some of the 275, which a UN investigation found, had been murdered in Khan Yunis by the occupying Israeli army. They also found that 111 had been murdered in Rafah refugee camp. During the occupation 8 employees of the UN were also murdered by Israeli soldiers.

When the occupation resumed, gratis President Johnson, in 1967 the terror did too, with attempts to frighten whole villages into leaving, while others were simply expelled and their homes demolished. Palestinian guerrillas were active and in response, Israel's army, as usual, retaliated against the civilian population, repeatedly destroying homes and telling the occupants if they didn't like it they could cross the bridges to Jordan. They also punished civilians by destroying fishing boats, wells, water pumps, and production facilities and of course with deportations. Amongst those deported there were Palestinian leaders who believed in Arab-Jewish reconciliation – eight of them on one occasion, dumped in the Jordanian desert in the middle of the night, one of them badly beaten with rifle buts: official Israel didn't want reconciliation. It wanted land.

One of the results of the occupation, despite claims otherwise, was the stifling of Palestinian economic life. Between 1967 and 1978, over 100,000 Palestinians fled from life under occupation. Amongst them were many of the educated and skilled.

Imperial Israel was published in Britain in 1990, but isn't out of date: Israel's behaviour hasn't improved. With death and destruction all around them – it is all they have ever known – Palestinian children suffer from a range of traumatic stress disorders, including nightmares and bedwetting and being too afraid to sleep alone. I would guess that their stone-throwing at the soldiers and their tanks is a self-administered "hit-back" therapy – for which some pay with their lives: the occupying army shoots children.

The many, in Britain and America, who believe an idealised version of Israel, time spent with the children of the Occupation would be a valuable experience. They would benefit from talking with the thousands of children who lived in the homes demolished by Israel's bulldozers. Most were given minutes to get out by the soldiers who suddenly surrounded their houses. Immediate notice to quit is often reinforced by gunfire, and fleeing families lose almost all of their possessions. And occasionally, some family members are killed.

The Palestinian Post is published in Britain, as far as I can tell, by independent Israeli citizens, who campaign against home destruction. In a recent issue it quoted an army bulldozer driver admitting that he had no mercy and would erase anyone with his bulldozer and that when he was told to demolish a house, he would knock down extra houses.

That soldier fits in with Israeli Army culture. Jonathan Rabin, Israel's assassinated Prime Minister, talking about how the Palestinians in the occupied territories fared at the hands of his army, said, "Believe me they suffer". He was attributing officially sanctioned brutal behaviour against civilians to the need to hit back for the attacks by Palestinian fighters. This is the constant excuse. Some of Israel's leaders have been more forthright than Rabin. Lieutenant-General Eitan told his officers that they had to do everything to make Palestinians so miserable they would leave. Eitan later became Deputy Prime Minister under Netanyahu.

And Major-General Zeev, once responsible for Israel's Answar concentration camp in South Lebanon and now assassinated, also said that life in the occupied territories should be made so difficult that the inhabitants would flee. He has been a minister in more than one of Israel's governments. Such attitudes have shaped Israeli army culture.

And there was the senior Labour politician, Yigal Allon, who had broken with Ben Gurion in 1948 over the latter's insufficient zeal in "cleansing" (his word) Palestine of the Palestinians. When Israel later took Gaza, Allon wanted to expel the population to make way for settlers.

The bulldozers have destroyed thousands of acres of orange groves, olive trees and other crops, which families need to survive. And they have levelled greenhouses and ripped up sewers, water supplies and electricity infrastructure and knocked down mosques and even bulldozed a zoo, which was considered to be a place of therapy for Palestinian children.

(The Answar camp, outside Israeli national territory, run by surrogate Lebanese, held innocents as hostages, outside the Geneva Conventions, without trial for years, reducing some to mental wrecks. Their families didn't know until they were released whether they were dead or alive. Some were dead. Such a place induces revulsion. Yet the Guantanamo prison in Cuba, beyond American national territory, was almost certainly "inspired" by Answar.)

A licence to kill

A recent Guardian article by Chris McGreal reported that a growing number of children have been hit by Israeli snipers. He said that two girls from the same school were shot in the head in their own homes within the space of a few hours by sniper-fire.

Apart from the watchtowers, there are army sniper posts on the upper floors of seized Palestinian buildings. Palestinians can be shot from any of these places. Children have been hit at their desks in school. One thirteen-year-old girl, after being shot from an army post, was riddled with bullets from close quarters by an Israeli officer. Her body, at post mortem, was found to have over seventeen bullets in it. The army claimed that the girl had gone too close to the army post, and it had been feared that her school bag contained a bomb. It didn't. Other soldiers, unusually, have since refused to work with the officer, who wasn't punished.

For a close look at Israel's soldiers, some journalists have visited checkpoints, with revealing results. One visitor was Chris McGreal. He witnessed a soldier keeping a man unnecessarily for more than an hour, to wipe the smile off his face. The man had produced his permit, which showed why he had been smiling: he was on the way to his own wedding. The soldier was unmoved. A father who had been let ahead by the queue was also held up. McGreal told the soldier that he had been allowed forward because otherwise the fresh cream on the birthday cake the man was carrying for his son would spoil in the sun. The soldier let McGreal know that he didn't give a shit.

The same soldier was just as harsh in his treatment of a 70-year-old man on his way home from hospital after heart surgery, who was finding the wait in the summer heat difficult. And a student who tried to explain his permit in English was told to either speak in Hebrew or shut his mouth. He couldn't speak Hebrew and so was detained for 4 hours. A Palestinian who could speak Hebrew, apparently, tried arguing and was told to shut his mouth or he would get a bullet in his head. The soldier pointed the gun at the man's head and cocked it. The man shut up.

There have been many similar reports of harassment: some of people who needed medical treatment being prevented from leaving to get it. Palestinians returning to studies or jobs abroad have been kept for days *from leaving*, presumably to deter them from ever coming back. One could put together from journalists reports, just from checkpoints, a catalogue of persistent abuse of a people.

Visitors also get the army's attention. Conservative MP, Crispen Blunt, reported that while he was part of a parliamentary delegation travelling in marked UN vehicles, Israeli soldiers fired on them. Less than forty-eight hours earlier, Save The Children representatives also received Israeli army fire.

Unjust settlement = no settlement = continuing violence

Both JFC Fuller and Liddell-Hart, the fathers of 20th century military thinking, insisted that the most important factor in waging war was that it be morally right: that it be a just war. And they argued that moral behaviour in war produces the most fruitful results: that military operations should be directed only at necessary targets, avoiding unnecessary destruction and suffering on the enemy side, both for military efficiency and so as to leave no legacy of bitterness or desire for revenge. They also argued that an unjust outcome to war wasn't peace: it was a halt before a resumption of conflict when those suffering injustice would seek to overturn the injustice.

Although both Fuller and Liddell-Hart had been deeply affected by their experiences of the slaughter in the trenches of WW1, their arguments weren't based on an idealistic wish to reduce the casualties of war. Each presented his arguments only after a thorough study of the history of war. For example, they showed that the North's devastating military campaign through Georgia near the end of the American Civil War, so destructive of the morale of the South, left a lasting legacy of bitterness and violence.

Another example they gave – even though little money was actually paid – was the humiliating imposition of reparations, by the Treaty of Versailles, on the defeated German people, after WW1, without which, arguably, WW2 might not have happened.

Although they weren't blind to the realities of unjust wars and the short sighted use of gratuitous violence in war, Fuller and Liddell-Hart's thinking was, in a sense, idealistic because in an age dominated by the struggle of imperial powers for global power, rather than justice, they served an imperial power. Nevertheless, their arguments were logical and realistic, winning widespread theoretical support, although in practice their core philosophy of just war, minimum use of force and just treatment of the defeated has too often been ignored.

Had they lived through the second half of the 20th Century,

they would have witnessed a vivid demonstration of the validity of their arguments as Israel heaped injustice upon injustice in a series of wars of land seizure, full of gratuitous violence against civilians, that has left, not defeated opponents accepting abject defeat, but communities of victims still yearning for justice and willing to resist, some of whose members have seen so much suffering and are so psychologically damaged, they commit suicide to hit back at those who have taken their land.

If Fuller and Liddell-Hart were alive today, they would witness successive American Presidents producing a recipe for lasting bitterness, humiliation and violence, as they tell the Palestinians that they must accept the unacceptable: that they have been permanently ethnically cleansed from most of their land. And they would, as a result, be witnessing the alienation of much of the Muslim world from America.

November, 2005